The Green Reaper

The Green Reaper
Memoirs of an Eco-Mortician

Elizabeth Fournier

WiDo Publishing
Salt Lake City

WiDo Publishing
Salt Lake City, Utah
widopublishing.com

Cover design by Steven Novak
Book design by Marny K. Parkin

ISBN 978-1-937178-89-5
Library of Congress Control Number available upon request

Printed in the United States of America

For those who shined their light during my darker days

Chapter 1

Because Why?

Early one Sunday morning, when I was eight years old, my mom died after a long illness. I woke to hear my brother and father talking about her in the other room. They said she was in a better place. When my dad finally came to my room, I asked where my mom was.

"She's in Heaven. I'll let you just think about that for a while."

Think about that? I had no way to "think" about it because I had no idea what he was telling me. "But why?" I demanded of him. "Why?"

"Just because."

And then he was gone.

"Just because"? What the hell did *that* mean? Who was she visiting? When would she be coming back? Who could I count on to make my favorite pancakes that morning?

A lady from our church came over, and Dad left the house. My brother, Nick, and I played a game of Monopoly while the church lady kept herself busy in the living room. He was one year older, and I really needed him.

After a while Nick asked, "Aren't you sad?"

"About what?"

"About Mom."

"Why?" His question sounded so odd. She would be back at some point, wouldn't she?

The next day we went to the funeral home. My mother was there. She was dead.

"Are you scared?" Nick whispered. But there was my mother, as if asleep, and I felt more comfort than I had since my father walked into my room with the news.

"No," I told him. "I like it here with Mom."

The next night I asked if we could go back to the funeral home.

"No," my father said. He seemed sad.

"Why not?" I asked.

"There's no visitation today. Other people need to use the funeral parlor."

"Why?"

"Because they do."

"Because why?"

"Just because they do, honey. Eat your pasta."

❧

Years before, after realizing my mother was chronically ill and would be in and out of hospital care, Dad had given Nick and me a set of Bert and Ernie puppets. My father felt they would be built-in best friends and comfort creatures during that rough period. Nick and I had a kinship with our rubber puppets, and Bert and Ernie's likenesses were firmly affixed to our left hands with their striped shirts flowing down to our bony elbows. My brother's puppet twin, Bert, had a unibrow crafted into the head, and my sassy Ernie had a merrily frizzed sprout of hair. These *Sesame Street* dummies slept with us, ate our Rice Krispies with us, and accompanied us to science camp. They were our closest childhood friends. After Mom died, it just seemed natural to go on using my imagination to cope with my loss.

I developed a rich fantasy life. When I answered the phone, I told callers they were speaking to the Lady of the House. Sometimes I would close my eyes, spin around and around, and tell myself when I opened my eyes my mother would be sitting on the couch in front of me.

But she was never there. Just because.

One cold morning, during breakfast and *Sesame Street*, Big Bird was passing out drawings he had made of his friends. Mr. Hooper had been a friend of Big Bird and often made him birdseed milk shakes. Big Bird was excited to share his drawing with Mr. Hooper and headed toward Hooper's Store, but the *Sesame Street* adults called Big Bird back. We learned Mr. Hooper had died, but Big Bird did not understand and announced he would just wait for Mr. Hooper to come back. The adults explained: people don't come back after they die. Big Bird demanded to know why things had to be this way.

"Who is going to take care of the store?" Big Bird asked. "And who is going to make my bird seed milkshakes and tell me stories?"

The adults reassured Big Bird they would take care of everything and look after him, but Big Bird was still troubled. "Well, I don't understand!" Big Bird said. "You know, everything was just fine! I mean, why does it have to be this way? Give me one good reason!" No one had a ready answer at first, and then Gordon stepped up.

"Big Bird, it has to be this way. Because."

"Just because?"

"Just because."

Boy, had I ever come to hate that little non-answer. Was that really the best grownups had to offer? I looked down at my soggy cereal and wondered how they could feed such crap to poor Big Bird. It wasn't fair. Big Bird deserved a better answer than that.

So I sang Marie Osmond's "Paper Roses," hoping once again to hear my mother's voice join me in our special duet. The result was predictable.

❧

At my tiny suburban Catholic school, I suddenly stood out because everyone knew my mother had died. Kids would come up to me and say, "I heard about your mom."

"So?" I would reply. And that would be it. It may have been a lousy answer but it ended the conversation. What was there to say?

Nick and I had to figure out what our lives were supposed to look like. My father had to leave for work early each day so my brother slipped into the role of prodding parent. With Mom no longer there to help the two of us get ready in the morning, my brother and I fended for ourselves.

"Get up!" Nick would scream down the hall. "You gotta get ready for school!" But a powerful depression I had never known before took me in its grip. I would burrow further under the blankets.

"Get up, Nancy!"

I had never liked my name, and now it became a label I hated to wear. At the last second I would spring out of my bed, put on anything that came to hand, and race to the bus stop cursing the fact I had a first name I hated and a life I hated even more.

At school, I'd hear it again: "Nancy!" one of the nuns would call out at lunchtime. "It looks like you had quite a morning," she might say, taking in the ratted mop on top of my head and my mismatched clothes. "Did you bring lunch?" Invariably, the answer was no. "Let's go over to the convent," Sister Ann Francis would say. "I'll make you a peanut butter and jelly sandwich."

I knew I was pathetic. As soon as I finished my sandwich I would run to the playground. I wanted to crawl in a tire swing and die.

Why couldn't I die and be with Mom? Then I could be like one of the angels from the paintings in the convent—I had the long blonde hair. I practiced looking ethereal. Sometimes I imagined I was Christ—suffering with wise repose, misunderstood, beloved, and divine.

I watched burial scenes on TV with great interest and played Funeral with my dolls in the sand box. It didn't strike me as weird. I simply developed an interest in funeral play, the same way a boy might become obsessed with building a fort in the backyard.

"This is the dead one," I explained to my friend Kelley one afternoon. "Line up the cars for the procession while I dig the grave."

Kelley conscientiously lined up half a dozen toy cars. She was a good little worker.

"Okay, but we need more," I instructed.

"Why?"

"So the other dolls can see how many people came to pay their respects to her. Only six means not popular."

This would turn out to be good practice for when I was called upon to officiate at real funerals, although at the time it didn't seem like preparation for the future. It was merely my attempt to cope with the dreadful reality of the present.

A neighbor my age, Denice, had a tiny cat named Pinky that she carried with her everywhere. One day her father started his truck and realized, too late, that Pinky had been sleeping in the engine compartment. Denice placed what was left of Pinky in a box on the kitchen table and sent her brother to get me.

"I'm watching *CHiPs*," I said, by way of refusal.

"She needs you to give the cat a funeral."

Okay, that was different. I still hated to leave Officer Poncherello, but duty called. I got off the couch, grabbed a shovel from the garage, and headed to the neighbor's. When I got there, my friend Denice looked like her soul had been pulled out, stomped on, and replaced with a retread version.

Peeking into the cardboard coffin, I announced, "We need to find a proper burial space."

I scouted the grounds and then directed Denice's brother to dig a grave right in the middle of their mother's garden. "This is a pretty place to lay Pinky to rest," I said, now an authority. Denice agreed.

Pinky was lowered reverently into her shallow grave. I said a prayer or two of contrition and turned toward home, hoping to catch the end of *CHiPs*.

ɕ⁊

Since Dad was overextended by the duties of being both mother and father, I often directed my angst toward my brother and all the cool stuff he owned that was not "appropriate" for me. I compared my dumb Baby Beans and Silly Putty to my brother Nick's super grown-up Erector Set, fuming that he got all the best toys. The red metal box holding his Erector Set became my heart's desire. I started sneaking it out of the house so I could strut my stuff, while wearing a Bee Gees t-shirt and carrying that red box up and down the sidewalk of our cul-de-sac. I always hoped someone would ask what important stuff I was up to. No one ever asked.

The words on the side of the box were tantalizing. It read: "Choking Hazard—Small Parts. Not for children under 3 yrs." I swallowed a rubber pulley just to see if the warning was a bluff, washed it down with warm Fresca, and waited to wrap up the experiment. What if I died? They'd be sorry when they found my body. Big surprise, nothing happened.

Sometimes, though, Nick let me join him in playing with the Erector Set. We always ended up building a bridge. The bridge had no name, no destination or purpose; it was just a bridge on my brother's floor surrounded by sunshine yellow walls. We didn't care. We turned up our *Jaws* soundtrack and worked the girders and gears. Done for the day, I was ordered to "go away and leave it alone."

But he was out of luck with that. I was full of torment over our loss, so much that I was completely unable to appreciate that it was just as much Nick's loss as mine. Of course I snuck back in after he left for Boy Scouts or whatever, to give the bridge a slight adjustment. However, he never noticed, so what good was that?

One morning my brother was intensely contemplative at the breakfast table. I wondered, would this be the day the bridge would finally lead somewhere? We downed seconds of Post Super Sugar Smacks, and then Nick announced he had other plans for the day and I was not allowed in his room. Maybe he sensed that I was unfairly taking out my grief on him.

The grief, however, was not so easily thwarted. I resorted to sabotage, and hunted down Nick's GI Joe with the Kung Fu Grip. Joe's soft, pliable hand was perfectly formed for holding a pair of binoculars, or something fierce like a bayonet. I slipped a dainty, glittery Barbie clutch purse into Joe's grip. That would really cheese my brother's crackers. I sneaked into the garage and took sandpaper to the sleek Pinewood Derby car Nick had been working on with our father. With my Captain & Tennille LP on the phonograph, I spent the rest of the afternoon rearranging Chef Boyardee cans. I pulled them all out of the cupboards and grouped them under the sink for a better, more fulfilling placement.

Nick got home from Boy Scouts, flung open the cupboard, and the confusion on his face quickly turned to anger. I could hear him fuming. "Why do you feel the need to relocate my lunch?"

"Beefaroni, SpaghettiOs, and the Chef's Ravioli are best observed in a deep cabinet in long lines!" I called back.

If Nick went ahead and told on me, I'd wait until the next day to exact my revenge. Instead of a cupcake, I'd eat the Twinkies, because that was my brother's favorite choice in the Hostess Snack Pack.

But I also threw Nick's football around in the backyard in hopes he would notice.

❧

Grandpa, my dad's father, was a big help to us and to me. He waited at our house after school each day to watch us until Dad got home from work. One afternoon, Grandpa met me at the door and followed me into my bedroom.

"Nancy, what is this on your dresser?"

"It's a cemetery. See the gravestones?"

Grandpa nodded. "I see. You did a pretty good job."

"Thanks."

"What's it for?"

I shrugged and straightened a couple of the rock tombstones nervously. "I just liked it. I like making things." I knew I needed to do these things, but some deeper intuition kept me from wanting to look at the reasons with an important family member as my witness. Or maybe it was just the instincts of an ostrich compelling me to hide from my own reasons for these rituals.

"I see," Grandpa repeated. The concern in his voice sent up all kinds of red flags, but something in my behavior caused him to back away from the topic. "Do you want a cheese sandwich?" he finally asked.

"Yes!" I said, and shimmied out of there on the double. When the sandwich was ready and I came back in, we both pretended nothing happened.

Sometimes we would go to Grandpa's house on Saturdays. Nick occupied himself playing with his muscle-bound friend, Stretch Armstrong, or hung out with neighbor boys. I followed Grandpa around, helping him with household chores. He showed me how to replace washers in the kitchen sink faucet and how to tighten loose drawer handles. Sometimes he asked me to sew a button on one of his church shirts, because his big hands made threading the little needle frustrating. I whiled away time going through his "junk drawers," which he had a lot of. They were crammed with jumbled odds and ends, small tools, keys that no longer fit any lock, bits of string, old stamps, and the occasional black and white snapshot of people he couldn't remember. Then I'd organize the cans in his cupboards, grouping them by type and lining them up according to their expiration dates.

"You were born with a gift for arranging canned goods," Grandpa remarked one day. I beamed.

Grandpa had pictures of my father and my mother on his walls. My father was an only child, so Grandma and Grandpa fully accepted my mom as their daughter. In her high school graduation picture, she looked perfect. Her complexion was flawless, and not a hair was out of place. Grandpa once explained it was a black and white photograph that had been painted to add color. Her beauty was tantalizing. I could not walk into the living room without looking at that picture. When I was alone, I gazed at it until I was on the verge of breaking down in tears, then I would run away.

I wanted to ask Grandpa if he was sad his wife was dead, but I didn't have the guts.

Then Grandpa died, too. That weekend he was buried next to Grandma in the pristinely-kept grounds of St. Anthony Catholic Cemetery two rows from my mom. During the graveside service, I couldn't keep my mind on what Father Vince was saying. I looked around at the neatly-ordered head-stones and thought how weird it was we were leaving him in such a tidy, tightly-shorn place. *What did all this orderliness have to do with my grandpa of the delightfully messy junk drawers?*

"Why was Grandpa buried there?" I asked on the way home.

"To be next to your grandmother," Dad replied.

"Why did she pick that place?"

"It's where most of the burials from our church are done."

"Why?"

"Nancy!"

"It's so phony," I muttered.

☙

Eventually, at the age of ten, I was sent to a grief counselor—not so much because of my strange obsession with death or my juvenile harassment of my brother—but because my father was dating. He felt we needed a mother. I wasn't having it. When he prepared for a date I would come down sick, going so far as making myself throw up if that's what it took to keep Dad home. I demanded his help with every single homework exercise and threw gargantuan fits if he didn't give me his full attention. I went out of my way to act outrageously as often as possible, including at the counselor's office.

The sessions were filmed so specialists could watch them and assess how I was doing. My father could see me through a TV link. Three weeks into the sessions, the therapist left the room, probably to discuss something with my father. I suddenly thought it would be a good idea to pull down my pants and dance.

The therapist burst back into the room, told me to pull up my britches, and sent me to rejoin my father. At ten years old, I had to watch myself strip tease with my father and the grief counselors. Why had I done this? I had no idea.

"Because," I said.

"Because why?" one of the counselors pressed.

"Just because," I insisted, trying to think of something to say that would appease them—sure that if I said anything, the great cinder block of shame and sorrow in my chest would split, expand, and blow us all up.

My father and I were silent all the way home to our house in suburban Portland. We went inside and life went on. Just because.

Chapter 2

Dance of the Not Dead

I CONTINUED TO MARCH TO THE BEAT OF MY OWN HERKY-JERKY, mournful drum. I had been unsuccessful at preventing my father's remarriage, which ticked me off. I hated how everyone acted like it was all fine when it was obviously so bogus.

"How can you stand this new family?" I asked my brother.

He shrugged and said, "It's not *that* bad."

"I hate it!"

"Why don't you try giving us all a break?"

"For what?"

Publicly, I did my best to act like my step-mother and this new marriage didn't exist. Privately, I was just confused about everything and wanted to be left alone.

I delayed my return home from school as long as possible. Fortunately, there were a ton of kids in our neighborhood. We rode bikes and played until the street lights came on, which was the universal signal for suburban children of our era to go home. On rainy days, the girls would hole up in somebody's bedroom and pour through issues of *Tiger Beat*. Leif Garrett was beating out Shawn Cassidy for heartthrob of the moment, but I was steadfast in my loyalty to my hunka' hunka' burnin' love, Erik Estrada.

"He's all right," my friends would say dismissively, "but Leif is way better looking."

"*Whatever*." I refused to let on that stung. Did it matter if other girls didn't approve of your choice of boyfriend?

"You're so weird sometimes."

"You're not so cool yourself!"

"At least I don't play with dolls that are always dying, dork." God, I hardly even did that anymore!

"I'm not a dork, you're a dork!"

"See ya later, alligator."

"I didn't want to hang out with you guys anyway!"

If only Frank Poncherello would knock on the door that very minute looking for me. Who would be the dork then? I knew my mother would approve.

When I didn't want to go home and couldn't go back to a friend's house, I rode my bike to a cemetery some ways down the road. It was quiet there. The dead make few demands and the living tend to leave you alone in a cemetery, under the assumption you are there on solemn business with the dearly departed.

Sometimes, I would seek out quaint markers—one with a carved lamb, or angels, preferably. I'd make up elaborate stories of grief, starring myself in an invisible black veil. I carried a linen handkerchief that once belonged to my mother so I could dab the tears from my eyes. I practiced looking picturesque in grief.

Or I would pretend to be a private investigator, hot on the trail of a murderer, sussing out clues amongst the tombs. I dearly wanted to gain entry to an actual mausoleum.

Occasionally I would try talking to the dead. Since we didn't live close enough to where my mother was buried for me to visit on after-school forays, I reached out to someone who might be able to carry a message to her. When I came upon that grave, the person who seemed like he or she might be sympathetic to the concerns of a motherless daughter, I respectfully asked them to tell Mom to try to reach me. "She could just send me a sign," I suggested. "Any sign will do."

For days afterward I'd watch for anything that might be a message from beyond the grave, but like Bess Houdini, I eventually gave up waiting for my dead love to speak to me.

One Saturday, my neighbor saw me at the cemetery. It turned out her parents were buried there. When I arrived home for supper, my dad made inquiries. "What were you doing at the cemetery today, Nancy?"

Would it have killed the neighbor to keep it to herself?

"Just hanging around," I told my dad.

"Why weren't you playing with the other kids?"

I shrugged. Like I was going to tell my dad other kids thought I was a freak. Besides, I could tell he already thought I was kind of weird.

"Oh, Nancy," Dad said, looking sad again.

Nick walked in and immediately knew something was up. "What's going on?" he asked.

"Nothing," Dad said. "Let's eat. Pasta's ready."

ℭ

On September 13, 1980, *Solid Gold* made its television debut, giving me a new daydream to chase.

Every week the show served up audio clips of the Top 10 songs of the week. It was hosted by people like Dionne Warwick, Rick Dees, and Liberace-ish Wayland Flowers with his puppet, Madame—an outrageous old broad who spouted double entendres and witty comebacks.

Musical tracks were augmented by choreographed routines that were pure '80s excess and Jazzercise moves. I loved the *Solid Gold* dancers. I was smitten with their sleek look, attitudes, and headbands. I wanted to look like that and dance like that. I loved to shake what my momma gave me—still do.

As long as I can remember, I was always dancing around the house. Mom and I were fans of *Donny & Marie*, so I always got up and danced when they came on TV. My mother would be lying on the couch because she was always sick, but my dancing would make her smile. I danced my heart out for her.

One time, I shook, shook, shook my booty and Mom's smile disappeared for a moment.

"Good girls don't do that, Nancy," she warned.

What! It seemed so natural to move my butt when I was dancing. Why not?

I tried not to do that move any more, but it was hard.

My formal dance training in tap, jazz, and ballet started at age four. Dance class was super fun because I had a natural talent for it. When the music started, most of the girls hung back, uncertain. Not me; I pushed to the front, eager to perform. Having practiced all week, I could execute every move with confidence.

After Mom died, I danced for anyone I could press into watching. Our garage was the scene of many an elaborate performance. I always hoped to be discovered, so up went the garage doors on Saturday, Captain & Tennille blasting, and goofy me dancing for the people and dogs passing by. Whenever I danced, I imagined my mother watching and smiling at me from some celestial balcony. Surely, she would be proud of me if I became a *Solid Gold* dancer, right? I studied their choreography carefully, trying to decide whether or not they kept their butts within the good girl boundaries. If I was going to be damned, I would at least be damned on the *Solid Gold* center stage. So worth it, and Mom would understand.

☙

Despite my dreams of glittery fame, my preoccupation with death continued. I scoured *National Geographic* articles about death rituals in other cultures. Pyres seemed interesting: imagine going up in a dramatic wall of flame! That's an attention getter.

Once I could drive, I went to funerals of people I didn't know—like in *Harold and Maude*. First I went to a nearby mortuary, but eventually I branched out across Portland's metropolitan area. Saturdays often found me lurking around a back pew dressed in black. I knew all the classic dirges by heart and sometimes found myself unguardedly humming "Blessed Assurance" or "Just a Closer Walk with Thee." The Protestants really have it going on when it comes to funeral hymns.

Other people's funerals were comforting, to a degree, but often left me dissatisfied. Obviously, I am fond of processions, but compared to some of the customs I had read about, the generic American funeral seemed sterile. Detached even; the body in a box wearing Sunday-go-to-meetin' clothes. Service was recited, eulogy delivered, and then we walked past the casket off to the church annex for ham sandwiches and deviled eggs. Where were the age-old rituals that prepared the bodies of the recently deceased for their journey to the afterlife? I missed keening or lamentations. We were just expected to sit there politely and passively while the professionals handled it. It wasn't working for me.

It's not that people weren't grieving. You could see the desolation of the nearest and dearest, the sadness of close friends, and discomfort of co-workers. They hurt, plainly, but they were lost and at loose ends and there was no solace for them. It was like watching Big Bird learn Mr. Hooper had died. Not fair; they deserved something better than that. I wanted to provide a better emotional setting/ritual for mourners but, at my young age, didn't quite know how to do this. Maybe get up and say something thought-provoking about the decedent? About the beauty in the circle of life and death?

I left one stranger's service stewing over these thoughts and failed to make my escape before being noticed. My escape through the vestibule was interrupted by a tiny, ancient woman in a shiny black suit. "How did you know Magda, sweetie?" she asked.

"Uh, from the church?" Actually true, I had met Magda at the church just an hour ago. She was the lady lying in the coffin, after all!

"That's nice you came," my gentle interrogator said, patting my arm. "You're a good girl."

I blinked hard to keep from crying, nodded and fled. After that, I spent less time at the funerals of strangers; but as graduation approached, I began talking about a career in funerary services.

"I thought you were going to be a *Solid Gold* dancer," Nick teased.

"Mortician is not a good job for you, honey," Dad warned. "You think it sounds like a good idea now, but you're young and you'll probably change your mind."

When I insisted I knew what I wanted, he upped the ante, "You'll never get a date, because it's strange!"

"Lots of funeral directors are married," I replied. Were they? I wanted to get married. Someday . . .

"Funeral directors probably marry other funeral directors," my friend Denice said the next day. Seeing the look on my face, she added, "I mean, it is a little scary, but you're cute. You'll get dates."

☙

To ease Dad's concerns, I majored in communications in college. Secretly, I watched the newspaper classifieds for opportunities at a local mortuary.

Until something opened up I did odd jobs, occasional voiceover work or radio gigs.

One day I spied a listing in *The Oregonian* for a dance instructor job at Arthur Murray Dance Studios in Beaverton.

"That job will be mine!"

Although I had no ballroom experience, I knew I had excellent rhythm, timing, movement, and execution. I'd learn the rest as I went along.

I spent most of the morning staring at my closet. What would a ballroom dancer wear to interview for a teaching job? I channeled Debbie Allen from *Fame* and chose a simple top and flowing skirt with the nearest thing I had to dance heels. I realized my costume was just a coif and rosary shy of a nun's habit and switched to a more figure-skimming long-sleeved black top with a ballerina neckline. Better, but still too sober.

"I can do this," I whispered to myself. I thought of my mother. She never would have had this problem. She always knew how to make clothes work for her. Not for the first time, I wished I could call her for advice.

I tried to remember how Mom approached assembling an outfit. I'd sit on her bed, watching her dress. In my mind's eye, Mom slipped into one of her simple, well-cut outfits, then went to her dresser and sorted through her jewelry and scarves to find just the right combination for the occasion before her.

"Accessories," I said aloud. "I need something with a little sparkle."

On the back of a closet shelf was my childhood pink jewelry box. It contained some of my mother's jewelry. I retrieved the box and found Mother's rhinestone bangles and a crystal choker just long enough to skim across my collarbones without overlapping the neckline.

Perfect. Fabulous!

"Thanks, Mom," I whispered to the mirror. I was bedazzled!

The dance studio was on my side of town, only ten or twelve minutes away. I dashed out of the house.

I walked through the door and was greeted with a huge smile. I hadn't filled out the application yet, but I knew I had the job. I introduced myself as *Elizabeth*. I had been toying with the idea of starting to use my middle name, so I threw it out to see how it stuck. The applicants were led to a small room to learn basic waltz and foxtrot steps. I could already do a box step like nobody's business—I was hired. A dancer named Elizabeth was born.

"A dance instructor," my father mused, "what do you have to do to become a dance instructor?"

"In my case, dance the waltz, foxtrot, and swing for an hour," I explained.

"Well, it's a start," Dad said, and for once he didn't look worried about me.

"Oh, so you are going to be a *Solid Gold* dancer one day after all," Nick teased me when he heard the news.

I scowled. *Solid Gold* had been off the air for a couple of years and he knew it.

"Well, congratulations there, *Elizabeth,*" Nick laughed, popping the top on a Moosehead Pale Ale. "For a minute there, I thought you were going to end up as the Morticia Addams of the Pacific Northwest."

I scowled harder.

I liked Morticia; she was musically inclined and fiercely loyal to her family.

Chapter 3

My First Funerary Forays: Living in a Cemetery Shotgun Shack

I COULD HAVE HAPPILY GONE ON DANCING *La Vida* TRADITIONAL-Professional forever had Opportunity not knocked upon my door with a bony, welcome hand. I was at the Pi Kappa Phi Beach Bash party when I learned a local cemetery desperately needed a night keeper. I looked at the cute boys in tank tops and surfer shorts, drinking beer from red cups, and despite the charm of it all, I took off. My first death job was waiting!

I chucked my pukka shell necklace and flip flops in the corner of my room, threw on a new pink suit in record time, and drove forty-five minutes to interview for night keeper at one of the most prestigious cemeteries in the city, Dyrland's Memorial Gardens.

Getting hired meant living alone in a cemetery. Sounds scary, doesn't it? Well, it was, but not for the reasons you might expect. I didn't have a problem with the deceased; it was the living that terrified me. High school kids would hop the cemetery gate to get dead-drunk. It was my job as gatekeeper to get them in the hearse and haul them out. Really blotto fellas liked to sneak back and peek into my trailer window while I slept. It was a massive un-perk of the job, both personally and professionally.

My solution? I slept with a shotgun under my bed.

Evenings were consumed by funerary duties: answering the phone, washing the hearse, emptying garbage cans. My days were about waiting in my stifling cemetery trailer at the end of the property, hoping to get thrown some extra scratch for being sent on a job-related mission.

Very little liveliness, charm, or surprise to my life that summer. I could walk the grassy graves barefoot and look at names for a half hour, or drive my Jeep to the far back, undeveloped area. I'd emerge and roll my body down a long hill like a five-year-old. I'd get up quickly to look around and make sure no graveyard employee could see me. After all that excitement, I'd return to the hot toaster-oven trailer to see if I missed a call from the office.

My living shack was about two hundred feet from the office. It was separated by a long drive that was super creepy at night, behind a row of even creepier tall shrubs. Occasionally, I would leave night shift headquarters to refill my Super Big Gulp, or head to the local library for a thick stack of magazines since I spent so much time alone.

One hot day, I stretched out in my bright pink swimsuit with a chilled soda close by, sunscreen applied, and a ukulele tuned. I couldn't play much on it, but I was able to pull off something close to an E chord and an A-flat minor. With only one chord or note, I managed to pluck out something that sounded, remotely, like "Love and Happiness" by Al Green.

Very remotely like Al Green. I stunk at ukulele, but a girl outside a cemetery trailer in the dead heat of summer does avoid complainers. I could plainly see how unmusical I was, but fate decided to put my lack of talent to the true test—an audience!

Richard, the funeral director who had the misfortune of working that weekend, rang me up that same afternoon. "There's a funeral in the chapel and somebody needs to step up, *pronto,*" he blurted out.

"What's up?" I asked.

"The soloist is a no-show and the family is getting itchy. Put on some clothes and get down here; I need you to sing something before they start to riot."

"Sure thing! I'm your gal!"

I entered the back of the chapel without a clue of what to do. A man spoke at the microphone, there was silence, then Richard gave me my cue. I gingerly walked up the aisle to the familiar opening of "Wind Beneath My Wings."

I couldn't concentrate on the notes; I had to make sure I got the words right, not to mention the melody. To help me focus, I kept my eyes on a woman's ugly hat, mid-row on the left. My vocal stylings were over before they began. I made the mistake of looking at the audience and caught expressions of horror. I nailed it, but not in a good way, and my awfulness was reflected in their faces. I finished up, gave Richard a huge, toothy grin, and scooted out of there before they could start throwing tomatoes.

The next time I saw Richard, his feedback was brief: "You suck."

"Singing at a funeral is hard!" I whined. "Everybody's so emotional."

"What did you have to be emotional about?" Richard demanded. "You didn't know the deceased."

"Look, I'm just some poor schlub who happened to be living in the trailer at a cemetery, minding my own business, until you begged for a favor. Did you honestly think you were getting Elton John under those circumstances?"

"Wise-ass," Richard snapped. "Here's a tip, kid. You can be a funeral director without knowing how to sing a note. I sound like Yoko Ono when I sing, so I don't, but you're musical. Practice a few hymns to have something on tap next time the soloist flakes."

Holy crap! Richard thought I had it in me to be a funeral director! Did you hear that, Mom?

ɛɔ

Some nights the phone rang. Usually it was a crank: "I'm locked inside the cemetery and I need you to get me out" was a big favorite. Yawn.

Other times it was a bereaved family member. "My brother is there and I need to know he is all right," one woman cried. I could spend an hour on the phone with people, trying to bring them some comfort. But grief is messy, and I wasn't always up to the job.

"Why does my little girl have to be behind a locked gate all night?" one inconsolable mother asked me.

"I'm sorry," I replied. "We have to lock the gates to prevent vandalism."

"I get so lonely for her at night. It feels like I can't go to sleep because I haven't hugged her good night. Why do we have to bury people off somewhere away from us like we're trying to get rid of them?"

"Well, because . . ." I had nothing. Just because.

The heartbroken mom on the other end of the line confessed, "I feel like I'm failing her."

I could relate.

After we hung up, I walked over to the grave of the little girl who had been interred earlier that week. My poor dad, I thought. He had done his best when I'd asked this tough question of him. I wondered if he had felt as empty and angry with himself that day Mom died as I had on that phone call. I had given this mother the same worthless answer I'd received years earlier.

"Mom?" I whispered. "I'm sorry I am so troubling for Dad. I'll make it up to him, I promise, no matter what." I cried all the way back to my trailer. I hadn't told my dad about the cemetery job—or that I was considering mortuary school—so I mixed that into my guilt stew to make it a long night in my hot trailer.

☙

I called my dad in the morning and offered to treat him to lunch at Greenway Pub. "What's the news, Nancy? Or I should say, *Elizabeth*?" he asked. Geez, what was with my dad having a sixth sense all of a sudden?

"Nothing," I lied. "I miss you."

"Well, I can't turn that down, can I?" he replied.

At the restaurant, I played it cool until Dad had a little cheese fondue in him.

"Are you dating anyone these days?" he asked. Oh sure, with my schedule?

"Mmm . . . a little," I said. "There's nobody special." That was true.

When the time was right, I took a deep breath and plunged in. "Dad, there is something I want to talk to you about."

"I figured," Dad said, sopping up some beef sauce with the end of his French Dip.

"You know how I talked before about being a funeral director?"

Dad put his sandwich down and sat back.

"I got a gig with Dyrland's Memorial Gardens this summer."

Dad brightened. "Oh, you mean like that commercial you did for the oil change place?"

"Not exactly," I said.

"What then?"

"It's helping out at one of the big cemeteries, you know, just to try it."

"Like answering the phones?"

"No."

"Elizabeth," Dad said with a sigh. "Why don't you cut to the chase before these sandwiches mold?"

"It's no big deal, I'm just the night gatekeeper at Dyrland's, but I'm kind of thinking of looking into getting licensed."

"What does a night gatekeeper do?"

"Mostly run drunken kids out of the place."

"And you like this?"

"No, but I like helping people, and I think I would like being a funeral director."

"I thought you liked being a dance instructor."

"I do, but it's different."

"Tell me about that," Dad inquired.

"I don't know what to say, except I feel more like myself when I do this work. I feel like I'm where I'm supposed be. I know you're worried about me, but I swear I can do this."

There was a long pause. Finally, Dad said, "If this is what makes you happy, Elizabeth, try it. All I've ever wanted is for you to feel right."

A warm rush of love ran over me. Somehow, awkwardly, I made my way around the end of the table and wrapped my arms around his neck. "Thanks, Dad," I said.

He hugged me back and patted my shoulder, which probably meant he was concerned I would cry. "Would it have done me any good to try to talk you out of it?"

"Probably not," I admitted with a sheepish grin.

"I didn't figure. Eat your West African Chicken Peanut Soup, whatever that is. It's getting cold."

☙

When I got back to the memorial gardens, I hunted down Richard and asked him what I would have to do to pass the state licensing boards and become an actual funeral director.

"Write twenty obituaries, parallel-park a hearse, and run a hundred-yard dash pushing a casket," he quipped.

"Wise-ass!" I called to his retreating back. Maybe my local librarian could help me.

Sure enough, the library had a book. Just one: *The History of Funeral Directing*. The pictures were more interesting than the dry descriptions, but I plowed through, searching for golden nuggets of information that would unlock the secrets to my funereal career. What did I need to know? I brainstormed a list: *Funeral home ethics, general principles as they related to customs, religions, human relations, and social behavior. Requirements for burial and cremation, of course. Anatomical donation process? Sure. Would I need to know how to do a burial at sea or did the captain do that on days he didn't have to perform a marriage or steer clear of an iceberg?* My list looked tidy but daunting.

In the interest of being thorough, I called the Oregon Mortuary and Cemetery Board. Alas, I couldn't take the test until I had a degree, and there was a year-long apprenticeship I had to complete before I could be licensed. Embalming licensure required graduation from a mortuary sciences program, the road traveled by most aspiring undertakers. I was a senior at a prestigious private college. Pumping dead bodies full of formaldehyde didn't seem like the kind of thing one could learn through a correspondence course, though. Did I want to embalm people?

I learned that modern embalming in the US got its start during the Civil War but wasn't popular with the general public until the 20th century. Before that, the dead were bathed and dressed, placed in the coolest room in the house for visitation, and buried quickly. Eventually, morticians took over the care of the dead; the new, national railroad system meant extended family and friends could travel to funerals, if the body was preserved for several days. This gave rise to what most of us now think of as a "traditional" funeral.

During the second half of the century, the environmental movement picked up steam. More people questioned the wisdom of using so much land to bury people and opted for cremation. The environmental impact did concern me, but I loved cemeteries. Where would the living go to visit their dead if cemeteries disappeared? What if one of my great-great-grandchildren was an odd little girl who needed to escape the living every now and then? Where would she go?

To embalm or not to embalm?

I ran the question by Richard, who was his usual cheery self: "That's a great idea. We'll stop embalming and let Grandma leak all over the carpet."

"We didn't used to embalm the dead," I reasoned.

"Right, we could go back to filling the room with flowers and holding perfumed hankies over our noses. That would be great, and it ought to be a real gas watching the children scream and flee the visitation rooms."

"Maybe we should bury people faster, like they did in the olden days."

"Maybe we should perform the service people want us to perform, so people can have a memory picture of the dead to give them solace in their grief." That sounded reasonable. "Elizabeth," Richard continued, "you need to understand that people don't want to look at the dead. Families are grieving. We have a responsibility to present the remains in a way they can handle."

"Okay, okay," I said. "I'll check out mortuary school."

I turned in my trailer key at the end of my summer cemetery gig and headed south to the Harvard of Funeral Education.

Chapter 4

Education of a Young Mortician and the Moon Maidens

S AN FRANCISCO COLLEGE OF MORTUARY SCIENCE WAS IMPRESSIVE. Considered the best in the country, it stood in a yellow, Romanesque building on the corner of Dolores and 29th streets. I was rather impressive the day I toured it, as well, but not in quite the same way.

Decked out in a pink sundress and white high-heeled sandals, my long hair flowing down my back, I felt pretty grand. The large wooden door required some force to open, so I gave it a strong pull and entered, then tripped. My sandal caught under the metal flashing of the door and caused me to lunge forward. A distinguished-looking older gentleman, who was in the best possible place at a most embarrassing moment, caught me. Turned out, he didn't only look distinguished, he *was* distinguished. I had fallen into the arms of Donald Dimond, the school's esteemed President.

Mr. Dimond helped me right myself and seemed pleased I was there, despite how I burst on to the scene. I thought perhaps he appreciated the diversity I would bring to the school—I wasn't "one of the boys." The students wore business attire, to reinforce the notion they were attending class in a functioning mortuary. A bereaved client might round the corner at any time. If I could have gotten away with it, I would have dressed like Marilyn Monroe every day of the week.

Mr. Dimond asked me for my complete funeral work and education summary. My recent summer job was all I had to show for myself, but he seemed satisfied I was there for the right reasons. Laura was summoned to conduct my tour. Laura had one ear. The right side of her head had gotten lopped off somehow. I didn't want to stare, but I was fascinated.

We started down the hallway and I walked a few paces behind her, still staring at the right side of her head. Was she born that way? Did an accident happen? Did this accident happen here at mortuary school?

Laura took me past pictures of former students, all white males. "Most students in the school are apprentices at funeral homes in the city and live above them. There are about seventy-five to eighty students every year. Tuition here is ten thousand dollars for a full-year curriculum that includes classes on anatomy and pathology, as well as accounting and marketing. The associate in arts degree in funeral directing and embalming can take from twelve months to sixteen months to complete, depending upon a student's previous academic record."

When she glanced at me, I made total and focused eye contact with her so she wouldn't catch me staring at other parts of her head; missing parts that obsessed me. She was clueless, thank God.

"This is the anatomy lab. In this course, the student will be expected to dissect and identify the major anterior and posterior muscles, blood vessels, and nerves. It's really an introduction to basic human anatomy, with special emphasis upon cells, tissues, organs, the skeletal system and its articulations, as well as various definitional terms. Did you take anatomy in college?"

"Nope. I'm a Mass Communications student." She was *this* close to catching me.

At the Restorative Art Laboratory, Laura explained the practical lab application of the principles learned in Restorative Art I and II. Students apply modeling techniques to reproduce, in clay, the four features of the human face: ear, nose, mouth, and eye. Ironically, Laura was the top student in this class.

"That is where we do the reconstructive pieces after the basic procedures." Laura explained. "Students come here without basic skills, such as how to set features. They must learn the art of using perforated caps under the eyelid to grip the skin and hold it in place; next the mouth is wired shut so the jaw won't go slack. So many don't know how to glue lips together or fix the corners into an expression of serenity. They have no idea how to fill wounds with a putty-like compound."

Suddenly I was glad I hadn't stopped for a cheeseburger on the way to the school.

I wanted to ask questions, but I couldn't get over my fascination with Laura's disfigurement. Did she sense my inappropriate interest?

Laura blithely continued, "Students here are seriously exposed to the extremes of the trade. The school always needs corpses, and often that means taking weeks-old bodies that have been abandoned and mangled by advanced decomposition. We are proud of our low-income service program. About two hundred bodies pass through the school's downstairs mortuary each year at a cost to their kin of about five hundred dollars each."

I decided to grow up and let go of my ear mania. I said, "I hear they call the San Francisco College of Mortuary Science the 'Ivy League for Death.'" She smiled smugly.

We walked to the very end of the building, to a vast chapel that had the stale quality of an old ballroom. It was awash with the light from Hollywood-Moorish electric candelabras. It was lovely; I had a sudden urge to waltz. Pews that were originally designed to accommodate the packed houses at longshoremen's funerals stretched on and on. The chapel could seat more than four hundred.

"There is something else we are really proud of," Laura said. "Our application fee is only twenty-five bucks."

I was dying to be in the death industry, and obviously it was a great school—an institution that would go down in history—but the thought of starting over when I was so close to my degree left me cold.

Nick always did things the right way, so I swallowed my pride and called him for advice.

"I catch your fantasy to be the ersatz ferrywoman for those crossing over the River Styx, Morticia," my brother said, "but if you want my opinion, no, I don't think you should interrupt your current education to start something else. Finish your degree at Linfield and if you still want to go to mortuary school, you still can, but if you change your mind you haven't lost anything."

"Well, if you want to be sensible about it . . ." I mused aloud.

"What have you got against being sensible?" Nick asked. "Too bourgeois?"

"What! No. You're just jealous because some of us have an imagination," I shot back.

"I have an imagination. I'm imagining you as a famous—or infamous—funeral director who wears glittery headbands and dances to Elton John songs before the eulogy."

"Don't be an ass!"

"Oh, oh, or you could do 'Knockin' on Heaven's Door'; can you dance to that?"

"Stop!"

"'I've Got Friends in Low Places.' Now that would be hilarious!"

"I'm hanging up now, Nick."

☙

After my hermity—not counting the dead—hot trailer summer, it was good to be back among the very alive at college. I found a "Roommate Wanted" ad on the bulletin board in the student lounge and arranged to meet "Willow" to see if she could stand to cohabitate with me.

The rental was a mother-in-law house in somebody's back yard. Willow met me at the door wearing a hemp dress and smoking a clove cigarette. She was an anthropology student who had recently returned from a summer fighting deforestation in Ecuador. Her living quarters were draped and layered with colorful fabric, rugs, and tapestries. Plants cascaded off bookshelves, and tiny white Christmas lights crisscrossed the ceiling. It was the polar opposite from the stark and stinky cemetery trailer; I wanted to live there immediately.

Willow cleared a cat and a couple of throw pillows off a denim-covered sofa and invited me to sit down. "Would you like some rose hip tea?" she offered. "It's excellent for boosting your immune system."

"I would!" I said, as if I was not an inveterate soda addict.

She brought our tea on a round wooden tray that had been decoupaged with exotically-patterned paper and cut-out elephants. She was barefoot and wore a silver toe-ring with a tiny turquoise bead hanging off it. I cursed my stilettos and hoped she would like me anyway.

"You're a student at Linfield?" Willow asked.

"Yes, Mass Communications and Broadcasting," I said. Did that sound shallow? "I think I'm getting a volunteer gig at KBOO this semester," I added. KBOO-FM is Portland's ultra-progressive community radio station.

Willow beamed. "What are your plans after graduation?" she asked.

"To become a mortician," I blurted out without thinking.

A tiny crinkle appeared in Willow's forehead. "Really? Are you aware the funeral industry pumps hundreds of gallons of toxic chemicals into dead bodies every year? Chemicals that will eventually leech into the environment?"

"Well, I'm not sure I'm going to become an embalmer," I said. "It's not required to help people."

"In Ecuador, people are traditionally buried the next day. They don't embalm," Willow said with a hint of superiority in her voice.

"I think that's the better way," I replied, somewhat apologetically.

Willow brightened and continued, "The body is driven around the streets of the neighborhood, then taken to a viewing house for a wake. The family stays with the body, and friends come. There is music and everybody wails to show their grief. The next day the casket is placed in a type of mausoleum called a *boveda*, spiritual places where you can communicate with the dead. Ecuadorians aren't as inhibited about their dead as we are."

"Actually," I said, "I think that sounds beautiful."

"You do?"

"When my mom died, I would have liked to be with her all night and dance for her."

"Your mom died?"

I nodded. "When I was eight."

"Oh, you poor thing," Willow cooed. Suddenly she was all compassion and second helpings of rose hip tea. I let her minister to me and hoped her sympathy would smooth my way to a move in. To seal the deal, I organized a couple of her chaotic cupboards before I left and promised to finish the rest after I moved in.

"You certainly do bestow a harmonious aura upon canned goods," Willow observed when she saw my handiwork. "I get the distinct feeling you were the town merchant in a previous life."

☙

My days became vivid again, despite the Oregon drizzle. School and my volunteer gig at the radio station kept me busy, and for the first time ever, there were friends at the house. Growing up, I rarely invited people over; my mother was sick, of course, and after Dad remarried, I didn't want anyone over. Willow was very social and had a large circle of friends who were in and out at all hours, spending the night if we stayed up too long talking. I was grooving on the abundant female energy.

One Friday night, the house was full of Earth Mamas, and somebody asked Willow's friend Tabitha if she and her housemates had synced yet. "What does that mean, synced?" I asked.

"We live cooperatively in rhythm with the cycles of the moon to restore harmony in our bodies and lives. This synchronizes our moon flows, which helps us manage our communal energy."

"Moon flows?"

Tabitha looked at me with a knowing smile. "It has been shown that calendar consciousness developed first in women, because their natural body rhythms corresponded to observations of the moon. The great Maya calendar was based on menstrual cycles. To bleed together on the new moon and ovulate during the full moon—it's perfectly in tune with the women in our community." Her voice was so gentle I felt mesmerized.

Something must have been working for them because all of them were naturally quite sexy and full of wisdom. I tagged along with Willow on a visit to the home of the lovely ladies.

A mural painted on the side of their big old house read: "Musical Maidens of the Moon." The goddesses spent a lot of time sitting cross-legged in a circle on braided rugs and making mind-blowing hippie, sand-art jewelry. They sold it from booths at cool festivals, wore it to their yoga classes, and hung it around the house in accordance with their collective artistic energy.

They took frequent moonlit walks and ate local foods.

I had only heard women talk about their periods with disdain: *I'm on the rag, Aunt Flow came to visit,* and *I'm riding the crimson pony.* My own period had been a traumatic surprise, followed by an unwelcome explanation and a supply of maxi pads from Sister Ann Francis. These Pacific Northwest divinities were a coven of bloody wonder. They lived a romantic astrology of womanhood made divine. I wanted to learn their secret.

One special evening was supposed to start with a drum circle, but Petra's djembe had some issue so we were all just sitting around. I seized the moment to ask Tabitha how syncing worked.

"We start by spending nearly every day and most weekends together but to complete, syncing requires swallowing the moon energy in full force."

They faced the moon when it was rising and gently breathed in the lunar energy. That was followed by a barefoot chant repeated twenty-nine times, the number of days in a lunar cycle.

Raven heard us talking and drifted over. Raven was a strong-willed, persistent woman who spoke her mind incessantly and held herself out to be the leader of the bloody babes. She was a Cancer, the sign ruled by the moon.

She gave us the moon/sync story: Moon flows have been tied to the moon and the lunar cycle for thousands of years. Before the age of hormones, it was generally accepted that a woman's periods followed the lunar cycle. After all, the moon controls the ocean; why not women's bodies?

"The dark new moon is the perfect backdrop to support our going inward and attending to the needs of our soul. You are obviously out of sync with our natural rhythm."

Her statement dismayed and challenged me. I was determined to prove to them that I, too, could establish a bleeding rhythm that matched the energy of their environment. I would show them I was powerful and mystical enough to take in the moon energy and become a Musical Maiden of the Moon.

I left and rode my bike to the closest bookstore on Hawthorne Boulevard to get an action plan together. I sat in the aisle with my ankle bells and a half-eaten spinach feta pocket I had grabbed from the co-op next door. I focused on memorizing the chapter called "Attuning to the Natural Forces: Harmonize our Body with Nature's Cycles."

That night when the sun set and the moon was bright, I stated my intention out loud. I wanted to bleed during the new moon and ovulate at the full moon. I walked barefoot in my backyard for about an hour and focused my energies on that statement. I said it loudly and clearly, but not too loudly because my duplex-mates in a neighboring kitchen kept looking at me, thinking I was trying to raid their garden.

For many a moonlit night, I met the moon at that very spot and resumed my intention-setting. I promised to create a Moon Lodge with women friends, to create a sacred space together on the new moon, possibly my backyard. I swore I would avoid foods that contained endocrine disruptors such as growth hormones, or food packaged in plastic or BPA cans. Even my beloved Super Big Gulp refills might disappear if I was granted the supreme gift of becoming a Musical Maiden of the Moon.

In three months' time my power cycle kicked into the flow gear. I talked to the moon, letting the light into my womb. I slept in a completely dark room and got up daily at six a.m. I sat under the sun and let the warm and gentle morning sunlight caress me while I had my spirulina breakfast smoothie.

When I was sure I had synced, I slipped on my Birkenstocks and walked the holy path to the house of the Moon Maidens to share my news. The first tip that something was amiss was the smear of white paint over the "Musical Maidens of the Moon" sign. No one answered when I knocked and through the porch window, I saw an empty room devoid of grain sack upholstered chairs, beeswax candles, and wild tapestries. Where had all the dried flowers gone?

Weeks later at the Food Co-op, after some minor shelf-straightening of organic beans, I ran into Raven. She saw me as she loaded a large jar of soy powder into her bicycle basket. I asked her what was up with the Maidens and the house.

"We broke up," she said and then, without another word, glumly pedaled off to Qigong practice in her loose-fitting batik clothing.

Oh well, I thought, pretending not to be disillusioned. It's Winter Solstice. A new year and a fresh slate and I wonder if any of the mortuaries are looking for an apprentice yet.

Chapter 5

Babe in the Woods without a Drum

THE LOSS OF THE MOON MAIDENS DIDN'T KEEP ME AWAY FROM PORT-land's bustling Earthy community. I refused to stop shaving my legs, but Willow could always count on me to attend anything with a drum circle. That is, when I wasn't working on a story for KBOO or on my never-ending search for funeral work. I was always on the go, but it was exhilarating. Before I knew it, I had graduated college and the rest of my life was spread out before me like a funeral buffet. Unfortunately, my search for a mortuary apprenticeship was going nowhere.

Frustrated, I called Richard over at Dyrland's. "Nobody is hiring," he said. "I thought you were going to Frisco to mortuary school."

"I decided to finish at Linfield," I clarified.

"Mortuary school would help your prospects," Richard advised. "And there might be jobs down south."

"That's true, but I'm involved in a lot of things here I don't want to leave."

"It's your funeral," Richard chuckled, and I could tell he was busting up at his own joke.

"You kill me."

Richard laughed out loud. "You're all right, kid," and hung up.

I thought Richard had a point, but I was involved at KBOO and volunteering with environmental justice groups. I had a big circle of like-minded, progressive friends; I couldn't imagine leaving Oregon or my home with Willow or my dad. Maybe I'd eventually need to move, but I decided to put off the decision at least for a few months. Maybe something would open up in the meantime.

"If it's meant to be, a position will come," Willow counseled. "If it hasn't happened yet, it's because it's not the right time. The universe knows what it is doing."

While I waited for the universe, I called Arthur Murray to see if I could pick up some hours. Fortunately, I could. It looked like the universe wanted me to keep eating and living indoors for a while, but it remained foggy on my dream fulfillment plans.

A couple weekends later, Willow and I went to a Shamanic Journey drumming circle, and the universe opened right up and nearly swallowed me. Standing amidst the sea of hippie guys and gals was a tall, dark-eyed preppy in a blue blazer. He was straight out of my Catholic schoolgirl dreams. I checked to make sure my denim cut-offs and peasant tunic were arranged modestly and migrated toward him. His name was Anthony and, to my great liking, he had a degree in Environmental Science. Fresh out of college, he had come west for our relaxed lifestyle and the company of other tree huggers.

"Are you here with anyone?" Anthony asked.

"Just my roommate, Willow," I replied to his evident satisfaction.

Little by little, we edged away from the drums so we could hear each other better. We had the same taste in food and music and movies and the stuff that makes you feel like you've met your soul mate when you're in your twenties. It was late by the time we managed to tear ourselves away. I couldn't find Willow, so I floated home alone, sure that the stars were brighter than they had ever been before.

I slept until well after ten the next morning and arose to find Willow in the kitchen making falafel with our friends Ryan and Kevin. They were an item, but Ryan wasn't ready to come out yet. They hung around at our house a lot since it was one of the few places Kevin could get Ryan to go.

"Rise and shine, early bird!" Willow joked when she saw me. "Where were you last night?"

"I met the most amazing guy."

"Do tell!" Kevin said eagerly, handing me a Diet Coke from the cooler he had brought. Willow seized the vile can, told me to sit down, and started fixing a cup of tea. Kevin and Ryan were watching me eagerly.

"Well," I said, "Imagine the best parts of Tom Cruise and Mario Lopez."

"Honey, I imagine that several times a week," Kevin said. Willow chuckled and batted his shoulder with a crocheted potholder. Ryan blushed.

"He's an environmental scientist, gorgeous, and he's Italian," I bragged. "And he likes sushi and he loves his family."

"Sounds like a ten plus," Ryan said.

"Definitely goes to eleven!" Kevin agreed.

I smiled and took a sip of Willow's steaming water and bark blend. "We're going to dinner tomorrow night."

"Does he know you're going to be a mortician?" Ryan asked.

"No," I said. "But I'm sure we'll talk about it."

"Does that make you panicky?" Ryan asked.

"No, it will be fine." I flashed back to my dad's early concerns for my love life. But no, it would be fine, right? I looked around at my friends and asked "Right?"

Willow said, "If he's the right one for you, it will be all right."

Kevin winked my way and said, "If it's not all right, have some fun and throw him away. There will be another one right around the corner."

Ryan, concerned, added, "That's not nice."

"He's not serious," I said, patting Ryan's hand. "Besides, I'm not that kind of girl and this is only a first date."

"So?" Kevin asked.

"So, first dates are for getting to know each other, not for going too far."

"Wait, what are you saying? You *never* do it on a first date." Kevin looked incredulous. "Not even if you just want a little fun?"

"No. I'm not looking for a little fun. Well, that's not true, I want to have a fun time, but you know."

"Afraid you'll ruin your reputation and boys will write nasty things about you on the men's room wall?" Kevin teased.

"You can be a real pill, you know that, Kevin?" Willow interjected. "A woman is allowed to set her own sexual boundaries. Lay off."

"I'm just not interested in hooking up, or whatever they call it," I said.

"Ooh, you're the marrying kind!" Kevin exclaimed.

"Yeah, I guess. I want to find somebody to spend my life with. You know, grow old together and take care of each other."

"I think that's sweet," Ryan said. "Don't listen to him. I understand completely."

"You'll have to walk out of the closet before you can walk down the aisle," Kevin told Ryan.

Before they could start bickering, Willow asked Kevin to get the tzatziki sauce out of the refrigerator and set Ryan to slice the cucumbers. By the time pitas hit the table, we were chatting about the hot topic of the year: the ethics of Africanized Honey Bees and whether or not killer bees would migrate as far as the Pacific Northwest.

☙

Anthony took me downtown to Vat & Tonsure for our first date, and we picked up the conversation from the night before.

"What did you study in college?" he asked at one point.

"Mass Communications."

"Oh, you're going into broadcasting? The KBOO thing is a foot in the door?"

"Um. No, actually, I want to be an undertaker."

"That's funny!" Anthony said with a laugh.

"No, I mean it," I said.

Anthony stopped laughing. "But you're a girl."

"I'm glad you noticed." I gave him a warm smile and flipped my long blonde hair back over my shoulder like I was starring in a shampoo commercial. His smile came back.

"Historically, women were the first caretakers of the dead," I said. "They washed and shaved and dressed the corpses for the burial services."

"I've never heard of a woman doing that job," Anthony protested.

"That's only because mortuary education became formalized. Boys went to school back then, girls didn't. So, men took over caring for the dead."

"Don't you think it's kind of gross?"

"I have seen some gross things. I worked at a funeral home last summer, and there was one body that arrived in an advanced state of decomposition. It wasn't the nicest thing, but it's usually not that bad. I think I'll be able to handle it."

"I guess women these days do everything else they want to," Anthony remarked.

"Actually, I think it fits well with our nurturing instincts and our knack for details."

"I do like a nurturing woman," Anthony said with a hint of suggestion in his voice. "Just don't be coming home smelling like some dead guy."

Coming home? That sounded promising!

The next afternoon I called Dad to tell him about Anthony.

"Sounds like a decent fellow," Dad said. "Do I get to meet him some time?"

"If we keep dating, absolutely."

"Make him treat you right, sweetheart. If he doesn't treat you right, leave him and find somebody who will."

"Sure, of course, Dad."

"Is he Italian?"

"He is!"

We talked for a while about the Public Service Announcements I was writing and voicing for the radio station; I could tell Dad was happy about how well I was doing. He told me about a job he'd heard of at one of the local television stations.

"I'm still hoping to find an apprenticeship at one of the mortuaries," I said.

"Well, maybe for in the meantime," Dad suggested. "You'd be a good journalist; you like to write."

"My heart's not in it, Dad, I'm sorry."

"I understand," he said.

Once off the phone, I found Ryan sitting in the living room window seat. "Where's Kevin?"

"He's helping Willow unclog a plug in the washing machine." Sure enough, I could hear sounds of thumping, and possibly cussing, from the utility room behind the kitchen.

"What are you doing out here alone?" I asked.

"Just thinking."

"Want to talk about it?"

"Kevin is getting tired of hiding," Ryan whispered.

I nodded. Willow and I had suspected that.

"The thing is, he's really brave. I am not that brave. I could never tell my parents; it would kill them."

"Are you sure?" I asked. "Sometimes parents surprise you with what they can accept. Yours love you."

"I'm sure," Ryan said, soberly. "I can't do it. I want my dad to be proud of me."

"Of course, you do," I said.

"But I think I'm going to lose Kevin if I don't come out," Ryan said.

"Is he your Mr. Right?"

"Yes."

I didn't know what to say, so Ryan and I just looked at each other sadly until Kevin and Willow walked in. How does somebody choose between Mr. Right and the rest of their life? Isn't Mr. Right supposed to *be* the rest of your life? But what if the two things don't fit together?

I gleefully congratulated myself on finding a nice Italian boy who seemed okay with my aspirations. I continually talked to my mother about him; she would have loved him!

❦

Anthony and I started seeing each other almost every day. He had lived in Montana for a while and had a great appreciation for national parks and natural settings. We hiked a lot and took pictures of ourselves hiking. We camped nearly every weekend. Most days, after I got home from the dance studio, Anthony stopped by. Willow and I fed him vegetarian suppers, and then we'd take long walks in the neighborhood.

When winter brought the rains back, we spent more time at his place because it was close enough to stroll to the movies. We had friends over for wine and cheese, or we hung around with each other for company. Occasionally, I'd find Anthony at the local bakery, writing in his journal or playing guitar in the pub on the corner. We attended my brother's wedding together. My whole family liked him, even my cousin Isabella who never thinks anybody is good enough for me.

His family was not as enamored with me. Anthony was a very rich boy from a very rich family on Long Island Sound. They saw me as a weird, funky, counterculture hippie liberal who wanted to kibbutz with the dead. As far as they were concerned, Anthony was wasting his time with me. He and I talked about that a little but shrugged it off, thinking they would come around eventually. Besides, everything else was so easy between us, as if we were always supposed to be together. By New Year's, I rarely went home any more.

One spring Saturday, Anthony disappeared early. He returned about noon and explained that he had taken my father out to Elmer's Pancake House for breakfast. They had a good chat, apparently. I quickly rang my dad as soon as Anthony made his way into the shower.

"I heard you and Anthony shared a pile of hotcakes. Anything I should know?"

A long pause, then, "Honey, he just thought it would be good to take the old dad out for a short stack."

Dad didn't have to tell me he had always been waiting for a fine, young man to take him out for a short stack and ask for my hand; I inherently knew. Suddenly I was floating in warm, syrupy gooeyness.

"Anthony is going to ask me to marry him," I reported the next time I was home.

"How do you know?" Willow asked.

"He took my dad out for breakfast the other day."

"What are you going to say?"

"Yes, of course! I can't wait to have a life with this guy."

Willow gave me a long hug. "I'm so happy for you," she said, "but Kevin and Ryan are coming over. Please don't mention it in front of them because they're fighting again."

Poor Kevin and Ryan. Sometimes, when I compared my relationship with Anthony to theirs, I wondered if they were really meant to be together. I was smug.

I also was on tenterhooks the next couple of weeks. Anthony and I would be doing our usual thing, poking through the bins at Hippo Hardware or strolling along the river bank, but I could barely pay attention. All

I could think was, *Is today the day? Is he going to ask me here? When is he going to do it?*

Just when I could no longer stand the waiting game, the game changed. Toward the end of the month, Anthony told me his parents sent him a plane ticket. He would be going home to New York for Memorial Day weekend. There was no plane ticket for me.

"I thought we were going to Crater Lake for Memorial Day weekend," I whined. "Remember, hiking and camping?"

"We can go to Crater Lake any time; my family is getting together for a sailing trip," Anthony said. "I need you to watch my place while I'm gone, okay?"

"Oh, so I'm supposed to sit here while you go off sailing because your mommy and daddy don't like me? How does that work?"

"How it works is you cut me some slack. My parents are under no obligation to provide you with plane tickets or sailing trips. Their money is not your money," said Anthony.

I was flabbergasted. "I never said it was!"

"Then stop acting like an entitled brat!"

"Why are you yelling at me? Why are you being mean? I don't think I like what this says about our relationship." I was nearly in tears.

"I don't think I like what it says about you! Do you think you can spend the rest of your life working part time and having other people support you?"

I was floored; I had never asked him or anyone else to pay my bills. He was supposed to be proposing to me, not belittling me. I left before I broke down completely.

Anthony took the plane to New York, and I went to the Bay Area to see my favorite cousins in California. I needed to be around people who loved me unconditionally.

Late in the evening, Monday of Memorial Day weekend, my cousin Gene called me to the phone. It was Anthony. He phoned to inform me that his parents would like him to break up with me and that, in fact, he was breaking up with me. We were no longer a couple. When he arrived back in Portland, he would probably be moving back to New York, so I needed to get my things out of his house.

After I hung up, I sat on the floor in Gene's den as the light got dimmer and dimmer. The room was filled with Willie Mays memorabilia. I looked at the figurines and statues of the legendary baseball player and felt like a worthless failure. *How would I break the news to my dad?*

My cousin Sue finally came and found me. Sue and I had worked at her family's agriculture resort in Hollister during summers in our youth. We were a rowdy pair then and had weathered many storms together over the years. She put her arm around me and asked what was wrong.

"Anthony broke up with me. It's over," I said.

Sue held me and rocked me and I cried while the sun went down.

When I arrived back in Portland, I went straight to Anthony's house and removed everything that was mine, a couple of boxes' worth. As I threw my waffle maker in my Jeep, I broke down and sobbed right there on the sidewalk. Little did I know that the pancake breakfast with my father had consisted of nothing more than a short stack of cakes and some coffee.

I went to my father's house.

"Your cousin called," Dad said at the door.

"So, you know?" I said. He held me and told me how sorry he was for building up my hopes, that he really liked Anthony, but somehow this was for the best.

"How about a small glass of Two-Buck Chuck?"

I followed my dad to the kitchen. I couldn't manage a smile, but watching him pour me a glass of his Catholic singles group's sacramental wine was a very sweet moment.

"Your cousin says there's an ad in the paper down there for a job with some funeral home," he said, handing me a slip of note paper where he had jotted down the phone number. "Why don't you try for it? The change of scenery will do you good. I can help you out with moving expenses if you need."

My eyes welled up. "Thanks, Daddy."

"Sure thing, honey. Do you want some peanuts with that? I got some peanuts over here."

Chapter 6

Taking My Heart South of San Francisco

SAYING GOODBYE TO MY FRIENDS IN PORTLAND AND MY LITTLE HIP-pie home with Willow was nearly as painful as losing Anthony. Willow took it with her usual gentle grace while I gave her canned goods a farewell organizing. In return, she loaded me up from her shelf-full of books extolling the irresistible power of a Refuse to Lose attitude.

"This is not an end, it's a beginning. You have work to do. People need help to understand why current burial practices are unsustainable."

"This is an admin job—typing up death certificates."

"But it's a foot in the door. Speaking of which, I think I hear Kevin and Ryan."

I peeked out the window. Sure enough, the guys were coming up the driveway. Kevin had an insulated bag in his hand, and Ryan was carrying their familiar pale blue cooler. I rushed over to the door and threw it open.

"We brought Thai!" Kevin said, holding his burden aloft.

"And Mimosas," Ryan chimed in. "It's a bon voyage party!"

At the door, they sat everything down so they could smother me in hugs and sentiment.

"You're killing us."

"But we're so happy for you."

"But you're killing us."

"We're going to miss you."

"But you're going to be a fabulous funeral femme fatale."

"And we can come see you in San Francisco!"

"You will?" I said, teary and mascara-smeared.

"Girl, are you kidding?" Kevin said. "You know we're in San Fran as often as we can get there. We'll take you to a couple of bars we like: Crowbar, Hot 'n Hunky, Twin Peaks. Do you own any leather pants?"

It felt good to laugh.

"We could go leather pants shopping for you," Ryan said with a twinkle in his eye. Where was his usual blush?

"Are you making gay jokes?" I asked Ryan.

Ryan shrugged. "Why not?"

"You should have seen him last weekend," Kevin said. "He wore his 'Nobody Knows I'm Gay' t-shirt to the Silverado."

"No way!" I said.

"Way," Ryan confirmed. A hint of color rose to his cheeks, but he looked proud.

"He's going to be okay," Kevin said. "Let's get this party started."

We carried everything to the kitchen, big hugs 'round to Willow, and unpacked carry-out containers. Kevin popped the champagne cork. "A toast!" he declared. "To the best looking grim reaper to ever get one shiny black heel inside mortuary doors! May your dreams come true, and may you always be better looking than the people you serve. Salute!"

"Salute!" we all chimed in, clinking our Libbey Flower Power glasses.

"True friends are the best," I said. "I can't believe I'm leaving."

"No more tears," Kevin said, brightly. "I've been collecting death jokes. Ready?"

We groaned, but said okay. There was no stopping him anyway, once he decided to lay his latest joke collection on you.

"A skeleton walks into a bar and says 'Barkeep, I'll have a beer and a mop.'"

Kevin kept us giggling over his corny comedic offerings until the threat of tears passed and our good cheer could sustain itself. I need a man like him, I thought. Someone who can make me laugh when life feels too big to handle.

Later that night, Ryan and I drifted to the patio. "Does this new comfort with yourself mean you've told your dad the truth about who you are?" I asked him.

"Not yet, but I'm closer. I know I'm gonna do it, I just haven't figured out when."

"What changed your mind?" I asked, checking out a pot of geraniums that looked too dry.

"Kevin is sick."

My head shot up. "No."

"Yeah," Ryan said. "Don't say anything; he doesn't want anyone to know."

Blood was pulsing so hard in my head I felt dizzy.

"So, I have to tell my dad," Ryan continued, "because I have to be there for Kevin when he dies."

"Maybe he won't die," I said. "They have medication now."

Ryan stared at me like I was out of my gourd. Of course, I was. How could I even say that? I held my arms out and Ryan sank into them. We held each other silently for a long time.

"I'm here for you," I said. "Anything you need, please call me." Against my chest, I could feel Ryan nodding. Somehow, we didn't cry. I guess it was too horrifying for tears.

We heard Kevin calling from the living room, "Get in here, we're going to play Charades!"

We sure are, I thought, as Ryan and I straightened up our faces for our return journey to the denim-covered couch.

୧୨

My death certificate typist job was for a mortuary under the broad-reaching umbrella of SCI, Service Corporation International. I shared a smallish office in the back corner of a giant funeral home, in the middle of a giant cemetery. There were three other women on a rotating schedule who puffed on their Camels and Pall Malls more than they tinkled the typewriter keys.

Every morning, I headed through the outdoor typist smoking section, floating on nicotine fumes. My corner chair was wedged between the copy machine and the wall. I typed, I transposed—names and dates of the lives of decedents, plus other vital info: education, parents' names and birthplaces, last address. Then, off to the doc for a signature. Somehow, I never got lost in the big maze of the parlour; I believe I had a guardian angel for a Thomas Guide. Thanks, Mom!

Even though it didn't have the same homey feeling as Dyrland's, it was rather unbelievable to stroll down huge corridors, passing gargantuan bouquets of gladiolas, stopping in the many slumber rooms for a peek at the decedents, and to see a fleet of hearses ready in the back lot for a loved one's final ride. To be working as part of a huge funeral service network would fill a huge plate of my funeral buffet of knowledge I so craved. SCI was the largest funeral and cemetery owner in North America. SCI firms were everywhere, and I bounced around to a few of them.

I was sent one day to another of SCI's funeral homes, Green Street Mortuary, in the North Beach section of San Francisco. This parlour sits in the traditionally Italian section of the city, but Green Street Mortuary is San Francisco's largest Chinese funeral parlour. More than three hundred Chinese families a year hire the Green Street Mortuary Band to give their loved ones a proper musical send-off through the streets of Chinatown. An open car, a black Cadillac once owned by John Wayne, follows the band and carries a large, framed photo of the deceased. The hearse is next in line, and then the family rolls by in a Lincoln Town Car.

My assignment that day was to drive the limo for the huge funeral procession. It would wind through fifteen blocks of Chinatown. The route was dependent on where the person lived, if they had a business in the area or were well known in the community. I could hardly believe I would be part of a celebrated Chinatown funeral procession.

I sat alone for a while, parked inside the stifling black limo. At the end of services, the vehicles began the lengthy procedure of lining up for takeoff. Driver Larry moved his hearse into formation; green placards identified all cars in the procession, which would end at the cemetery.

The family loaded into my car, and I moved forward but couldn't see any action because of the tall floral sprays in the convertible at the head of the line. Family members held up a large picture of the deceased, Dr. Fa. He looked like a man suited to taking his last ride up high in a sleek, low vehicle.

A group of chanting monks floated out the chapel door. Bells were ringing, brethren were singing, incense was in the air. It was show time! I was giddy with excitement.

As the coffin was placed in the hearse, there was a drum roll and "Amazing Grace" wailed through the rows of triple parked cars. Enormous sticks of incense were lit, and the mourners took their final bows in honor of

Dr. Fa. A motorcycle escort stopped traffic. I had both hands on the wheel, waiting for a quick hand signal to make my move forward.

I was part of something I had seen only while shopping in Chinatown. Cymbals crashed, and loud drums with green Chinese characters led a procession that snaked for blocks in honor of this beloved citizen on his last journey.

We passed the Willie "Woo Woo" Wong Playground on Grant Avenue; apparently, this was significant in Dr. Fa's life. As we rode on, attendants burned incense and threw paper "spirit money" from the funeral vehicles. At his business, the back door of the hearse opened and more paper money went flying in the air. The action was just as intense behind me.

We continued through Chinatown with a noisy farewell to Dr. Fa. Passing his home on Taylor Street, windows from a walk-up townhouse were thrown open so any traces of Dr. Fa's spirit could be released. The timing was impeccable, making it look as if the flow of age-old ritual had been choreographed.

Everyone turned to look at us on the densely packed streets. People peered out of city buses, men removed their baseball caps.

Back at the garage when it was over, Larry asked, "What did you think?"

"I am completely stoked!" I said. "That was wild. I'm glad the police were there to direct traffic, or I don't know how we would have maneuvered through the crowds."

Gary laughed. "Those weren't police."

"What? Yeah, the motorcycle cops who were stopping the traffic for us."

"Sweetheart, do you know how much it costs to get San Francisco PD to work a funeral?" Larry asked.

"A lot?" I ventured.

"More than most families have. Those were hired escorts, but it's the one time you're guaranteed to stop traffic, kid—the day we carry you to the boneyard."

☙

I spent two full days searching for my dream rental in San Francisco and learned the meaning of sticker shock. The possibilities looked bleak that I could swing the high cost of housing in San Francisco by myself, so I found a house share south of the city. As a bonus, I often got to drive through Colma, the cemetery capital of the nation. There was well over a million people in Colma at the time, but only about 1,500 of them were alive.

My commute was worse than it had been in Portland, but I got to live in a beautiful old house with a Market Street address near Santa Clara University. It had a revolving door of loveable but oddball roommates ranging in age from thirteen to forty-five, and the diversity didn't stop there.

Stu and Sarah were boyfriend and girlfriend, straightaway my least favorite housemates. They spent their days hogging the basement furniture, lying around and complaining about nothing. Sarah was financially supported by Stu. They hailed from Alamo, a ritzy, San Francisco East Bay Area community. Why they left the comforts of the 'burbs was hard for me to guess. I was never sure what they did for work, since I was busting tail for long hours in a funeral home.

Stu bragged about his party connections. "Earlier yesterday, I totally managed to ingest all the audio that we recorded at the rave." Catching my unknowing look, he said, "A rave? A big, bad-ass dance explosion rave, which takes place at some random space? Like you Rave On?"

My favorite adult in the house was Rand. He took my career seriously, probably because he had an eccentric job himself. He had left the drudge of spreadsheets and accounting at a good firm in Oakland to take a six-month paid apprenticeship as a cheesemaker. He explained what he did at the Cribari Creamery, and I was fascinated. He asked me if I'd like to visit; baby goats were about to be born. I was in! After an hour drive past rolling pastures, Victorian farmhouses, and rows of fragrant eucalyptus, we arrived at the creamery on the east shore of Tomales Bay in Marin County. I couldn't help but notice how similar "creamery" was to "crematory."

There was also a law student in the house with a delightful son, thirteen-year-old Andy, who I fell in love with. I imagined myself having a small person like this one day. He was bright, asked fun questions, and was always happy to see me. We loved rolling our eyes at Beth, another roommate and the owner of the house.

Nothing in the house was quite right for Beth until it had a fresh shot of spray paint or string of beads hanging from it. It was immature of me, but Andy and I disdained her craftiness and rubber stamp collection. Each stamp had a baby kitten name like Precious, Angel, Jem, and Ju Ju.

"Can you imagine what she would do if she could get her glue gun and craft box inside a funeral home?" Andy would say. "It would be so creepy, but in a Beth sort of creepy way."

I loved that kid.

I loved Beth, too, because despite her peculiarities, she was a gracious roommate and she made peach cozies for the doorknobs.

So, it was The Raving Lumps, The Cheesemaker, The Kid, The Aspiring Undertaker, and The Bedazzler. Together, we would have been perfect on a season of *The Real World*.

Life seemed pretty good, except I was still grieving my newly single status. To supplement my low wages at SCI, I managed to land a job as a DJ at a small radio station. I was supposed to be serving up platters of light rock, but my playlist was nothing but heart-wrenchingly sentimental and sappy songs. Before long, management decided they'd heard Debby Boone's "You Light up My Life" one too many times and kicked me out on my miserable can.

I tried dating. For a while, I went out with a high-tech entrepreneur from San Jose; but I wasn't willing to compete with his real girlfriend—the cell phone in the left pocket of his Armani button-up. Because of our work life, we could only get together on weekends, when he couldn't shut off his phone long enough to have dinner with me. Wherever we were, his pocket would ring. I would sit for two minutes—or twenty-two—while he conducted important business. When he asked me to move in for a trial relationship, I rolled my eyes and told him to lose my number.

I couldn't help but brag to the basement full of housemates about my ridiculously cool date at the House of Genji. I met up with a man who loved preparing animal skins and stuffing them into a lifelike form.

"He wore buckskin pants and a hunting shirt, with buckskin fringes along the seams of the legs and sleeves."

Their eyes widened.

"Nah, just kidding, you dorks! He was wearing jeans and a polo shirt."

A stale chunk of nachos got tossed my way, courtesy of the male couch lump, Stu.

"Tanner shook my hand firmly and let on that he was in a feisty mood. He knocked back a Wild Turkey in record speed and told me about his day at the salt mine, or the butchers block, if you will. He says, 'Some city slicker comes in and tells me I recently mounted a deer head for his hunt-ing buddy, and asks how much I'll charge for the six-point buck he just shot. I give him my price. He says it's too high. He tells me that his buck is so big I'd be amazed to see it, so I tell him to truck it over to the shop. I take a look, quote a higher price, and then he says I should mount it for free just for the advertising I'd get from it.'"

"And then what?" huffs Stu, who's clearly bored but mostly drunk.

"Hold your pants on, Snarky. I'm telling a story here. So, he tells me, 'I put the animal back in his truck bed and sent him on his way. I use high grade synthetic materials to prevent bugs, molds, and odors, and have never received a complaint. I've been around over twenty years and know my trade. Everyone wants their game trophy right this minute, and don't understand why it takes so long. It's an art, just like embalming.'"

"Your soulmate, dream dude, totally," declares The Lump. "My pick up line used to be that I love long walks on the beach until the LSD wears off and I realize I'm just dragging a stolen mannequin around a Wendy's parking lot."

The uncomfortable silence is as subtle as a flying brick.

"Why do I even bother?" I asked Beth one night.

"Because you want a man?" Beth suggested.

"Ugh. Why? Mary Tyler Moore didn't have a man and she was just fine with it."

"Yeah, but not too many of us are Mary. Most of us are her boy-crazy neighbor, Rhoda."

Chapter 7

The McDonald's of the Hereafter

M Y SHARPLY OBSERVED ATTENTION TO DETAIL WAS REWARDED with steady employment at a mortuary relatively close to my home address. Each morning, I was assigned to little jobs at another SCI affiliate, the Little Chapel of the Souls, like making sure the external lights were turned on and the music switched over in the music room. Then I strolled through the chapel to the rhythm of melodic dirges to pick up any leftover remnants of tissue and forgotten hankies. When finished, I tidied the arrangement and visitation rooms. Later in the day, I might wash a hearse or two, fetch coffee for people, change a light bulb—all this in a suit and heels. I limped home every night.

"How do you like your new job?" Dad asked one night on the phone.

"I love it, but the hours are brutal."

"Are you doing all right with working on dead bodies?"

"I'm in my first year. I mainly work with Kleenex," I explained.

"You'll get there," Dad assured me.

"I promised myself I would, no matter what."

"That's my girl."

Andy was the other person I could count on to take an interest in my career. He was a bright kid who knew too much about heartache, and needed more attention than his dad could give him at this season in life. He asked a thousand questions:

"Why are you a mortician?"

"Are you afraid of the dead people?"

"Why do some people get buried and some people get cremated?"

We spent many early evenings together in the cemetery near our house. I power walked; Andy rode his scooter. He was fascinated by headstones. "What does R.I.P. mean?"

"Rest in Peace."

"Why do some of them have sheep on them?"

"That's a lamb. It represents the Lamb of God."

"Who's buried in Grant's Tomb?"

"Now you're just messing with me!"

Andy started reading about death and funeral customs. I wasn't sure if it was because his mother had left him, a death of sorts, or because of our friendship, but I didn't want to risk making him feel self-conscious by asking. Andy made our beautiful house feel less lonely. Sometimes we would plug in all my Virgin Mary nightlights to cast a soothing glow over my bedroom. He would quiz me on my current funeral home general price list, and the kid really dug this.

When I had time off on weekends, I soaked up some family lovin'. Sometimes I went to Uncle Joseph's, where the table and the pasta pot were always full. Uncle Joe came from my mother's side of the gene pool; he was the most colorful person I ever knew. His lovely and vibrant lady friend, Roxy Montana, welcomed me in like I was a long-lost refugee.

"You're getting skinny," Roxy would fuss. "Dancers like us need to have more muscle."

"I only eat processed food from 7-11."

"They're working you too hard at the funeral home. Come have some homemade gnocchi."

"Would love to."

"There she is!" Uncle Joseph called across the house. If he wasn't watching the San Francisco '49ers in his easy chair, he'd be at the dining room table playing dominos with his cousin, Primo. "Have some gnocchi. Roxy! Get her some gnocchi." I ate the gnocchi—happily.

It was impossible to be lonely or hungry at Joseph and Roxy's. We talked about family we'd seen lately, ate, played cards, and danced late into the night. Roxy would put on an old record, and we'd dance like we'd been called to worship. When I stayed over, Cousin Sue and I would sleep together in the bed, just like we used to as kids. On my way home the next morning, I'd sing mariachi songs at the top of my lungs; it's what happened when my love tank felt full. I knew "Guantanamera" from childhood, and songs such a "Cielito Lindo" were sung at every Mexican burial. To scream out the chorus of "*Ay, Yai, Yai, Yai*" at full volume was heavenly.

If I had a bad day at the parlour, I would ask Roxy and Uncle Joseph to meet me in San Jose at the Saddle Rack Country Night Club. Joe loved to dance and had helped found the Hollister Dance Club in 1959. In 1985, he was inducted into the California Southwestern Dance Hall of Fame. They called him Three-Shirt Joe in dance circles, because of his habit of dressing in layers. We would dance until his third shirt turned to sweat. He was an epic "spinner." He won a Swing dance contest at the Hyatt in Monterey by zipping through fifty spins on the dance floor. I never quite knew what to do while he spun and spun. Should I count? Get a drink at the bar and return before he finished?

Later in the week, Kevin and Ryan visited bearing a care package from Willow. "Look at this, she sent homemade goat's milk soap and some cookies."

"I think those are flax seed. She's on a huge flax kick right now," Ryan explained, "and she's been dating a very hot Guatemalan who is probably undocumented. At one of her women's groups, she heard flax seed has a lot of plant estrogens and antioxidants. She met the Guatemalan while campaigning for immigration reform," Kevin clarified.

"So not much has changed in Portland then," I said. Kevin looked thin, but I didn't want to say so. "How are you two doing?" I asked.

"I told my parents," Ryan blurted out.

"How did that go?"

"Mom says Dad will come around."

"She likes me," Kevin said with a knowing smile.

"Who doesn't?" I asked.

"In the meantime, I can't go to the house," Ryan continued.

"Oh wow," I said. I put my hand over his. "How are you doing with this?" Ryan dropped his gaze and pushed his eggs around on his plate.

"He is so brave," Kevin said, wrapping his arm around Ryan's shoulder, dropping an affectionate kiss on Ryan's temple. "Eat your eggs. I want to show you Harvey Milk's old camera shop, and then we're going on the *Tales of the City* walking tour to Aquatic Park and Russian Hill. Liza, my darling, you can be Mary Ann; Ryan will be Mouse."

"Who will you be?" I asked.

"I'll be Maupin, guiding you through your San Francisco adventure."

"He's been trying his hand at writing fiction," said Ryan. "Last week we had to go to where Celilo Falls used to be, since the Native American in *One Flew over the Cuckoo's Nest* was so bothered by it being flooded when they put in the dam. The week before that we threw a 'Come as Your Favorite Supporting Character from Classic Literature' Party."

"So, nothing has changed in Portland then," I said.

℣※

My prior life in Portland had a free-flowing vibe. I had gotten away with sundresses and bare legs at work, which was nowhere near my new work uniform. "How can you wear pantyhose in this heat?" Sarah asked one blistering August day while I was passing through the basement.

"I have to when I'm working at the funeral home," I said. "Navy or black suit, nylons, closed-toed shoes, no pants for women unless it is their official pantsuit."

"That's repressive."

"It's a conservative industry. We're supposed to always look ready to stand guard at a funeral."

Sarah looked me up and down, not bothering to conceal her disdain for my costume. "I think you've mastered that."

"Glad I meet your approval," I said lightly. "Gotta dash!" I was off to see my favorite Bay Area colleagues, fun fellows I'd met driving the Chinese funeral. Larry was Italian and eighty-five, Gary was seventy-three, both confirmed bachelors. They were sassy, and they'd been working at Green Street Mortuary for years.

"Hey, you two, been to Chinatown lately?" I called to them as I entered their garage.

"Just yesterday," Larry said, grinning. "Processions through Chinatown are our specialty."

"This guy got in the movies for it," Gary said, nodding at Larry.

"You're kidding!"

Gary shook his head. "Watch *The Fan* with Robert DeNiro. In the scene with the Chinatown procession, you can see Larry at the wheel of a hearse."

"That's pretty stylish," I said. Larry's grin swelled along with his chest.

"Hey, I got something for you," Gary said, reaching inside his coat. He handed me a pen from Evergreen Mortuary of McAvoy O'Hara.

"Uh, thanks," I said.

"That's to start your collection," Larry explained. "They're the oldest parlour in the city."

"My collection?"

"Your funeral home pen collection," said Gary. "We have hundreds." He pulled three or four more pens out of his coat. "See? We pick 'em up on the job."

"When you get as many as we have, you'll know you're an official oldtimer in the business."

"I'll do it!" I said, resolving to pick up pens from random parlours and surprise them at our next funeral.

They helped me load the orange cones I'd come for and waved me off.

Twenty minutes later, I was scrubbing the cones in the back parking lot of Little Chapel of the Souls, wearing my suit and heels on this lowly job. I made the best of it by singing Sheryl Crow's "All I Wanna Do." A little too loudly; when I got to the line "hosing and scrubbing as best they can in skirts and suits," I saw one of the managers standing over me.

When Mr. Douglas said, "Miss Fournier, pipe down and come with me," I figured I was about to be given my pink slip. Did they use pink slips in the funeral business? Maybe something more sedate—a pale gray on thick paper with a black edge.

He led me to the conference room where my other co-workers were already seated. They were ominously silent as I worked my way around to an available seat. Mr. Douglas got right to the point: "Phil and Andrea are no longer employed with this funeral home. I'll keep you posted as to who will handle their duties."

What the heck? Both funeral directors were gone?

"They left this weekend," the bookkeeper announced to the room, but that was all the information he had. Everybody went back to their work.

This put Little Chapel of the Souls in a desperate position because all our affiliated parlours were very busy. We wouldn't be able to "borrow" a funeral director from another mortuary.

"Elizabeth," Mr. Douglas called from his office door. "Will you please step in here?" Oh crap, I thought, memories of my parking lot performance flooding back.

Mr. Douglas closed the door behind me and told me to sit down. "I'm going to need you to step up until we replace Phil and Andrea," he said.

"I can do that," I declared. "Just tell me what you need."

He had me sign some paperwork to cover the funeral home's legal arse and marched me to the embalming room as the new unofficial embalming apprentice. "The features need to be set on Mrs. Navarette for her service tomorrow. Do you think you can manage this?

"I'm your girl," I said. "You can count on me." Though my head was screaming—*Uh, really?*

"I have some things to attend to. If you run into trouble, come find me." Just like that he was gone, and I was in charge of readying the body to be viewed by its loved ones.

I fished around on a shelf full of small boxes and found one containing eye caps—small rubbery domes with tiny hooks across them. Eyes flatten after death, so eye caps are used to recreate the look of a living eye. The hooks ensure the lids will stay closed. It's tricky to apply this process correctly, but I worked steadily, cleverly using a crochet hook to position everything correctly. Mrs. Navarette was all set with her eye caps.

Now I had to get her mouth guard in place to give her an expression of stately repose. The procedure is to wire the jaw shut, then superglue the lips closed. That took me most of the afternoon, but by the time I walked out of there, I was no longer a glorified janitor; I worked hands-on with the dead.

To celebrate, I stopped by a wacky gift shop on my way home and bought a card with a picture of Morticia Addams on it. I wrote "Congratulate me!" inside—no signature—and dropped it in the mail to my brother. A few days later, the florist delivered a large bouquet of roses from Nick. Attached to the ribbon that encircled the vase was a pair of scissors so I could snip off their heads.

Chapter 8

Chemical Odor and Carlotta

THE SUREST WAY TO DETERMINE IF YOU WANT TO BE A FUNERAL director is to work in the prep room. Things are very . . . real, we'll say . . . in there. Real in ways few people want to hear about. "I managed to get the correct tension on the mouth sutures today," is simply not welcome dinner conversation.

Every day I suited up in gown, apron, shoe covers, gloves, and goggles to reverse the ravages of death and decay—work so intimate it seems wrong to discuss the details. Every night I went home and pretended I hadn't done anything profound that day. It was a strange, bifurcated existence.

Shortly after Phil and Andrea left, a trade embalmer named Toby was contracted to help out if things got busier than the new funeral director, Mr. Ingraham, and I could handle. The two of them set about teaching me the art and craft of preserving bodies and setting features. I had many questions to ask but didn't feel a great connection with Mr. Ingraham. He was serious, never smiled, and I was sure he thought I was of no value to him. When we passed in the hall, he would look straight ahead, never answering my hello.

One day I saw a thick white binder on a shelf in the funeral director's office. It was the complete and current-year California Cemetery and Funeral Bureau Laws and Regulations, printed directly from the website. I flipped through the pages voraciously for an hour before Toby asked what I was looking for. I shared that I wanted to learn the material for the licensing exam. It seemed the right time to get licensed as a funeral director because of the current staff situation. He reminded me that I was being groomed to work in the back of the building, not the front.

"How do you do this every day?" I asked Toby. Trade embalmers work for several funeral homes and that's all they do. They don't get involved with the families; they don't transport the bodies. Their entire job is embalming.

"It's funny," Toby said. "Nobody ever asks the coffin maker that, even though we're both artisans in our own right."

"Yeah, but the coffin maker isn't draining the blood out of dead bodies and pumping them full of preservatives."

"No, but he also doesn't make it possible for clients to travel in from out of state for the funeral and still see their grandma or grandpa looking almost like they did in life."

"Doesn't it get to you after a while?"

"Some cases do," Toby admitted. "But then I have one where the clients didn't think they could have an open casket, and I make that possible for them and it feels great, frankly."

I hated that word, "cases." It felt equivalent to saying the people we cared for were nothing but a number to write in a file, rather than a person with people who loved them. It's the industry term, though. Wherever funeral directors gather they say things like, "How many cases does your funeral home do a year?"

"I don't know if I'm cut out for this," I admitted to Toby.

"You're doing fine."

I don't feel fine, I thought.

"You'll learn. Many people think embalming is a topical application of oils to the skin and some sort of disinfectant that's rubbed on. They don't realize how invasive a procedure it is."

"So, blood is drained through a major artery and replaced with highly toxic chemicals?"

"Including formaldehyde, which is an irritant, a volatile acid and a known carcinogen. Then, blood that has pooled in organs and other bodily fluids is removed with a vacuuming device called an aspirator. Elizabeth, didn't you go to mortuary school?"

He makes an exit before I can answer. Do I want to spend my days wearing a mask while working with cancer-causing solutions? Restoration—the art of making the deceased look as if they are sleeping—is achieved through a variety of wires, prosthetic devices, fillers, and cosmetics. Even though we do everything possible to be respectful and gentle with the bodies we serve, the process then left me uneasy and sometimes queasy. The fumes from the embalming fluid permeate your clothes and hair. Many days, I left for home feeling heavy and grim.

"You smell weird," Andy said the first time he met me at the door after a day in the prep room.

"It's embalming fluid; I'm headed straight up for a shower," I said.

"Is it neat working in the embalming room?"

"Um. Neat? No."

"It seems like it would be really cool."

"You know how you said you thought McDonald's seemed like magic before your cousin went to work in one and told you about what happens in the kitchen?"

"Yeah?"

"My job is the same. Seeing what happens behind the scenes kind of takes the magic away."

"Oh," Andy said, deflated.

I felt bad about disappointing him. Later, I told him about one of my favorite parts of working in the funeral industry in the San Francisco Bay area: the churches. "There's this one that really blows my mind called Grace Cathedral," I said. "It's on the top of Nob Hill, and there are labyrinths inside."

"Like in that myth about the half-human, half-bull guy?"

"Well, they're not caves. The mazes are in carpets."

"What are they for?"

"For people to walk the labyrinths and pray or meditate to reach a higher state of blessing."

"That is so cool! Could I do that?"

"Anybody can do it. I'll take you sometime. On Friday nights, they have candlelight labyrinth walks. They play music and everybody prays for peace."

"Awesome!" Andy shouted. "That sounds rad!"

"Right on," I said. I could use a little extra peace in my heart.

❧

I would often hear that I didn't look like a mortician. What I preferred hearing was that it took a special person to work in my industry, and it's true. Not only is it a harsh reality to be in the presence of people in mourning, but funeral directors are basically on call 25–8. I don't think 24–7 cuts it. We never know when we'll be needed on the phone or in person, ready with the right words to say.

I would randomly be jarred from a sound sleep by my cell phone. I might need to dress in the middle of the night and creep silently down the hall. Occasionally a wacky housemate would be up making tea or staring longingly out the window, probably searching for their dharma. Into my Jeep and off to the funeral parlor I'd go. I'd swap my vehicle for the death van and be on my way to a private residence, a nursing home or hospital. I would drive in the dark, pre-dawn hours, wondering why my life had taken this turn behind the wheel, and if my friends and family were proud to know me.

After finding the address, I would unload the gurney and make my way to the decedent I was to bring into the funeral home's care. An hour or two later, I'd be back in my bedroom lit only by the moon. I'd undress and hope to get a few hours' rest. It was an interesting life, but I was ready for some wackiness and adventure. There's only so much death a girl can take at a stretch.

Inspired by Kevin's *Tales of the City* tour, I convinced my cousin Sue to join me for a *Vertigo* tour.

"I've never heard of that one," said Sue.

"That's because I made it up," I explained. "Meet me Saturday at my house and wear your hair like Carlotta's so we can buy bouquets and end the day at the museum." Believe it or not, Sue went for this. She didn't hear the kidding in my voice, probably because we were huge fans of the film, and she knew I was crazy enough to do this. No movie shows off the City by the Bay more gloriously than Alfred Hitchcock's *Vertigo*. Sue and I had seen it a dozen times together. Somehow, each viewing was more haunting than the last.

We started our tour in front of the townhomes on the 1300 block of Taylor Street. The movie opens with detective John "Scottie" Ferguson and his partner chasing a fugitive across those very pricy Nob Hill rooftops. Unfortunately, Scottie, aka Jimmy Stewart, loses his footing and ends up dangling from a gutter. While trying to save Scottie, his partner plunges to his death. From then on, Scottie suffers from acrophobia, which causes vertigo. We weren't sure we pinpointed the exact spot where Scottie would have been hanging from the roof, but who cared? We were doing the *Vertigo* tour, living out loud on a beautiful San Francisco autumn day.

In the movie, you can see the Brocklebank Apartments behind Scottie as he first climbs onto the roof. Later, he will tail the female lead, Madeleine, there; we walked over to 1000 Mason Street to check it out. It hadn't changed much since Hitchcock filmed it. Across the street was the Fairmont Hotel where Alfred Hitchcock stayed during filming.

We wanted to lunch at Ernie's Restaurant, the one with the red silk wallpaper where Scottie first sees Madeleine. Ernie's was a favorite of Hitchcock's but alas, more expensive than women of our modest means could justify. We made cinematic history by grabbing a bite at a more reasonably priced taco bar blocks down the street, then headed to the apartment of Scottie's college friend and former fiancée, Midge. The exterior of this apartment was shot in the 200 block of Union Street on Telegraph Hill. Were the interior scenes shot in Hollywood? We would never know, since we were shooed away by a lady and her broom.

At Mission Dolores, 16th and Dolores Street, we passed the adobe-walled chapel and headed straight to the graveyard, as Madeleine does. We spotted a groundskeeper who looked like he might have been on location for the original shooting.

"Excuse me," I said, interrupting his raking. "We would like to see the Carlotta Valdes gravestone."

"From the Hitchcock movie?" he asked. Sue and I nodded. Now we were getting somewhere.

"That was a prop," the old man said and returned to his raking. Damn, why didn't we think of that? No matter; we toured the chapel and went in search of a florist.

We had something similar to Madeline's bouquet of posies made up at the shop, then boarded the street car for the long ride to the California Palace of the Legion of Honor.

En route Sue said, "Carlotta's portrait won't be there; that would have been a prop, too."

"I know, but the one near it called *Portrait of a Gentleman* is still there."

"You've done this before?" Sue asked.

"I just visited the museum. A date took me there." Sue flashed me a look that said she didn't 100% believe me. I was too self-conscious to admit how many lonely days with time on my hands I'd headed north to the bench at the Legion. My rich fantasy world was always my own.

At the museum's main gallery, we sat on that famous bench, looking up at the art display.

We left after a security guard walked by and sniggered.

"Some people have no imagination," I remarked as we crossed the grounds to catch a ride on BART.

"Next time we should reenact the chase scene from *Bullitt*," Sue said. "Any chance you could borrow a couple of hearses?"

❧

I wanted to go home for Thanksgiving, but my apprentice-sized paycheck wasn't up to the trip. I accepted an invitation to my Aunt Mary's in Hollister. I had enough cash to drive down but to save money, I prepared hamburger patties stuffed with cheese and onions, swathed them in bacon and aluminum foil, and popped them onto the manifold of my old Jeep. According to Nick, this was genius grillwork. Sure enough, when I stopped at a scenic viewpoint for lunch there was an excellent hot meal waiting for me under the hood.

Arriving at Aunt Mary's, my lively cousin Isabella had a robust laugh over my car-be-cueing story.

"Your grandfather used to do that," Aunt Mary told me, meaning my mother's father, the famous Bay Area heart surgeon.

"You're kidding!" I shrieked.

"No. Back when he drove up to his hunting ranch at Mount Hamilton, he used his old Army Jeep to cook his lunch since he had a lot of driving to do. He used to make a foil packet of ham and beans or stew or something, and he'd throw it under the hood so it would be hot at lunch time. Your grandmother was horrified by it."

"My mom used to talk about that old Jeep," I said.

"Did you know we have it here?" Aunt Mary said.

"Come on," Isabella said. "I'll show you."

Mary and Isabella lived on a huge hill surrounded by green rolling pastures and dotted by black cattle. Parked in the far corner of their property, my grandfather's legendary Jeep was slowly rusting away.

"He used to take my mom for rides up to the ranch on Sundays after Mass," I said. "Just the two of them. It was their special time together."

Isabella put her arm around my shoulder and we stood there for a long time. I silently told my mother it didn't seem fair to be there in the actual embrace of my actual precious family and still feel lonely.

I left early on Saturday morning so I could study. My Uncle Joseph and Auntie RoMo were out of town for the holiday weekend; I knew they wouldn't mind if the lonesome family funeral worker parked her Jeep near their citrus trees and read about state bylaws. After two hours of studying, I was feeling full of funeral facts. I packed it in and got on the road home. I was dying for a Diet Coke.

Back in Santa Clara, the house was abuzz with its own Beth brand of cheer. She had purchased a bread maker from Williams-Sonoma and was turning out little loaves studded with dried fruit. She spent entirely too much time trying to recreate Christmas decor featured on *The View*.

"We're getting out the lights," Beth said Saturday afternoon. "Want to help?"

"No," I grumbled. "The holidays blow."

"How can you say that?" Beth replied. "I love hanging the lights."

"I abhor Christmas lights, especially the red and green twinkly kind. And I'm sorry to be such a buzz kill, but Christmas reminds me of death and my mother dying."

"Oh, my god! Did your mother die at Christmastime?"

"Yes. I can't stand the commercials and shows and everything geared toward families. And the cards! The frigging cards with everybody else's beautiful family picture on the front. It reminds me she's dead, so I didn't have that; and I'm alone, so maybe I won't ever have it."

Beth looked morose and I felt ashamed of my rant. Who was I to wreck her enjoyment of the season? She ought to be able to play carols and string lights and make cocoa without being harassed. "I'm sorry, Beth," I said.

"So, I guess you don't want eggnog, then."

We started to giggle. "I guess I don't."

"It seems like I should give you your Christmas gift now."

"You got me a Christmas gift?"

Beth left the room and returned carrying a box wrapped in snowflake paper. I unwrapped it self-consciously, careful of the homemade paper. I didn't want her to think I was ungrateful as well as a Grinch. Inside the box, I found two dozen funeral pens from mortuaries around the country.

"Oh, my gosh! What did you do?" I asked.

Beth laughed. "I called funeral homes and asked them to send me a pen."

"And they did, just like that?"

"Not exactly."

"Seriously, what did you do?"

"I told them my grandma had attended a funeral there and brought home one of their pens, but she lost it and was sad, so I wanted to know if they would send her another."

"That's hilarious! I didn't know you had it in you," I said, looking at each pen to see where it had come from: Lady Lake, Florida; Kalamazoo, Michigan; Polk, Nebraska; and my favorite of the bunch, Bizzarro Funeral Home in Troy, New York. It was like a tour of the United States via stops at the local funeral homes.

"What did the morticians say?"

"Most of them laughed and said I'd made their day." Beth looked pleased with herself. I gave her a hug and said I'd help get the knots out of the Christmas lights. I didn't want to, but I couldn't avoid it after her thoughtful gift.

We were going through the boxes of holiday decor when Andy walked by. "What do they do with the body if somebody dies on a cruise ship?" he asked me.

"It's stored in a big refrigerator until they get back home."

"Cool!"

"Literally," I said.

Chapter 9

Going Back to My Future

SHORTLY AFTER MY FIRST ANNIVERSARY AT CHAPEL OF THE SOULS, Mr. Ingraham tracked me down at my desk while I finished an intake report. I was now an officially licensed funeral director, sans any work promotion. The report documented any personal items brought in with the deceased, details of the body, cuts, bruises, etc. This information is invaluable if a family brings a suit against the mortuary. I finished listing the jewelry Mrs. Sherwood had been wearing on arrival, and Mr. Ingraham glanced over my work.

"You do good work, Miss Fournier. I like your sense of organization," he said. *Was he really saying this to me?*

"You should see what I can do with canned goods," I shot back, feeling awestruck we were having a conversation. "Maybe I could come by and straighten out your pantry some time," I jested.

"I would never ask an apprentice to do such a thing," Mr. Ingraham said seriously.

"It was a joke." I smiled really big to prove it.

"Oh. Well, thank you for the offer, but my wife wouldn't like anyone else fooling around in her cupboards."

"Did you want to check this embalming report, or did you need something else?" I asked.

"I'd like to discuss your future plans. You have practical experience preparing bodies, sitting in with families, working funerals, and processing the paperwork, have your license on the wall; but I notice you have not attended a mortuary sciences program yet."

"That's true," I said humbly.

"You'll need to before you can apply for your embalming license," he advised.

I only needed a mortuary sciences degree if I was going to become an embalmer. There was no way I wanted to be an embalmer, but I wasn't sure I should say that to Mr. Ingraham. A few nights ago, I had discussed this with my father; it was pretty clear he hoped I'd reconsider journalism.

Mr. Ingraham must have seen the doubt flash across my eyes. "You don't really want to be an embalmer, do you?" he asked.

"I prefer not to," I admitted, without meeting his eyes.

Mr. Ingraham sat back and thought for a long moment. "I'm the son of a funeral director," he finally said. "My dad likewise was the son of a funeral director. I grew up in the business and as far as anyone was concerned, I was going into the business. When my dad passed on, he left me the funeral parlour."

"Then what are you doing here?" I asked. "Why aren't you running your own place?"

"I lost it."

I didn't understand what he was getting at so I asked, "Where?"

"This was never a calling for me," Mr. Ingraham explained. "I don't exactly have the kind of personality people gravitate toward. People started going elsewhere and after a while, I couldn't meet the bills. I had to sell the parlour that had been in our family for three generations."

"I'm so sorry," I said.

"I don't have another line of work," Mr. Ingraham continued. "This is all I've ever been, so here I am and I have no idea what it's like to enjoy a day of work. You have a calling for this, Elizabeth. You're excellent with the clients, and you know how to add nice little touches that make the service more personal. You'll find a place for yourself. If you don't want to be an embalmer, don't do it."

"Really?" He was sharing all this personal stuff with me, and he called me by my first name. I could not have been more shocked if he had announced he was going to be performing at open mic night at a comedy club.

"Really. This business is going to wear out your body and kick your heart around and mess up your family life, and that's enough to give to any line of work. If embalming is going to wreck the rest of it for you, don't be an embalmer. You are special, kid. Go work for a family funeral home or something."

Still unable to believe this was coming from my grim boss I said, "Are you joking?"

"I wouldn't do that," Mr. Ingraham said.

&

My head reeled over Mr. Ingraham's advice. I slipped out of work early and drove to the Green Street Mortuary garage.

"Why the long face?" Larry asked as I approached.

"I'm just thinking," I said. "How come you never became a funeral director after all these years of working for a mortuary?"

"Didn't want to. I'm a driver; I'm good at that," Larry said. "It keeps me out in the fresh air, and I don't have to deal with so much of the crying and hand holding. I can't stand to hear women cry; it breaks my heart."

Gary overheard us and came over. "Why are you asking, sweet Elizabeth?"

"I'm pretty sure I don't want to be an embalmer," I said.

"Well, that's no problem. They're on their way out anyway," said Gary.

"You think so?"

"Cremation is the thing these days," Larry explained.

"You'll do fine, darling girl," Gary said. "You're a good soul. You don't have to do any throat slashing if you don't want to. That formaldehyde is nasty stuff, anyway. I think it's the reason so many of the old timers in this business end up with cancer."

"Oh, speaking of which," Larry interjected, while reaching into his jacket, "I have another pen for you. I had to drive to Carmel, where an old friend of mine owns a parlour. I don't think he'll be there much longer. I guess they decided he has leukemia."

When I got home I sat in the Jeep for a while, looking at the house. I could see the light from the TV blinking through the basement windows. It looked like Beth was in the front room bedazzling something. I didn't want to go in, so I started the engine. Suddenly, Andy's face popped up in my passenger's side window. I shut off the engine and motioned for him to jump in.

"Where did you come from?" I asked.

"I just came back from my friend Alex's house," he said. "What are you doing out here?"

"Trying to decide what I'm going to do in the next phase of my life."

"What's to decide?" Andy said with a shrug. "Just make yourself happy."

I looked at the house and back at Andy. "What if making myself happy means I have to leave here?" Andy's face tightened, and I immediately felt guilty.

"Are you serious?" he asked.

"I think so. I don't think I have the right job. I think I want to go back to Portland. I miss my dad and my friends there." I could see Andy's lower lip was starting to tremble. "I'm sorry, buddy."

"It's okay," he whispered, then looked at me. "Maybe my mom will want to come back one day, too. Maybe she misses me."

I felt like the worst person in the world and wanted desperately to make it up to him. "Do you want to go for a ride in a hearse this weekend?" I offered.

"No," Andy said, opening my Jeep door and stepping out. "Leave me alone, please."

I went to bed thinking Andy would feel better in the morning. He was just a kid and I'd dropped a pretty big bombshell on him, but we were buddies. He would forgive me, wouldn't he?

He wouldn't look at me the next morning. I pulled away from the house muttering, then shouting the f-word. Why did I have to screw up everything? *I always am such a failure!*

At the parlour, I went straight to the phone and called Dyrland's. Richard wasn't there, but they said they would page him and have him call me back. I stomped to the break room and put more ice in my Super Big Gulp. Then I stomped back to my desk to work on an obituary I had promised to finish the day before. By the time the phone rang, I was so worked up I nearly jerked it off the desk.

"Little Chapel of the Souls, Elizabeth speaking," I barked.

"You rang?" Richard replied, his sardonic voice snapping me back to my emotional senses.

"Hey, Richard, how's tricks?" I said wearily.

"Oh, everything is coming up roses and lilies and chrysanthemums, as usual," he said. "What's up?"

"Do you know of any small funeral homes up there hiring? Some place that would need a shiny, new funeral director?"

"Actually, yes and no."

"Me no follow."

Richard laughed. "No, there are never any family funeral homes ever hiring, but yes, I know a corporate place taking their time to hire a funeral director, and something tells me you could be their girl."

I cringed at the word "corporate," but I was ready to face my fears and make the move. After all, I had worked at a huge conglomerate in the San Francisco Bay Area. Anything in Portland would be small by comparison.

"Really? Which one?"

"Western View. I have a friend who works there. Want me to put in a good word for you?"

"Would you?"

"What are old friends for?" he asked. "Just don't embarrass me over there and sing Bette Midler. And good job on that test, kid. Next time I see you, I'll buy you a cold one to celebrate."

I promised I would be the best funeral director Western View had ever employed, hung up, and rang the Oregon Mortuary and Cemetery Board to see what I had to do to register for the Funeral Service Practitioner exam. I would have two licenses in two states!

It took a month before I knew I had the job, and Andy barely spoke to me the whole time. Beth figured out something was up and tried to mend fences, but that only made Andy avoid both of us. I spent more time with Joseph and Roxy. It was comfortable to be with them, plus I wanted to see them as much as I could in case I was about to move back to Portland.

Finally, Western View Funeral Home made me an official offer, and I packed for my move to the City of Roses. Bedazzlin' Beth and Cheesemaker Rand took me out for dinner to celebrate, and Aunt Mary and Isabella planned a nice going away fête for me. Mr. Ingraham was sincerely congratulatory when I put in my notice, and the good man instructed the secretary to order a cake for my last day. Larry and Gary took me out for a drink at their favorite bar, the Top of the Mark, and toasted me heartily. I felt like I was leaving triumphantly, except for one young man whose pinched little face haunted me day and night.

Finally, I got fed up with the silent treatment and hunted Andy down at his favorite skateboard park. He was sitting on a low wall, watching some kid with scraped elbows practice kick flips. I walked up to him and declared, "You're not being fair."

Andy turned his head away from me but didn't leave. I figured that was something, so I sat down beside him. "I know you're mad and I know you're sad, but we're friends. We're supposed to talk about things."

"But we're not going to be anymore, are we?" Andy said. "Because you're leaving, so now who is not being fair?"

"Just because we're going to be apart doesn't mean we can't be friends."

Andy rolled his eyes. "You know what I mean."

"That's true, I do."

We sat in silence for a long time before Andy said, "The house is really going to suck without you."

"But, you could take up fruit bread making," I suggested. To my relief, that got a giggle out of him.

Andy held up one hand, pinky extended. "Instead of taking walks in the cemetery with you, I can go antiquing with Beth and start my own collection of tea cups!"

"You could build a chicken coop in the back yard with little drawers under the nesting boxes for tidy egg collection!" I crowed.

Andy suddenly became somber. Were his eyes tearing up? I put my arm around his shoulder and he let me keep it there.

"I'm going to miss you," I said. I felt him nod. After a moment I said, "I could come visit you when I'm here to see my cousins. I don't know how often I can afford the trip, but sometimes."

"Okay," Andy said glumly.

It wasn't fair. Andy deserved more than a crappy substitute for a mom who was just a temporary roommate. I wondered if I had done the wrong thing by encouraging his friendship. Anybody could have predicted this day was going to come. Had I been selfish because I was lonely? Are we insensitive when we let kids love us, knowing they are going to lose us sooner or later?

☙

The day finally came when I loaded my boxes in the Jeep, put some potatoes and a packet of salmon on the manifold, and turned in my key to the beautiful Market Street house. Andy walked me out to the street and gave me a long, hard hug. How the heck was I going to drive away from this kid? Beth saw us from the living room window and came out for a hug, too.

Then she put her hands on Andy's shoulders and said, "We'd better let Elizabeth get on the road, it's a long drive." Andy nodded and I climbed into the driver's seat. I felt like I was kicking a puppy as I started the engine and slowly pulled out. In my rearview mirror, Andy and Beth waved a last goodbye. My eyes were getting hot, so I turned at the next intersection and pressed the gas a little harder. Like ripping off a bandage, I thought, better to do it quickly. When my chest refused to loosen up, I channel surfed the radio, looking for some deliciously funky song to take my mind off the situation.

Nothing. I gave up and let myself hurt for a while.

Chapter 10

A View into My Future

S AN JOSE TO PORTLAND IS ABOUT A TWELVE-HOUR DRIVE AT A decent clip, counting bathroom breaks and meal stops. I'm a right-lane driver, even when I'm not being paid to participate in a funeral procession, so there was no way I could make it home in one day. Springing for a motel room was out of the question but no matter, since the entire route was studded with glorious camping opportunities: Mount Shasta, Six Rivers National Forest, and the Rogue River. I decided to go out of my way to camp at Hellgate Canyon, just west of Grants Pass, Oregon. It had appeared in many classic movies and TV shows—Rooster Cogburn and Eula Goodnight had floated through, back when John Wayne was still alive, and Marshall Matt Dillon once escaped outlaws by jumping in the icy river. It was, and still is, a popular white water rafting spot, and the natural star of *The River Wild*.

It turned out to be too popular. I arrived to find there were no camping spaces left. The manager at Indian Mary Park told me I could camp on Bureau of Land Management land, which sounded like a great idea in the light of day. I followed his directions to a wide spot in the road, where a sign directed me to a camp about a quarter mile down a steep trail. No problem there, I was a good hiker and wearing sensible shoes for the trip.

I lugged my manifold meal and sleeping bag down the hill. Feeling like a brave pioneer woman—better yet, a young Native American skilled at living off the land—I gathered some twigs and limbs and built a camp fire. Then I sat down to eat my car-be-que. After supper, I thought I'd meditate in the hopes of entering Portland in a higher state of being. I couldn't wait to tell Willow about my overnighter at the edge of the Siskiyou National Forest.

I was finishing up my scrumptious, Jeep-poached salmon and baked potato when I heard something, or someone, lumbering through the trees. I froze. Were they friendly? Suddenly, I remembered how *The River Wild* turned out: Kevin Bacon and his friend were really scary bad guys in that movie. I suddenly remembered lots of other movies I'd seen where camping alone turned out to be not such a great idea. Probably nobody around like those *Deliverance* guys, right? But what about bears? Were there still bears in Oregon? My heart was pounding so loudly in my ears I couldn't recall.

No, no, no! I thought. You are not a stereotypical wimpy girl! Logically, chances are it's just a raccoon or something that smelled your dinner. You do not need to run. Stay near the camp fire, and it will never come close to you. Until you go to sleep, and it snuffles its way over to see if there are leftovers. But what if it's a person? Probably coming to camp here just like you did . . . and of course, having other campers around will make it more fun . . . unless they are fugitives from justice, of course. . . .

I stomped out the fire, double-time, grabbed my sleeping bag and trash and smashed my way through the brush back to the trail. Oh, smart! Make plenty of noise so the predator can track you easily. Should I slow down to avoid looking like prey to four-legged forest dwellers? Or would that help a serial killer catch up to me?

The salmon wasn't sitting so well in my stomach anymore. I fumbled around in my pocket for the Jeep keys, to have them out and ready to open the door. *But where the hell were my keys? In my back pocket! Yes! Progress!*

I crested the trail, dashed to my dear old Jeep, threw myself and my sleeping bag in, and slammed the locks down. So much for communing with nature. Still panting, I drove back to Grants Pass, found a well-lit parking spot, and settled down in the driver's seat for a restless night under the street lamps.

A couple passed by, hand in hand, walking their bouncy baby Labrador. I watched them with envy, until they looked at me suspiciously and made me realize it would be wise to make myself less conspicuous. Discussing my vagrancy with the local sheriff would only lead to humiliating confessions.

The rest of my trip was long but uneventful. By the time I reached Portland, I was wilted and famished. My brother Nick and his wife, Phoebe, had offered to let me stay in their basement until I could find a place of my own. I drove straight to their house. Dad was there, too, waiting to welcome me home, and there was a spread on the table, thank goodness. It felt so good to be back! Dad was a little grayer, residual from his icky divorce. Nick had a more settled air, and Phoebe looked peacefully maternal carrying my baby niece around the kitchen. *Did I look more grown up to them as well?*

"How was your trip?" Dad asked.

"Uh. You know, boring," I lied. The details would only worry him.

"Let's eat, kiddo," Nick said. "I thought you'd never get here. We can unload your stuff after dinner."

I was thrilled to dig into salmon with fingerling potatoes that weren't cooked under the hood of my Jeep.

❧

Monday morning, I was back in black and off to my new job. Western View was a prestigious funeral home with its own cemetery gardens and a sweeping view towards the coast. A lovely combo unit—parlour and cemetery in the same location.

"Each section of the garden is named," a funeral director, Glen, told me on my walk-through tour. "You can see they are also designated by different statuary. That's Rugged Cross down there, Garden of the Apostles is here, and Nativity is down the way. You'll get their names down in time."

"I absolutely love the statues," I said.

"The ladies always do," Glen retorted.

There was another funeral director, Nathan; a lovely older woman who ran the office, Faith; and a young guy who ran the on-site crematorium, Michael. They all made me feel welcome and took me out to lunch at Skyline Burger to celebrate my arrival.

This is going to be great! I thought at the end of the first day. I felt at home looking at the rose bushes blooming across the rolling slopes of Western View.

I had a lot to learn, and I watched a lot of Western View training films on my computer. The type of films produced by corporate headquarters, and some so corny it took extreme self-control not to mock them aloud.

I couldn't help but think of Andy, so I zipped a quick email off to him after I took a practice quiz.

Western View wanted family service counselors and funeral directors learning a specific, seven-minute presentation to dazzle families. They taught the proper way to upgrade casket choices, and I had to master selling people on using the company funeral service and cemetery together.

Sales weren't my bag, but it was the only way to make any tangible cash. My base pay was minimum wage; everything else I received was commission from selling property, caskets, headstones, and other goods and services.

"Commissioned sales?" Dad said when I told him about the training program. I could hear the doubt in his voice. "Aren't you a bona fide funeral director?"

"In California, only. I figure it's the trade-off. They have to pay the bills somehow in order to keep helping people, don't you think?"

"Yeah, you're right," Dad agreed.

"I can do this," I said.

"You can do anything you set your mind to."

"Mind set, training films watched, ready to prove myself!"

"Go get 'em, Tiger!" Dad cheered.

"Eye of the Tiger, Baby!" I roared to my father.

At Western View, the pressure to sell was offset by my work with the families. A woman came in one day and asked to speak to a female funeral director. Glen introduced her to me, making it clear I was technically a Family Service Counselor.

"I need to plan my funeral," she said. I guessed, based on the head scarf she was wearing, that she was fighting cancer. Her name was Helen McHenry and she was there on behalf of her husband.

"He's won't be able to manage after I'm gone, and I don't have long," Mrs. McHenry confided. "So, let's pick out everything and get it all taken care of; because he's going to be lost, and my son won't be any help. He's a nice boy, but both my men lean on me."

I assured her I understood, and together we planned her service. She picked a modestly-priced casket, music, her pallbearers, everything. She was particularly concerned that I list the family lawyer and accountant in her file. The death certificates were to be sent straight to them and all details handled so her men wouldn't have to do anything. I asked if there was anything else I could help her do.

"Yes, that's why I asked for a woman to talk with me," Mrs. McHenry said. I raised my eyebrows. "When my husband gets here, you take him off somewhere alone. Tell him you want to help him straighten his collar or something." From her purse, she extracted a small bottle of Scotch whiskey.

What was I getting myself into where I had to take an old man somewhere alone, and we'd need booze?

"You give him a little shot of this. Tell him it's from me and say, 'Papa, you can do this.' Say it just like that and if he cries, pat his back a little. He'll stop pretty soon and be okay to get through the day. It's got to be you or some woman. He won't be able to hear it from a man, but he'll know it's me talking to him if you do it." She looked me straight in the eye. "Promise me you'll do it."

I solemnly promised.

Her quavering voice betrayed a bit of emotion. "It's just that he leans on me so much. I've been trying to stick around for him, but the doctor says I've lost the fight."

I reached for a box of tissue, but Mrs. McHenry was on her feet and all business again. "You'll take care of everything," she declared. "I know you will."

"You girls get it all settled?" Glen asked after I saw Mrs. McHenry to the door. His tone told me his mind was on the sale he had just been forced to hand me. I didn't want him ticked off at me, and I didn't want to discuss my conversation with Mrs. McHenry. I just nodded.

"That was pretty sexist, her assuming a man couldn't help her as well as woman," Glen snarled.

"Sometimes people have funny ideas," I said, holding her secret close to my breast.

༄

My first Friday home, Kevin and Ryan took me dancing. Since this was my homecoming celebration, they made a special point of choosing straight clubs. Salsa clubs, in fact, and it was fabulous! Ryan was an excellent dancer.

His mother had given him lessons from elementary school all the way through high school. Little did I know we could have been waltzing and doing the mambo together all these years.

"You should have seen how wracked with guilt she was over it after Ryan came out," Kevin said. "I honestly felt sorry for her."

"Oh, no!" I said to Ryan. "Now I feel sorry for her."

"I'd feel sorry for her if that was the worst of the stereotypes she entertains," Ryan said, "but honestly, she's known I'm gay for a while. It's time for her to tune in to reality."

"Wow. You sure have found your self-confidence while I was away."

"That's what happens when you decide being half in and half out of something isn't enough, and you really commit come hell or high water," said Ryan.

I wanted what they had. If I could have sawed off my arm right then in exchange for that kind of love, I would have done it.

Halfway through the night, we were dancing in one of those awkward but fun triangles you find yourself in when your third wheel doesn't have a partner. I spotted a stunning man checking me out from the bar. Kevin spotted him, too and started maneuvering us in that direction, so we would end up by Mr. Tall-Dark-and-Handsome at the end of the song.

Dante Perez held up his end of the deal by moving into position where we'd accidentally bump into each other as I exited the floor. Then, he managed to send me an expansive smile and a drink. By the time Kevin and Ryan came to collect me and drive me home, I had a date for the following evening and a good idea of who my next boyfriend would be.

Chapter 11

Odelay!

THE ENTIRE CITY WAS IN BLOOM; I HAD A NEW JOB AND A SMOKING hot romance on the horizon. The future was so bright it required dark glasses, while my brother's basement was a gloomy downer. It was nice of Nick and Phoebe to let me stay there but living out of boxes was hellish. I couldn't help feeling like a dumb kid in the midst of their very grown up baby world. I knew if I stayed I would start feeling lame because I didn't have a baby, marriage, or life of my own.

Most of the women I had grown up with were getting married and having babies. I bumped into one of them (she used to tease me about liking Erik Estrada), and she could hardly get her arms around her baby bump to steer her grocery cart. Dad informed me that neighbor Denice, the one with the cat named Pinky, had a serious beau as well.

Oh, for the love of cheese and wine, was I the sole remaining single woman in the city?

Last I heard, Willow was still unattached. Was she looking for a roommate? I paid her a visit.

"Liza Love!" she squealed, pulling me through the door. "Come in here and tell me all about California. Wait, I'll get the tea. I just got a new licorice blend."

If she only knew I only drank that stuff to appease her. Her place hadn't changed much. I settled in at the bright red kitchen table and gave her the nutshell version of my time down south.

"Your housemates sound awful," Willow said. "Well, except for Andy. He sounds sweet."

"Speaking of which," I interjected. "Do you have a housemate these days?"

"I had a student this winter, but she moved out. I'm not getting another one because I'm leaving for Bolivia. My grandmother died and left me some money, so I'm going to the Amazon to work to reduce deforestation."

Well, of course she was. "What are you doing with this place?" I asked, knowing I couldn't swing the rent on my own, but it did have two bedrooms.

"The landlady has already found a new tenant," Willow said. "A family with babies."

Of course she did. They were everywhere, and on a campaign to crowd me out of housing. I changed the subject to Dante.

"He sounds sexy!" Willow said.

"He is! And he's a lot of fun and he's a great dancer and he's introducing me to his family this weekend. He works in his family's construction company, and I am completely coo-coo for cocoa puffs over him."

"Oh, my God, I have to read your cards!" Willow declared, jumping up to get her well-worn tarot deck. She shuffled the cards to clear their energy, performed a connection ritual, asked the cards if I would marry soon, and dealt out my fortune.

"See this?" she said. "The Lovers, the Ace of Swords, and Justice."

"What does it mean?"

"When they travel together, it means you will marry."

Yes!

"But it won't be just any marriage. It will be a union of soulmates."

I knocked the cards over to hug her. A union of soulmates! "And I'm about to meet his family!"

"Hold up. We don't know who the guy is for sure," Willow said. "The cards don't give his name."

"Who else would it be? Do you have some hunky beast I should know about hidden in the basement?"

To start fulfilling my destiny, I shopped for a new house share on Craigslist. There were a few places in my price range, but they all looked shady and not in the tree sense. Apparently, I could afford a room split from the kitchen by recycled office cubby walls and curtains. All this in a "4/20 friendly" house. There was the room with a man willing to reduce the rent for "body rubs." I shut down my desk top. Reading Mr. Rub-Me's ad made me feel like the computer could watch me undress.

I brought our new ritual drink, Coke Zero, over to Kevin and Ryan's place to ask if they knew anyone looking for a renter.

"Depends," Kevin said. "How do you feel about a no-frills place with a love triangle of lesbians, one of which who probably has an addiction problem?"

"Well, I don't mind lesbians, but how is the rest of that a valid offer?" I asked.

"Paddington has space," Ryan said. "His lover left him and he can't afford the rent by himself. I'm pretty sure you could have the bedroom."

"Paddington?"

"His real name is Oscar, but he's a really sweet gay bear and everybody calls him Paddington," Ryan explained.

"You don't want to live with Paddington," Kevin said. "All he does these days is mope around. It will be completely depressing."

I tried again. "Do you know any ordinary people looking for a roommate?"

"Scott and David are normal if you're willing to be a surrogate mother," Kevin said.

"Please forget I asked."

"Alicia and her new girlfriend are pretty normal except for all those cats," Ryan pointed out.

"Forget it!" I repeated. Kevin and Ryan started giggling.

"You're screwing with me!" I shrieked.

"You were totally going for it!" Kevin howled.

"Actually, the thing about Paddington is true," said Ryan. "He's downright morose these days."

"Come on, you guys, I need to find a place to live that's not my brother's basement."

"What's wrong with your brother's basement?" asked Ryan.

"It's my brother's basement."

"Try Craigslist," Kevin suggested.

We were done here.

♻

One morning I pulled into my favorite 7-11 for a tuna sandwich and refill of my Super Big Gulp. There, in the parking lot, was my 7th grade arch nemesis, Nancy, wearing a nurse's uniform. I jumped out of my straight-up hooptie vehicle, called her name, and we hugged and ran through the usual questions: How is your family? What are you doing these days? Do you still line up dolls in your sand box to watch long funeral processions?

We laughed as we recalled meeting on the first day of 7th grade, both pissed we had to share a name with another kid in the class. We duked it out with rulers and became fast friends. She won by default all these years later since I legally changed my name to Elizabeth.

I told her I was looking for a place. Voilà, she was looking for a renter for her attic space. "I'll take it!" I said on the spot.

"You should see it first," Nurse Nancy warned. "It's finished, but the ceilings are pretty low and I have cats. Are you all right with cats?"

"How many exactly?" I laughed.

"Two."

"I'm short, plus I get along great with cats. Is it available now?"

We agreed I'd move in on Sunday. Saturday was booked to spend with Dante's family.

I was amped! Back in Portland, check. Gainfully employed, check. A home that was not my brother's basement, check. Gorgeous, sexy, wonderful boyfriend, check. All I had to do now was pass my state boards to become a bona fide Oregon mortician.

☙

I was going for a slam dunk on the state licensing test: I put my study guides into a binder and took it everywhere, just like I'd done in California. When the parlour was quiet, I hauled my binder to a remote area, took off my black pumps, and walked stocking-foot in the grass while reading and rereading the Oregon bylaws governing funeral directors.

The grass in that cemetery was perfect. The stones were flat to make it easy for heavy equipment and lawnmowers to move across the grounds. Sometimes I was tempted to roll down one of the hills. I didn't, for the sake of my ever-present nylons; I already had enough to do to hide the green stains on my feet.

Mr. Cremator, Michael, spotted me out there one day and came over to see what I was up to. "Had enough of the bier barons this afternoon?" he asked.

"That's not nice," I said.

"No, but it's funny."

"You make your living at the expense of grieving families, too," I pointed out.

"That's true," he admitted and dropped the topic. I stayed quiet.

"Well, better get back to it. Some guys and I are going over to 52nd Avenue for some beers tonight."

"Have fun," I said, cheerily.

"You like sports bars?"

"Not really."

"They have free hot dogs."

What a goof. How was that supposed to matter? I didn't want to hurt his feelings, so I just smiled until he finally slouched off.

"He sounds odd," Phoebe said that night at dinner, when I told the story of my interrupted study session.

"I suppose one shouldn't expect the very best social skills out of a man who hangs around alone in the bowels of a mortuary breathing in the smoke of the dearly departed," I said.

"He's probably just trying to be friendly," Phoebe agreed. "How old is he?"

"I don't know, young."

"What's the crematory like?" Nick wanted to know.

"It's pretty creepy. There are a lot of stacked boxes down there marked 'personal belongings' that haven't been touched in ages. People swear it's haunted."

"Sounds like your kind of place, Morticia," Nick said, winking at me.

"Speaking of, I found a place to move."

Nick and Phoebe made a sweet show of pretending to be sorry I'd be leaving so soon, but I was sure they were breathing a big sigh of relief. I couldn't blame them. If I was living the good life with my wonderful spouse and beautiful bouncing baby, I wouldn't want a kid sister in the basement, either.

Saturday I was up with the roosters—or at least the time I assumed roosters got up. Portlanders are only allowed hens in their backyard coops. I chatted silently to my mother while I was getting ready, a considerable amount of time. I wanted to look perfect when I met Dante's family.

Wearing my favorite pink sundress and best strappy sandals, hair cascading down my back, I sashayed through the kitchen. Even Nick was impressed; he whistled, I spun around, and my heart soared.

"Your hair is gleaming!" Phoebe said. "How do you get it so shiny?"

"Mayonnaise," I told her, popping the top off a yogurt container.

"That's what happened to the mayo!" Nick said. "I wanted a moist roast beef sandwich last night."

"I'm out of here tomorrow and you can have your condiments all to yourself," I said. "But for today, I want every advantage."

"They'll love you," Phoebe said.

"Sell the mom and you're in," Nick added.

"No sweat, moms love me."

And Dante's mom did love me. "Oh, she's beautiful!" Mrs. Perez announced, crossing the kitchen to greet us at the door. "Come in here, so the girls can meet you. Dante! The boys are in the yard and just about to knock over the chilies with their soccer ball. Move the table."

Dante kissed his mother and exited to do her bidding. I then met his sisters and aunties and most charming grandmother.

It was a day to cherish. Dante's family was welcoming, jovial, and best of all, large. His uncles and male cousins were sprawled on the patio, listening to Javier Solis and Ramon Ayala while drinking Tecate with Clamato. Dante joined them and every time I looked over, I would hear "Odelay!" and someone would raise a glass to toast. Enfolded in the bosom of that extended family, I felt the promise of the future I'd always wanted.

Dante didn't disappoint, either. His pride in me was obvious. He kept his affectionate gestures strictly appropriate, but I could tell his family's approval had electrified his desire for me. I spotted him looking at me like the grill wasn't the only thing that was hot in that backyard. He walked across the yard, never taking his eyes off mine. When we were face to face, he said in a low, serious voice, "*Que hermosa eres! Por tú silueta angelical me enamoré de ti.*"

I knew just enough Spanish to recognize that as a sweet nothing.

"You are so beautiful," he purred. "I fell in love with you because you have the shape of an angel."

When he saw me flush, he leaned in closer so his next words tickled my ear. "*Mi alma gemela.*"

Then he edged around so he could translate into my other ear. "My soulmate," he whispered, making me tingle right down to my perfectly pedicured toes.

This is it, I thought, looking around the yard. Together we will parent the next generation of this family.

Chapter 12

Roads to Perdition

O N SUNDAY, I HAULED MY LOVE-DRUNK HEART AND STILL unpacked boxes over to Nurse Nancy's. She lived in a funky little fixer-upper in the Clinton district, oh-so-Portland quirky, yet still affordable.

Her attic was stifling hot. I couldn't stand up straight in half of it, but it was mine, all mine. Nurse Nancy had outfitted it with a twin-sized futon and a make-shift wardrobe built out of modular shelving. Her cats, Dixon and Ticonderoga, came right up and made themselves comfortable on my bed. Although they might transform my decorous black suit collection to a furry mess, I was so thankful to have my own place I shrugged it off.

"Luke," Nancy called up the stairs, "you hungry? I made egg salad."

"You are the best roommate ever, Darth!" I called back. "I'm starving, and you're a supreme dork for calling me that." Those were our 7th grade ruler war names.

"Then come on down. I want to hear about your date and his Clamato."

We filled each other in on what had happened since we'd last seen each other a few years back. Since Nancy was a nurse, I could talk about my job without her getting grossed out at the first mention of a corpse. She also had experience in dealing with the pain families go through at end-of-life.

When Nurse Nancy's cell interrupted us, I cleared the table and did the dishes, glad for the chance to demonstrate what a superb choice of house-mate I was. Once I was finished at the sink, I turned my attentions to her pantry; Nancy's canned goods were in a terrible state of disarray and dread. They were all parked vertically in a parallel universe.

☙

I started my day Monday with the time-honored funeral directors' ritual of reading the obituaries. Not to see who had died, but to find out which funeral home is handling what "case," as they all say. There was one obit from Western View, so I clipped it and gave it to the secretary to add to the deceased's file.

Next, I sat down to pencil out my budget. Given my pitiful base wage and my lackadaisical attitude about selling merchandise, it was clear I needed to make extra money. There was no way I could make rent and still fill the gas tank on my thirteen-year-old heap to get me back and forth from southeast Portland to the northwest hills. It was an hour's drive each way. Fortunately, I did have an idea. It required funeral music, but that was no problem. Western View had a huge collection of instrumental CDs— everything from ancient dirges to popular modern ones. I ran down to Rite Aid and bought blank CDs and spent my usual study time burning some funeral favorites.

I was flying through the back hall to replace the mortuary's CD collection when, out of nowhere, a voice said, "You sure are busy today."

I shrieked.

"Hey, settle down! It's just me, Michael."

Of course. Creepy McCreeperson was always doing that: creeping around. "Sorry. You startled me is all," I said. "I have to return these."

"What are they?"

"Just some funeral music."

"Oh yeah, I can see why you'd want that," he sneered.

"Can I help you with something?"

"No, I was just leaving. I wanna catch the race this afternoon on my buddy's big screen—NASCAR."

"Well, exit the back door since that specific leather jacket doesn't exactly set the tone we're going for here."

"Yeah, I'll do that and I'll make sure not to screw with your *tone*," Michael replied, pulling himself off the wall he'd been supporting and ambling away.

Sheesh, sensitive guy.

I took my burnt CDs home and practiced a few numbers in my attic bedroom, but it made the cats anxious. I packed my stuff into a tote bag and drove over to Lone Fir Pioneer Cemetery, the oldest burial ground

The Green Reaper 97

in Portland. There were plenty of giant headstones I could hide behind. I settled down in the shelter of twin pillars that sat in the shade of an ancient oak tree and started my funeral hymns. I practiced till I could sing "In the Garden" all the way through—in tune. When I got home, I tested my skills on the cats. They didn't run, so I figured I was on to something.

At practice all Saturday, I worked to smooth out my delivery and put the emphasis on the right syllables. Now it was time to put my money-making plan into action. Richard worked weekends, and I hadn't seen a funeral announcement for that Sunday at Dyrland's. I took a chance and drove over there.

"I took your advice," I told him.

Richard raised his eyebrows. "That was wise. About what?"

"I have a small but growing repertoire of funeral songs I am available to perform."

"Oh, no!" Richard nearly shouted. "Fool me once!"

"Give me a chance. Let me at least audition."

"Why?"

"Because I can't make it on my base pay and I suck at sales. I need a way to pick up a little extra scratch."

Richard looked at me with dreadfulness.

"Please?" I begged. "Just listen? If I really stink you don't have to hire me. I swear, I will leave you alone about it if you actually listen and then tell me to get the hell out of here."

Richard sighed and considered his options. "All right, but if I motion for you to stop, you are to immediately cease and desist, and it will be the last time this comes up in conversation. Except over beers if I am making fun of you."

"Absolutely," I assured him.

At an unused chapel I handed over my CD. "Number nine," I said, and he cued up my digital accompaniment.

Richard listened to "The Old Rugged Cross" and "Abide with Me," but when he heard the first strains of "Wind Beneath My Wings," the song I had butchered the first time I soloed for him, he jammed his finger down on the off button. "Are you sure you want to go ahead, because I think I have PTSD from the last time you sang this."

"Don't be dramatic," I snapped. Richard tentatively pushed the start button and the game was on! I wouldn't say I hit a home run with my vocal styling, but I managed to get the ball over the second baseman's head.

When I finished, Richard looked, if not impressed, at least convinced of my competence.

"So, will you hire me to solo on weekends and evenings?"

"On an on-call basis only, when the regular soloist can't make it," Richard said. It wasn't much, but it would help.

"I promise I won't let you down. I'll keep practicing in cemeteries, and I swear you won't be sorry."

"Work on 'How Great Thou Art'; we get a lot of Lutherans in lately."

I let him know I was also available for other odd jobs: corpse cosmetology, body transportation, anything to bring in a few bucks.

I headed home, feeling triumphant. I rang the blue manse in Cali to tell Andy about my singing success, but no answer. We used to joke around and practice Run-D.M.C. in the cemetery together.

When I bounced into the house, I was in a fabulous mood. I explained my predicament and my plan for bringing my financial ends together to Nancy.

"I'm hoping after I perform a couple of times at Dyrland's, some other parlours will hire me, too. Then maybe word will spread like wildfire across town, if I'm lucky."

"If you need more side work, I was going to hire a housekeeper to come in a couple of times a month, but I'd rather reduce your rent for cleaning than hire a stranger off Craigslist."

"I'll pick up your filthy socks any day." We worked out a deal that would keep me out of the poorhouse, and I started immediately.

Nancy said, "Can you reorganize the upper cupboards?"

"Five steps ahead of you!" I shouted with a jar of Japanese horseradish powder clutched in each hand.

☙

That night, Dante took me out for a romantic picnic on the grass at Waterfront Park. I could tell by the menu that his mom had done the cooking.

Dante didn't strike me as a man who spent his days in the kitchen, yet there he was pulling warm tamales out of an insulated lunch bag and opening a plastic dish of fresh guacamole. There was even chocolate flan for dessert. Yeah, his mom totally approved.

"This looks delicious," I told him.

"You look delicious," he said, opening a cooler filled with icy bottles of Dos XX Lager.

We ate and watched the dragon boat teams perfect their rowing skills. He shared his dream of wanting to restore classic Chevrolet Camaros. I opened up about wanting to own a funeral parlour someday that catered to a simpler way of burial. The balmy night air had lured people to the park. They were strolling, roller blading, riding bikes, and playing with their dogs. To me it was just the two of us, alone under the night sky on a colorful blanket. We stayed until the food was gone and the beer cooler empty. We lingered on and hated to leave that blanket and our sweet talk; I was in love with the entire universe.

"Can I come in?" Dante asked later, outside my door.

"Uh, no, sorry. I can't," I said. His face fell and I reminded him I had a roommate. He seemed to accept this.

"Tuesday, then. I'll pick you up from work." My dark-eyed angel took off into the night.

I zipped up the creaky wooden staircase to my hotbox sleeping quarters and pulled down the shade. Off went my sundress so I could lay naked with a fan blowing on me while I got cool and cozy enough to read the treasure I had been anticipating all evening: Willow had bequeathed me an old 1960's paperback. *The American Way of Death* was written by Jessica Mitford, a pocket-sized Englishwoman who was a former communist. Mitford found the extravagances of the relentless salesmanship and pauses of sensitivity of the death-care industry a force to reckon with. In hopes of learning something from her searing depiction of the bloated funeral trade, my nude form struck a contented pose and I dug in.

"A funeral director in San Francisco says, 'if a person drives a Cadillac, why should he have a Pontiac funeral?' The Cadillac symbol features prominently in the funeral men's thinking. There is a funeral director in Los Angeles who

says his rock-bottom minimum price is $200. But he reserves to himself the right to determine who is eligible for this minimum priced service. 'I won't sell it to some guy who drives up in a Cadillac.'"

She was pithy, yet her dry English jocularity took on the so-called community plea for the end to sumptuous, costly funerals in sentences which were maddening, revealing, curious, and comical. It hit close to my work life. I finished the book in four hours, with an even deeper resolve to follow my heart and do the right thing.

☙

Down time at the funeral parlour was torturous, but to the company's advantage—I'd straighten newspapers in the break room or clean out the fridge, anything to make the hours go. I wasn't allowed to be an important cog in the wheel that was Western View.

One slow day I stood in the Rose Garden of the Savior, looking towards the Willamette River, when Michael "happened" by nonchalantly.

"Getting some sun in your golden hair?" he asked.

"Just listening to the motorcycles whiz by," I said. "I'll bet half the city is out on a speed boat today with drinks in their hand, and we're stuck here." I sighed.

"You seem kind of tense lately," Michael said.

I was not going to discuss my life with this youngster, so I changed the subject. "All these berry bushes on the property, it seems like somebody should be making pies."

"You want to make me a pie?" Michael asked, suggestively.

"You wish," I retorted, rolling my eyes.

"I do," he said, suddenly serious.

"I have a boyfriend," I pointed out, just as seriously.

"Yeah, but you don't have a ring and a date," said Michael, as he strolled away.

Where did that come from? I wanted to yell "I will! You'll see," but I had to get back to the slumber room. Mrs. McHenry had passed, and I had to make sure everything was in order for her viewing that evening.

I wasn't looking forward to Mr. McHenry's arrival. So far I had only met his son, Ian, who was relieved to learn his mother had handled everything before her death, including payment. I tucked the small bottle of Scotch whiskey Mrs. McHenry had given me in a drawer of the small conference room and sent a little prayer to my personal patron saint: "Help me know what to say tonight, Mom. Help me do this right." I considered bracing myself with a swig from the whisky bottle, but decided it was more appropriate to have Diet Mountain Dew on my breath when the family arrived.

Faith was in the break room, fixing herself a snack. "You look tense," she remarked when I walked in.

"I'll be fine," I said. "I'm just having a little trouble keeping my professional distance with the McHenry's."

"Professional distance is overrated," a voice said from behind me, making me snap my head around. Michael, again! How did he pop up like that—all of a sudden?

Before I could respond, my Nextel Walkie Talkie crackled: "Elizabeth, please meet your family in the cemetery office."

I scooted around Michael, gave myself a mental jiggle, sipped a bit of Diet Pepsi and went to find the McHenry's.

Helen had called it right: her husband was a straight-up mess. He looked like he had an upcoming appointment with the hangman himself. I gently steered him into the conference room and closed the second button on his shirt so it wouldn't gap to show his undershirt. Then I guided him to a seat and carefully poured a bit of whiskey into a Styrofoam cup. "Helen says you should drink this," I said, putting the cup in his trembling hand.

"Did you talk to her?" he asked. The hope in his voice about broke my heart.

"Not since before she passed," I explained. Mr. McHenry downed the whisky and I kneeled down so I could look into his eyes. With one hand on his shoulder I said, "Your wife said to tell you, 'Papa, you can do this.'"

He began to shake all over. What did she tell me to do when he cried? I patted his hand and nearly cried myself.

With tears rolling down his face, he told me he had married Helen when she was only fifteen years old. "I spent my whole life with her," he said. "She was my whole life. What am I supposed to do now?"

I pulled up a chair next to him and put my arms around him. He cried and cried. I had no answers. Finally, I began to pat his back and softly repeated, "You can do this, Papa. You can do this." After a long while, he pulled himself together and sat upright.

"I'm not going to make it," he said. "I'm going to make sure she's buried proper and then I'm going to be back soon and you bury me next to her."

What could I say? I opted for, "When the time comes, I'll be here."

"I'll be back before winter," he vowed. "You promise me you'll take care of everything and put me next to her."

"I will," I said.

"And plant some roses on top of us," he continued. "I want them so they grow together until they can never be separated."

"Okay," I said.

"Promise me."

"I promise."

When we left the conference room, Mr. McHenry was as stoic as a man in his frame of mind could be. Glen was lurking around the hall. "What are you doing?" he hissed as soon as Mr. McHenry was a safe distance inside the slumber room. "You have business to conduct."

I narrowed my eyes. "You have no idea what I need to do," I spat back.

"Are you sure you're up to this work? Emotionally?" Glen countered.

I opened my mouth and out popped, "Kiss my ass. I have a family here who needs me."

"This isn't over!" I heard him say as I marched toward the slumber room.

Chapter 13

War Is Hell

SURE ENOUGH, IT WASN'T OVER WITH GLEN. THE DAY AFTER Mrs. McHenry's evening viewing, I arrived to find Glen holding court in the break room. When they saw me approaching, everybody looked guilty and went slinking out. Glen and Michael remained.

"Good morning?" I said to Faith and Nathan as they quietly passed by. What was the deal here?

Glen poured himself a cup of coffee. He had a self-righteous look, and it set off alarm bells. Michael stood next to the coffee maker. His hackles were obviously up and he looked like he had something to say.

"Good morning?" I repeated, taking a glass from the cupboard.

Nobody said anything. I poured myself some hot water for the lemon I planned to slice.

"Need some of this to go with it?" Glen asked, sliding Mr. McHenry's Scotch whiskey bottle across the counter to me.

"Oh crap, I forgot to put that away," I said.

"Yeah," Glen said, as if he knew something.

"You're so full of shit," Michael growled in Glen's direction, then turned to me and explained, "Glen thinks you need liquid encouragement to do your job."

"What? No, that belongs to Mr. McHenry."

"Sure," Glen said, dripping with superiority. He walked out.

"It doesn't matter," Michael said. "Ignore him."

"No, really, that belongs to Mr. McHenry."

Michael put the whiskey bottle in his pocket, told me it didn't matter again, and left for the basement.

Well, this is a fine how do you do, I thought, but I figured Michael was right: it would pass. Glen would get his next big sale and get over it.

By mid-morning, it was clear The Case of the Scotch Bottle was under investigation. I got a call from our district manager, Vernon Travers, who normally paid me very little attention. Suddenly, he wanted a sit down with me during his visit on Friday but refused to say why.

Nathan and Faith were avoiding me. I hid in the Gethsemane Garden and tried to study.

I told my worries to Nurse Nancy.

"Substance abuse is a major issue in the medical field because of the stress of our work. Does the same thing happen with funeral directors?" she asked.

"I don't know, probably," I said. "Obviously there's a lot of stress working with death, and the hours suck and everything. Funeral directors get depressed and overloaded like everybody else."

"So, maybe Glen's concerned because it's an industry-wide issue?"

"I don't think so," I said.

"I don't either," she responded. "Why not have the husband explain it was his bottle of whiskey? That would clear everything up."

"How do I do that without humiliating the poor old guy? I'd be asking him to confess that his wife gave it to me because he's not man enough to get through this without Scotch. On top of that, a woman had to tell him what to do."

"I get it. Just don't worry about it. It'll blow over."

"Either that or tomorrow's burial will be my last at Western View, because the big cheese, Mr. Travers, wants to speak to me in person!"

She rolled her eyes and suggested a Diet Coke and an end to worry.

I was seriously nervous the next morning. Faith and Nathan were still keeping their distance, Glen was watching my every move, and the printer jammed up when I tried to finish Mrs. McHenry's service programs. Michael was sympathetic, but somehow his pity made things worse.

Mr. McHenry and his son arrived early. I heard my name paged and had my hands full, so it took me a few minutes to get up front. When I rounded the corner into the lobby, I saw Michael guiding Mr. McHenry into Faith's office. Panicked, I quickened my pace.

"I think you left this here yesterday," Michael was saying as he slipped the Scotch bottle to Mr. McHenry in full view of Faith. "We held onto it for you."

"Thank you," Mr. McHenry replied, dully. "I was wishing for that."

"Here's Elizabeth," Faith announced.

Poor Mr. McHenry looked relieved to see me. "She's a good girl," he said to Faith.

Michael looked me straight in the eye but thankfully didn't say anything. I hustled Mr. McHenry off to the chapel as fast as I could transport the dazed old man. My heart was pounding. On one hand, I hoped Michael's strategic move would be my saving grace. On the other hand, the idea of being indebted to him wasn't appealing. *Focus, Elizabeth, focus!*

Somehow, I stumbled through the service and interment and managed to tuck Mr. McHenry into his son's car. It was that gloomy point in time for him to return to his now empty home.

"Thank you," McHenry the Younger said to me before they left. "I don't know how you got my dad through this, but I'm grateful."

"I'm glad I could help." I said this in lieu of my first thought, which was: *You people may have cost me my job, but any time!* Of course that wouldn't have been fair, and I would never let Mr. McHenry know he had caused me any trouble.

৶৽

I was glad I had a date with Dante that night. He poured the wine and I poured out my troubles. "What a tool," he said of Glen, "but it sounds like that crematory guy got your back."

Yikes. Was Dante getting the wrong idea about some other guy looking out for me? It seemed smart to stay off the subject of Michael. I didn't want Dante worrying about it, because it was innocent with Michael—nothing Dante couldn't witness with his own heavenly brown eyes.

"Maybe," I said. "But the only person that matters in this situation is Mr. Travers. He is the one with the power to hire and fire at Western View."

Dante leaned over to nuzzle my neck. "I guess you better turn on a little of that old Elizabeth magic and charm him into keeping you." Dante's breath across my throat tickled a giggle out of me. "Wear one of those great fitting black skirts," he continued, making me squirm. "And those high heels you have and stockings with a seam up the back. Wait, do you have stockings with a seam up the back?"

"Wouldn't you like to know?" I teased.

I let him keep my mind off my troubles for several minutes before I tried to push him off.

"I have to go home. I need a good night's sleep before my meeting tomorrow."

"No, baby, stay here with me," he cajoled in his smokiest voice. Temptation loomed, big time.

But, "I really have to go."

"Stay the night, and I'll make sure you don't care what Mr. Travers has to say tomorrow."

"If you love me, you'll let me go." Where had that come from? Way to play it cool, Elizabeth.

Dante froze, shifted his weight so he could look into my eyes and said, "Oh, I love you."

Out of the melty puddle I had become, I heard myself say, "I love you, too."

I seemed like our next kiss would burn down the house. Alone that night, I dreamed of Dante and our beautiful sons and daughters.

Morning came; time to face my fate. I did what any sensible person would do and hid under the covers until Nurse Nancy finally shouted up the stairs. "Luke! Did you forget to set your alarm? Elizabeth! I'm about to leave. Shouldn't you be up?"

"I don't wanna!"

She walked up far enough to peek over the landing at me. "Don't be so lame about this. Even if your boss doesn't believe you, he'll probably only give you a write-up, anyway."

I growled, "If you're always going to be so logical we can't be friends." Then I forced myself out of bed.

Glen greeted me at the mortuary door with a cheerful, "Good morning, Miss Fournier!" followed by, "Do you feel all right? You look a little . . . rumpled." Always the consummate ass.

I cleaned the break room fridge to avoid standing around slack-jawed when Mr. Travers arrived. Since I figured it also wouldn't hurt if I could tell Mr. Travers I had a couple of appointments on the books, I made a few loathed sales calls.

When I couldn't stand dialing for another dollar, I trudged back to the break room for hot water and sliced lemons. For some reason, the fridge was always stocked full of lemons and tiny mayonnaise packets. Go figure. I spotted Michael and Mr. Travers down the hall conversing. Unfortunately, my invisibility shield failed and they spotted me. Mr. Travers gestured me into the corner conference room.

Mr. Travers was in his sixties and reminded me of Colonel Sanders, which was unnerving. He ostensibly spent his days in a plush, top floor office, sitting in a suede wingback chair. Unlike the rest of us, he wore tan suits. The tan indicated "regional manager" status, I suppose, instead of mere funeral directorship. I tried to imagine him as an earnest young man, just starting out in the embalming room. Somehow, the picture of him touching dead, unclothed bodies disturbed me, so I kept my early impression of him as a good ol' boy with an eye for opportunity.

"How do you like working for Service Corporation International, Miss Fournier?" he asked. "People treating you all right?" Hmm, trick question? Do I make like a nice team player and say how great everyone was or did I mention that Glen seemed determined to fit my back for a knife?

Good girl that I was, I went with: "Absolutely, this is a great team to work with, Mr. Travers. And I'm learning a lot. I'm very glad I chose SCI because the training is top-notch."

Mr. Travers browsed through a folder sitting on the table in front of him. "I see your sales numbers are rather low. I just want to remind you of the sales goals we have for you." He slid a paper across the table. It was identical to the one in my desk. "Now that you've been here a few months—had some time to get your feet wet—I need to see some progress toward these numbers."

"Yes, sir," I said. "I'll get there with a bit more practice."

"I'm sure you will. I've always said a pretty woman like you can be a perfectly good salesman if she puts her mind to it." He actually had the nerve to smile at me as if I would take this as a compliment. Unsure, I smiled back as if I had.

"I'd like to see everyone in the large conference room in twenty minutes," Mr. Travers concluded, lifting his bulky frame out of his chair and opening the door to let me know I was dismissed.

With my phony smile pasted on, I departed, nodding at him as I scooted past.

Michael was loitering at the end of the hall.

"Everything must have turned out okay," he said. "You're not being escorted back to your office with a cardboard box."

"I guess so," I said. "He didn't say anything about Mr. McHenry's bottle. I guess your efforts on my behalf paid off. Thanks."

Michael shrugged. "Travers asked everybody in the building this morning if they'd ever seen you drinking or drunk on the job. Nobody would have said yes, right?"

"Right."

"So there you go. Just get on with your job and don't let the bastards get you down."

"Solid advice," I said.

"I'm heading over to the conference room for the all-staff. You go ahead of me so Travers doesn't get the idea we're fraternizing."

Fraternizing? He wished.

I sat as far away from Glen as possible, hoping he would forget I was there. Mr. Travers let us wait for several minutes before gracing us with his presence. He thanked everyone "for their cooperation this morning." Could we just get this over with?

"I had a conversation with my superior yesterday, and we've decided to make a few changes." High alert sirens screamed in my ear. Was he going to fire me in front of everybody?

"Starting today," Mr. Travers said, "Glen will be the acting manager here."

Wait, what? I looked to Michael, slouching in his chair, wholly calm. Glen rose to a smattering of polite applause, self-satisfied and smirking. Mr. Travers went on: "I've tasked Glen with putting his sales management experience to work for the benefit of all of us, and I am tasking each and every one of you with giving him your full effort and support."

Damn me to hell.

At home, I crashed through the front door, and a startled Nurse Nancy asked what happened at work.

"Nothing I can't fix by throwing myself in the crematory oven!" I shrieked as I barricaded myself in my attic room for the night.

Chapter 14

Hearsing Around with
Lucrezia and the Dudes

M Y FIRST HEARSE WAS NAMED LUCREZIA. SHE WAS LOW, SLEEK, silver, and gorgeous. It was meant to be, me and Lucrezia.

I was walking in my neighborhood the first time I saw her roll by. I sighed over her classic lines and white velvet curtains. A week later while riding my bike, she whizzed past—a flash of icy beauty. Was she stalking me, or was it the other way around? I couldn't stop thinking about her.

Then dumb luck struck. Real dumb.

Just after two a.m. one Friday morning, not long after I introduced Dante to my family, I drove home from a date and stopped at the Plaid Pantry convenience store near my house. While digging through my ashtray for quarters to refill a mega soda, my obsession-on-wheels caromed into the next spot. Two dudes stumbled out, one carrying a guitar case. They entered the store and I watched them closely. Who, exactly, was driving my baby?

These guys plucked a twelve-pack of Heineken from the corner cooler and brought it to the register. I saw them digging through their ratty jeans. I presumed this was for money; it could have been for a gun to rob the place.

I sized them up easily: obvious stoners who bought a hearse because it's cool to drive one with your friends jammed inside, blasting the stereo and looking spooky. And now they were searching through every pocket attached to fabric to procure enough crumpled bills and coins to pay for the beer. Easy pickings, I thought, as I stepped out of my Jeep.

I waited for them in front of the hearse. The sight of a blonde in a mini dress and spiked heels in the wee hours brought them up short.

"Do you own this hearse?" I asked.

"Yeah, man," replied Dude Number One. "I bought it like a month ago."

"I saw you inside the store going through your pockets to buy this twelve-pack. Looks like you could use some cash. Want to sell it?" I barely recognized myself. I am not generally so bold, but my desire for the hearse had me getting down with my bad self.

Dude Number One looked at Dude Number Two, who shrugged his shoulders and looked back at Dude Number One. The eyeballing went back and forth for a while until I thought they might keep it up till sunrise. Finally, I asked, "What do you use this car for?"

They told me they were in a band and used the hearse to haul their equipment around to gigs. I laughed and remarked rather rudely, "You guys actually have gigs?"

Number One claimed he'd already had offers on the car but that didn't faze me. "Hang on, boys," I said, returning to the Jeep. Wallet in hand, I asked the Dudes, "How much?"

"Ah, I don't know like maybe, like maybe a thousand bucks?" Number One said, confused. He was off balance and I was in!

"What do I get for a thousand dollars? Does it have some sort of stereo?"

"Yeah, it's like a Blaupunkt and it jams."

Number Two, clutching his guitar case, interjected, "Dude, Jerry's gonna want that back if he isn't riding shotgun in the hearse, man."

"I'll need to give my buddy the stereo back," Number One clarified. "And my dad will want the jumper cables."

"How 'bout those curtains? Do I get to keep the white curtains or does Grandma need those back?"

Number Two demonstrated his grasp of my subtle humor and giggled.

"Okay, boys, I'm a serious buyer and I'm actually a mortician. I've seen your car drive though my neighborhood, and every time I see it I want it. This is your golden opportunity. I have cash and I'm going to buy that hearse. Right now."

"Dude! You're a mortician?" exclaimed Number Two. "Why do you look like a hooker?"

For that remark, I lowered the offer. "I'll give you seven hundred dollars; I'm going to have to buy a stereo and jumper cables."

Dude One tried to raise my price, but I wasn't having it. I figured any man who couldn't produce enough dollar bills to buy beer at a corner store would have a hard time resisting seven crispy hundreds. That was all I had on me anyway, I couldn't go any higher. I never carried that much cash, but I'd received under-the-table back pay from an undertaker who owed me for cosmetology work.

We came to terms, finally. The title was signed over on the spot and, since they were both handy with a screwdriver, I had them remove the stereo before seller's remorse set in. I handed Number One the jumper cables, took the keys, and drove the treasured hearse home.

I lived on a busy street, so I parked my gleaming ride a few blocks from my house. I didn't want the Dudes stealing it back after they'd finished their twelve-pack. Dante would get a call in the morning to see if his cousin, Javier, would change the locks for me. I walked backwards to my house, admiring the hearse all the way. A 1971 Cadillac! Even if she were a lemon, I could strip her down and sell the Caddy engine block for $500.

Javier changed the locks, and I took Lucrezia out for a maiden cruise; it was like steering a sumptuous velvet couch. Dante rode shotgun. "There's plenty of room for both of us to lie down back there," he pointed out. "Want to park?" I dropped him off at his car and he repeated his anytime, anywhere proposition. But Lucrezia needed respect, not a romp atop her upholstery. I did have him snap a quick picture for Andy before we parted.

Next stop, fill her tank. At the gas station, I strutted past the folks checking out my silver splendor. I had barely dressed for this ride, in warm-ups and no makeup, but I still felt like the hottest thing in town next to that car.

I got back in, turned the key, and nothing. Lucrezia wouldn't start—not a cough or a sputter. Of course I had given those little bastards their jumper cables back, so I was stuck. Humbly, I asked around for a jump.

Monday morning, I drove my hearse or "coach" as we say in the funeral business to Western View. Everybody came to the parking lot to see her. Even Glen thought she was pretty cool. At the end of the day, I was psyched to head into the sunshine and parade Lucrezia up and down Belmont Street and maybe stop at Its A Beautiful Pizza and grab a slice of pine 'n swine. I jumped in, put the key in the ignition. Again, no dice.

Michael walked up and asked if I needed a jump. "Want me to call somebody?"

"No! I'll handle it," I said, hammering numbers on my cell phone.

The mechanic said she needed a new starter, alternator, and about ten other things. I plunked down one hundred twenty-five dollars for a new starter, which would at least get me home where I could park her.

That was it for a while. I'd stare at her out my window. A week went by, then two or three weeks. The only action Lucrezia had was this car perv lifting the blinds to stare at her several times an hour. Other admirers included *The Rocky Horror Picture Show* patrons creeping past my window on the way to the movie nearby, ogling and stroking my beautiful dead coach.

I finally had to admit she was a lemon of a rig. Also, she got nine miles to the gallon and made my boyfriend doubt my judgment about major purchases.

ల

I wisely drove the Jeep instead of Lucrezia to Kevin and Ryan's housewarming party. Dante and I made the "Come as Your Favorite Ship Wreck Victim" scene as the parents from *The Swiss Family Robinson.* Dull choice—I wanted *The Blue Lagoon* and sexy teenagers, but Dante did not consider a loin cloth or a leopard bikini proper party wear.

Kevin was Ginger from *Gilligan's Island,* with seaweed in his wig. Ryan was cuter than the original Mary Ann. Dante was warmly welcomed. He was civil but obviously uncomfortable. He just needs time to get to know them, I told myself, and made it my mission to help him loosen up. For his part, Dante made it his mission to drink enough vodka so he didn't feel awkward anymore.

The guys had done a great job with the house, and the buffet was amazing. Ryan's mother was there and seemed sweet.

"Did your father come, too?" I asked him.

"No, he's never come around the way Mom thought he would," Ryan said.

"Give him time, dear," Ryan's mother said, but I could tell she didn't believe it either.

"I won't hold my breath, if you don't mind," said Ryan, "but you know what? I decided if I only get one parent, I'll be grateful for what I have instead of chasing what I can't have."

Dante was restless in this crowd. "Oh, look," I said to one couple, "you're the kids from *The Blue Lagoon*. We almost went with that idea ourselves." After a few pleasantries, Dante and I moved on. He asked me if they had been men or women.

"Does this really bother you that much?" I asked.

"Yeah," he replied. "I mean, I don't have anything against anybody, but my friends don't do this kind of thing. Let's not make this a late night."

Kevin was standing by himself in the kitchen; I thought he looked thin and little haggard. I asked how he was doing.

"Sweetie, I know Ryan told you I'm sick, but you don't have to worry about it. I got the insurance plan that will pay off the house for him."

"That's not what I'm worried about! I care about you. I asked if you are all right."

"I don't want to talk about it."

"But I'm your friend, Kevin. Why can't we be honest with each other about this?"

Kevin filled a glass of water from the tap and took a sip before saying, "Because it's my party and I'll talk if I want to."

"Okay, we don't have to talk about it tonight. Maybe we can get together later in the week."

Kevin sighed. "Sweetie, try to see it from my perspective. I have only one thing left I can give Ryan—he gave up his father and now most of his life to take care of me. The last thing I can give him is joy during the time we have together. I don't want to talk about being sick. I want to talk about happy things."

"You are the most wonderful husband in the world, you know that?" I said.

Before Kevin could reply, Dante called from the kitchen door: "Elizabeth, I have an early day tomorrow."

We said goodbye to our fabulous hosts and left. The ride home was quiet. I could only think about Kevin and Ryan while Dante was fairly buzzed. When I pulled up outside my house, I asked, "If you knew you were going to die, what would you want for me?"

"What?" Dante asked. "What kind of question is that?"

"Just a question."

"If I die, you can have anything of mine you want except my soccer jerseys. I want those to go to my nephews. Why do you ask?"

"No reason. Just because."

"You're a bizarre bird sometimes, Elizabeth," Dante said and kissed me good night.

"Yes, Dante, I am well aware I'm an odd duck," I muttered under my breath as he jumped in his manly ride and roared away. His black chariot trundled through the potholes of SE 75th Avenue.

Obviously, I'm working through my childhood issues with my job choice and all, but Dante, haven't you noticed I'm sort of lost and hope you can love me the way I am?

I stood in the middle of the street with my thoughts, watching him for eight blocks until I saw his tail lights turn right onto Foster Road.

Chapter 15

Upsales and Happy Trails

FOUR WEEKS AFTER PURCHASING LUCREZIA, SHE WAS STILL PARKED outside the house giving me the stink eye. "I get it, I really do," I told her. "You weren't meant for this life. You're a hot child in the city and you deserve better."

"Also, I deserve my seven hundred bucks back," I would mutter out of Lucrezia's earshot.

I figured my best chance of getting Lucrezia back on the road was to make a sale. I earned a bit here and there from freelance gigs soloing at funerals and filling in when a parlour was desperate, but I needed real cash to swing a car repair bill. I considered asking Dante for a loan, but he already thought I had been frivolous when I purchased the hearse. Besides, if I got a sale, Glen might cut me some slack.

All I had heard at Western View for weeks was "Upsell, upsell, upsell!" Never, "How did Mr. Higgins' burial go?" or, "Thanks for staying late to help the La Sene family." Each morning began with a sales meeting where Glen reviewed our performance and advised us/me on how to do better. Nathan outsold me every single week.

"Your problem, Elizabeth," Glen said, "is you are not *selling*. You are just *talking* to the clients." I was getting a tad resentful.

"What's the matter with you?" Michael asked one day, after watching me take my problems out on an orange cone.

"I need a few good sales."

"What's the matter with the sales you got?" he asked.

"They're not enough, and I'm sick of Glen harping on the subject. I didn't come here to smooth talk people into buying four hundred percent marked-up caskets."

"Then don't."

"It's not that simple. My base pay sucks, and I could really use a decent check. If I put a few repairs into the hearse, I figure I can sell her before she does any more damage to my fiscal solvency."

"You're going to sell Lucrezia? That's an awesome car!"

"Want to buy her?"

"No."

Across the vast lawn, I could see someone standing in the rain. "Who is that out there?" I asked Michael.

"It's Mr. McHenry. He's been coming just about every day. He usually brings a lawn chair to sit on."

"That poor man. I'm going to go talk to him."

Mr. McHenry looked like he'd aged ten years. He stunk of Scotch and there was a food stain on his pants. I stood next to him, gently patted his back, and asked. "Is there anything I can do for you?"

"There's nothing to do now but wait," he replied. I waited with him for a few minutes, then excused myself to get ready for an afternoon funeral.

"He'll catch his death of cold!" Faith fussed when I got back to the office. She'd been watching Mr. McHenry from a window.

"I think that's what he wants, Faith."

"That's not right. We should do something."

"What would we do? If we send him home he'll just pine there and besides, I wouldn't have the heart to keep him away from Helen's grave."

"I guess I wouldn't either, poor man. Maybe he should have cremated her so he could keep her ashes near him until he died."

"Helen wanted to be buried," I said matter-of-factly but with a dejected expression on my face. "I need to set up for this funeral, but if he's still there in a half hour, I'll heat up one of those bowls of instant soup for him and at least try to warm him up a bit."

"I'll do it," Faith volunteered. "Now, here comes a new family and you're the only person around. Nathan has a doctor's appointment and Glen had to go help pick up a body."

I stepped in and took care of the family on my own tender terms—before Glen got back to make the paperwork and business of burial official.

☙

I was outside inspecting Lucrezia's dents and scratches with a heavy heart, when a navy blue pickup truck screeched to a halt across the street. The driver pulled onto the neighbor's grass and ran to me, full speed. "How much do you want for that hearse?" he panted.

"Why do you think it's mine?"

"I can tell it's your car because of how you're looking at it."

"Fair enough. She's mine."

He ran across the roadway to his truck and back. "I'll buy it for three thousand dollars. I'm going to go home and get it, so please be here, okay? Oh my God, I have always wanted this car. I've seen it drive around the neighborhood. Oh my God, this is so great. Do me right, okay? You're going to be here, okay? Don't leave, okay, 'cause I'm going right now. I'll be back, okay, don't leave, okay?"

"Okay," I agreed.

I was floored. Utterly floored. I thought I'd never unload Lucrezia, my beautiful angel and scary monster. I felt the loss already. These would be my last remaining moments with her—if this guy came back.

To my relief (and disappointment) his truck whipped around the corner, and he came running out with a white envelope in his hand. I saw a whole bunch of hundred bills inside. Wow! Right there on a busy street in Portland, some guy comes out of nowhere and hands me a white envelope full of thousands of dollars—in exchange for Lucrezia. He was literally shaking from excitement. I gave him the keys and the title. Monty, the new owner, was naming the hearse The Silver Bullet.

"Well, Monty," I said, "It's been good doing business with you."

"Good doing business with you, too. Tell Michael thanks a bunch."

Michael? "What does he have to do with it?" I called, but Monty was already easing dear Lucrezia, aka Silver Bullet down the street. I glanced over at his left behind truck, which looked as unhappy as I felt. I almost cried, but the very green envelope stopped me. I had bought her for $700 and I was standing there free and clear with $3,000. "That damned kid," I muttered. "How did he do that?"

☯

"How did you do that?" I asked Michael from the bottom of the crematory stairs.

"Do what?" Was he being coy?

"Get somebody to buy Lucrezia."

"Because I'm amazing. Haven't you figured that out yet?"

"Seriously."

"Sales aren't rocket science, Elizabeth. You just need to know your audience. If you offer a guy with money what he wants, he'll buy."

"But how did you find somebody who wanted a broken-down hearse?"

"I already knew Monty wanted it. I was telling some of the guys at the bar about Lucrezia after you brought her to work. He was going on about how perfect it would be for his band."

"Okay, but how did you get him to offer so much?"

Michael gave me an infuriatingly half-charming, half-smug smile. "I can't tell you all my secrets, Lizzie, or you won't come down here to see me anymore."

"You are an ass," I said. "But thank you."

"Any time. Saving damsels in distress is my specialty."

At the top of the stairs I ran into Faith. She'd been searching for me; there was an at-need client in reception, and it was my turn. I hurried to meet Mrs. Bradley, who needed to plan a funeral for her husband, David.

She wanted a burial and traditional service. I showed her an oak casket with just enough frills to keep it from looking bottom shelf, but without a price tag that would give her a heart attack. Based on the way she was dressed, I figured she wasn't working with a huge budget.

"This is nice," she said, "but what about that one?" She pointed at the brushed stainless steel model; considerably more money. I stepped to the "Blue Majesty" casket and mentioned its price as soon as I could reasonably work it into my patter. I didn't want to sound like I was insinuating she couldn't pay for it, but I didn't want her to be disappointed if she had her heart set on that model. To my surprise, she continued to smile broadly.

"It has praying hands on the corners," she said. "So lovely. I just know Jesus would want him to have this one."

"And do you feel it fits within the budget you have in mind?" I asked, hoping I sounded considerate and not condescending. Mrs. Bradley looked at me, aglow with sweetness and conviction. "Oh yes," she said. "My husband was a plumber."

I wanted to ask what that meant exactly but decided not to. I also wanted to ask about her husband and how she was handling her grief, but she was too focused on her purchases.

"The Blue Majesty it is, then," I said, but Mrs. Bradley had already wandered off to the bereavement gifts display. "Oh, I want six of these photo frames that have the 23rd Psalms on them," she declared. "I'll put David's picture in it and give to our boys to remember their father by."

Well alrighty then, I thought, making a note on my planning worksheet. Mrs. Bradley wanted a very nice send-off, including a catered repast and the deluxe graveside tent. Before she left, she paid in cash. Holy first impressions, I thought as she pulled hundred dollar bills out of a vinyl envelope.

I saw Mrs. Bradley to her car and found Glen waiting for me at the door. "You missed the sales meeting," he snarled.

"Sorry, I was helping a family. I have to get her payment in the safe." Glen followed me back to the conference room, where I collected Mrs. Bradley's planning worksheet and the Ben Franklins.

"Nice work," he squeaked out after reviewing my sale.

"Thanks!" I chirped, neglecting to mention how small a role my sales skills had played in the situation. Why disappoint him after he'd dipped into his rather puny supply of graciousness?

While Faith locked up the cash, I asked if she knew the connection between plumbers and elaborate funerals.

"Have you ever had to pay a plumber for a weekend call?" she asked. "It's nothing a second mortgage won't cure."

My sale to Mrs. Bradley gave me some relief from Glen's badgering, and I honestly did try to improve my marketing skills without betraying my ethics. With this newfound insight, my checks improved enough for me to look forward to Christmas. Dante kept hinting he had a special surprise for me. I hoped it was something that came in a little robin-egg blue box.

The Western View office party had to be squeezed in between funerals. I couldn't wait to introduce Dante to my co-workers, especially to Michael. It would be a good idea for Michael to see that I was very much in love with someone else.

But Dante was not particularly enthused about my invitation. "The middle of the day on a Tuesday is not a great time for me, Elizabeth," he protested.

"I know, but it was the only time we could fit it in, and it means a lot to me," I said. "Please?"

"All right, *mi ángel.* You know I can't deny you anything."

ↄ

Corporate sprang for a catered lunch and even a few bottles of wine, which Glen warned us not to get carried away with. Did he think we were a bunch of high schoolers so excited over the prospect of wine at lunch that we'd lose all control?

"Is your boyfriend coming?" Faith asked, as I helped her put the finishing touches on the conference room/party space.

"Yes, he is," I gushed. "I can't wait for him to get here. I'm worried he might be late."

"He wouldn't let you down, would he?" Faith said.

"Well, it is a work day for him," I explained, while remembering the night Dante had arrived late and boozy to meet my family for the first time.

"Looking for me? How sweet," Michael said from the door. I rolled my eyes and Faith set him to work lighting the Sterno canisters. "Lighting things up is my specialty," Michael bragged with a wink.

Yes, I thought, it's past time for this one to meet Dante. I went to the front door, trying to look casual as my beloved strolled up the walk. In case Michael was watching, I gave Dante a hotter-than-an-office-greet kiss.

After Glen gave a corporate Christmas party speech that said nothing and meant nothing, we were released to mingle merrily. Faith's husband had brought their pint-sized granddaughter along, and I was cooing over her velveteen party dress when I sensed trouble. Glen and Dante were having what seemed to be intense words together. *What the hell?* I hurried over, but they both clammed up before I got there.

I took Dante aside. "What was that all about?"

"I just told him to back off you is all. I'm sick of hearing you complain about his shit."

"Okay, I appreciate you trying to defend me, but please let me handle it."

"That's the thing! You don't, do you?"

"Dante, please, let's not do this now."

"All right, all right." He kissed my forehead and got ready to leave. "Sorry, I just love you so much I can't stand the thought of anyone giving you grief." I rested my head on his shoulders and wondered if I should feel like the luckiest woman in the world or get a jump start on worrying about the fallout with Glen.

"You have a problem with constructive criticism, Elizabeth?" Glen asked from behind me.

"No, Glen, I don't. Sorry about what happened with Dante. He just misunderstood something I said the other night and was feeling a little protective."

"I'm glad to hear that," said Glen, "because if you can't take constructive criticism, you're in the wrong business." Something about his tone made the theme from *The Good the Bad and the Ugly* flit through my brain and I had to fight to keep from giggling.

"On the contrary," I finally managed to say, "I sincerely appreciate constructive criticism," which was absolutely true. Figuring I was in enough trouble already, I stopped short of elaborating that he might add something constructive to his criticism.

"I know you think I'm a hard ass, Elizabeth, but given the improvement in your sales numbers since I took over, I guess it's clear that's what you needed."

My mouth tightened into a tortured smile.

"You stick with me, you might get a head for business yet," Glen said as he turned to go. "You girls clean up the conference room."

The Good the Bad and the Ugly whistle started up again and I imagined myself as Clint Eastwood—lighting a cannon with a cigar, eyes squinty and unrepentant. In my head I said: "The way I figure, there's not too much future with a sawed-off runt like you."

But in the real world I schlepped off to help Faith pick up the mess from the Christmas party, dragging a big, stinky garbage can behind me.

Chapter 16

Testing for My Place in the Sun

The MONDAY BEFORE CHRISTMAS I WOULD TAKE THE OREGON STATE licensing exam. I wasn't up to dealing with any more drama. I pled finals week, but Dante apparently took the word "unavailable" as a challenge. He phoned relentlessly, knowing I couldn't shut off my phone in case something came up at work.

One night, when I was holed up in my attic bedroom with my nose buried in my study guide, he dropped in unannounced. When I insisted I had to study, we ended up arguing. I would often pretend I had to work late every night: the funeral parlour was my hideout.

Richard warned me that the test would cover little about the practical side of the job. "It's all about the rules and regulations," he said. "Don't think you're going to waltz in there and ace it because you've been doing this for a while. People who grew up in this business can't pass the test unless they learn the law inside and out, so study, study, study."

I did study, study, study. I was stir-crazy by the weekend, pacing the back halls of Western View like a Bengal in a cage. I promised if I studied until noon, I would treat myself to a Skyline burger and a phone call to Dante. Easier said than done, because Michael was in the building and kept making excuses to pass by. I could feel him checking me out. Why did it feel so smarmy?

Nathan, with a funeral about to start, was dashing around because he was late. "Elizabeth," he called, "would you please make a pot of coffee? I have to let the florist in." Relieved for the break, I agreed, although I had no idea how to run the industrial-sized coffee maker we used during receptions. Faith always handled it, but she was gone weekends.

I enlisted Michael. He didn't know how to run the gargantuan machine either but was willing to try and figure out it. We found the matching giant filters and took an educated guess about how many scoops of grounds to use.

"Where do we add the water?" I asked.

"You don't see this? The machine is plumbed into the water line," Michael explained. "Just push the button."

"Genius!" I hooted as the machine began to fill.

"So, what does your boyfriend think about you working here?"

"We haven't talked much about it, but I think he's proud of me. His family has a strong work ethic. Most of them are employed by his dad's construction company, Perez and Sons. Do you know it?"

"Kind of. I see their signs on commercial projects over on the east side—near a bar I go to a lot," Michael said. "What bars do you go to?"

Suddenly, hot brown water started spraying all over the counters and down to the floor. "What the hell!" Michael shouted.

I rushed to the sink to grab rags. We tried to make a cloth dam along the edge of the counter as burning hot water poured in a flash flood from the machine.

"Where is the pot?" I yelled. "Isn't there supposed to be something like a coffee pot or something to catch the water?" Michael looked at me like a deer blinded by headlights. "Get some paper towels!" I shrieked, knocking him out of his trance.

We mopped and mopped, using every sparkling white towel to contain the deluge of piping hot coffee. Finally, Michael spotted the big square coffee pot, drying upside down over a towel on a cart. He grabbed the pot and shoved it in place just as Nathan walked in. "What are you doing?"

"We had a user error," I said, pushing hot coffee toward the sink with the stained, sopping towels.

Nathan glanced at the mess with disgust and pulled the plug on the coffee pot. "Why didn't you just turn it off?"

Michael and I didn't answer; we were too busy staring like dolts at the plug.

"You guys are idiots," Nathan sneered on his way out the door.

Well, he did have a point. We stood in complete silence for a few more seconds while the coffee spit through the end of its cycle.

Michael finally broke our reverie, saying, "No sir, we are *complete* idiots." I started giggling, which caused Michael to titter, and before long it sounded like two hyenas had been let loose in the kitchenette. Nathan came back to hiss at us to pipe down because that's just how he's wired, and, well, we were in a funeral home.

Somehow the coffee got brewed properly and the break room was restored to its usual pristine condition. I put the stained and soggy towels in a trash bag, and we snuck past the funeral guests with our burden of guilt and incompetence.

"What are you doing here today?" I asked Michael once we were out of earshot of the service.

"Cremating someone, what do you think?"

"I didn't know you worked on Saturdays."

He shrugged. "It's busy right now. I have one this morning, and then I have to pick up someone for another location."

"You work at other locations?"

"Yeah, floating gives me extra hours; plus, I live over there."

"Over where?"

"Upstairs in the funeral home. At Finnegan's."

"You live in a funeral home?"

"Yeah," he said. In the basement storage room, Michael pulled a wheeled clothes rack from behind some boxes and we started hanging up the dirty towels.

"Why do you live in a funeral home?" I asked.

"Somebody has to make sure kids don't vandalize the place overnight. Little bastards get drunk and dare each other to pull some crap in the cemetery or to climb the building."

"I know," I said. "I used to be night groundskeeper at Dyrland's."

"You?"

"Yeah, what of it?"

"Just doesn't seem like work for a pretty girl, is all. Weren't you scared?"

"Only of the living," I bragged.

"Good to know," Michael said. "So it doesn't bother you down here?"

"Why should it?"

"It's pretty well known to be haunted. Wait until you see a black shadow down here some afternoon, or you turn on a light and it suddenly switches off. Ask around. Anybody who has ever worked here can tell you." He leaned over so his mouth was close to my ear. "Sometimes there are strange whispers when you know there is nobody else here. At least . . . nobody living."

Suddenly I was creeped out. "I have to go study!" I rushed up the stairs, with the sound of Michael's laughter trailing my high heels. Why was he always so exasperating? I took the rest of the afternoon to study out in Gethsemane.

"You're leaving?" Nathan asked as I headed toward the side door with my binder under my arm.

"I need to get some air," I said. "The atmosphere in here is just too close today."

❧

I am a big believer in looking my best whenever I need an extra shot of confidence, so the morning of the exam I began to dress for success: An ever-so-slightly-sexy dress, strappy little heels, and my hair brushed till it glistened. I pocketed a Mother Mary good luck charm and went downstairs for a bite to eat.

"Do you have a date right now?" Nurse Nancy asked as I sailed elegantly into the kitchen.

"Licensing test." I grabbed a pack of string cheese for brain food. "The last time I took one of these exams, I had to drive in the pouring rain two hours to Sacramento, circle the block for a half hour while freaking out because I couldn't find parking, and then run to make it in the door by nine a.m. I was frazzled, exhausted, and wearing ugly sweats."

"Knock 'em dead!" she called after me as I glided out the door, smiling. Nurse Nancy loved dorky puns.

When I got to the State of Oregon Building across town, my confidence soared. I parked in front of the testing room window. Inside, guys in sober suits were doing their best to act nonchalant, awaiting this chance to prove their worthiness as undertakers. All eyes turned towards me when I walked in. That's right, boys, I thought, I'm lookin' good and about to go straight to the head of the class.

The proctor, a woman, smiled thinly at me and pointed. "The beautician exam is across the hall."

"I'm here for the funeral director test," I reassured her and strode over to a seat in the front row. Beauty, indeed!

We were handed a booklet and answer forms with rows of little bubbles. Sharpened number two pencils were provided, and we waited for the long hand to hit the hour mark. I took a wrapped mint out of my bra and slipped my good luck charm into my palm. Another forty-five seconds crept by—finally, top of the hour.

"You may begin," the proctor said, hitting a digital alarm clock.

There were one hundred questions, true or false as well as multiple choice. Somebody at the licensing board had gone out of their way to write the questions in the trickiest way possible. Question by question, I worked my way down the list.

Unexpectedly, the proctor stopped in front of me. "What do you have in your hand?" she whispered. Uh, oh. I opened my hand to reveal a tiny Mother Mary rosary that used to belong to my mother. When she saw the crucifix and white beads, the proctor nodded and let it go. I forgave her for thinking I was a cosmetology student. Not that there's anything wrong with that!

I finished with a few minutes to spare and left before I could fall into the trap of going back and changing answers. We were told if we passed, we'd receive a letter on Wednesday. If we didn't pass, the letter would arrive on Friday since Thursday was Christmas and there was no mail delivery. I drove straight home, got my book, and looked through everything, marking it with stars and crosses to try and determine how many questions I had answered correctly. If I missed even a handful, I was toast. I couldn't tell; there was nothing to do but wait.

The cats were annoyed by my pacing, and the canned goods were already in their proper places. I called Dante to distract myself.

"Babe!" he said when he answered the phone. "Are you back among the living?"

"Yes, I just finished my test."

"Yeah? So what are you doing Wednesday night?"

"Hopefully celebrating that I passed."

"I've got something even better, be ready at eight."

"What could be better than passing my test?" I wondered aloud, but Dante had hung up.

For the next two days, I could hardly sit still. Wednesday I was so antsy I snuck out a half hour early, only to get caught in sluggish holiday traffic. *Don't think about it! Think about your date tonight!* Dante still hadn't told me what we were doing, although he'd hinted I should dress nicely. It was Christmas Eve, after all. I mentally scanned my limited selections and picked a green dress that brought out the color in my eyes and, of course, my mother's anciently gorgeous white coat to keep me warm.

Damn traffic. "Move it!" I shouted, slamming my palm on the steering wheel. An elderly lady in the car to my left gaped at me, alarmed. Feeling sheepish about screaming so loudly I could be heard through the plastic Jeep windows, I stared in the other direction and muttered, "Please. Move. It." This made no impression on the traffic.

Home at last, I checked the mailbox—nothing. Had my trusty roommate already picked up the mail? I rushed inside. "Nurse Nancy! Did you get the mail?"

"Yeah, you got a card from your Farmer's Insurance guy," she said. "It's on the table."

"That's it? Are you sure?"

"I'm sure. There was your card and a begging letter from some animal shelter addressed to me. Why?" Then her eyes widened and she said, "Oh my God, it's Wednesday. You're supposed to hear about your test." I bobbed my head. I didn't dare speak for fear I might cry.

"Maybe I dropped it by accident!" Nurse Nancy said and we rushed outside. A thorough search turned up nothing and I started whimpering.

"Listen to me," she hollered while checking behind the musty lounger on the porch. "You were completely prepared for that exam and you passed. The letter probably just got held up in the Christmas rush at the post office. Take some deep breaths; you are going to be fine, Luke. Use the force."

I breathed in and out, raggedly, a couple of times, and then Darth led me back to the house. "You're probably right," I said, "it was probably just delayed because of the Christmas mail." I had to hear myself say that out loud.

Lighting up a Marlboro, she comforted me: "Just put it out of your mind for right now and go have a decent time with Dante. Alrighta, arborvitae?" Her hokey puns always came at the right moment.

"It's just delayed in the mail, it's just delayed in the mail . . ." my new mantra, repeated in prayer. I numbly climbed the stairs and dressed for my date. By the time Dante rang our doorbell, I was ready. I picked up my mom's little white rosary from the straight-backed chair I used as a nightstand and went down to meet my brown-eyed handsome man. Nurse Nancy smiled steadily and mouthed "Just have fun." Dante grinned ear to ear at the sight of me. I resolved not to spoil his evening, even though it felt like there was a brick in my chest.

As we zoomed across the Morrison Bridge and I looked out the window at the twinkling holiday lights of my lovely city, Dante chattered away about something that happened with one of his cousins. I barely heard a word. It took everything I had to keep from crying.

Fortunately, he never bothered asking if I'd heard about the test results.

Chapter 17

Salty Mrs. Morton

DANTE HAD MADE RESERVATIONS AT THE PORTLAND CITY GRILL, a restaurant on the 30th floor of the US Bancorp building downtown. It's known for its spectacular view of the city and the Cascade Mountains. The place was packed with young professionals starting their holiday celebration with singles mingling. In no time the champagne was flowing at our table, with Dante waxing poetic about how much he loved me. I tried to pay attention; I really did.

"I can't take my eyes off you," Dante said.

"Uh, you too?" my mouth responded, while I mentally scanned the yard and house trying to visualize a rectangle of white paper Nurse Nancy and I had missed. I was relieved that Dante had ordered for us; I didn't have it in me to read the menu, let alone choose a meal.

Appetizers were followed by steaks and lobster. Dante, so wrapped up in what he was saying, didn't notice me listlessly picking at the beautiful dinner. Get it together, I told myself, taking another sip of champagne. Did I just hear Dante say I was most beautiful woman he had ever seen; could the letter have ended up going to the office by mistake?

"*Amor mio,* the babies we make together will be the most beautiful anyone has ever seen." What did he say? That got my attention and my mind focused, laser-sharp, on Dante.

"We are going to make babies?" I asked.

"That is my greatest wish," he replied. A waiter appeared from out of nowhere and placed a small plate bearing a tiny velvet box before me. Dante sunk to one knee, took my hand, and begged me to be his wife. A wave of euphoria rushed through me and flooded my eyes. This was the moment

I had waited for all my life. This was the man who would finally give me a family of my own. My head started bobbing up and down, and I must have managed to say yes, because applause erupted around us and Dante kissed me tenderly, then leaned his forehead against mine.

"You have made me the happiest man in the world," he said. Were those tears in his eyes?

The ring box! I was trembling too hard to open it. Dante helped, and we revealed a diamond that sparkled like the Christmas star. He slipped it on my finger and another champagne bottle cork popped. There was more applause and a flood of congratulations from the crowd around us. Dante stood and toasted me and everyone raised their glasses to our future. For a moment, I felt like the queen of everything. The envelope anxiety disappeared into the mists of my fairy tale moment. I was about to become Mrs. Dante Perez; I didn't need to worry about some rotten envelope—at least not on the night I became engaged. I was someone's fiancée!

The well-wishers turned back to their tables and Dante sat down. We savored our amazing dinner and drank and wondered if we should go to Maui or Mexico for our honeymoon. Dante ordered more champagne and talk turned to baby names we loved. By the time we noticed the staff trying to clean up the dining room, we were merrily pickled in love and bubbly.

"We need to call a cab," I said, as Dante placed my wrap around my shoulders.

"Sugar, we don't need a cab. I can drive us."

"We've both had too much to drink."

"I drive better when I've had a little to drink," Dante said with a mischievous gleam in his eye. "I pay more attention if I've been drinking."

"But it's wrong."

Dante was staggering, but sober enough to see the concern in my face. "Okay," he said. "Would getting a cab make you feel safer?"

"Yes."

"Then if it makes you feel safer, we'll do it. From now on, I'm going to make sure you feel safe every day of the rest of your life."

I am going to let him, I thought. What more could a girl ask for?

∽

Christmas Day opened at my dad's house. Nick let up on the teasing so I knew he was happy for me, and Dad added a present to my pile: a white, leather-bound Bible my grandmother had given my mother on her wedding day.

"You're going to make me cry!" I told Dad, and everybody laughed.

"Your mother wanted you to have it," Dad replied. "I just wish she was here to give it to you herself, because nothing would have pleased her more than seeing you this happy."

"She's here," I said. "I know she is." I could feel her presence all around us. It was so strong sometimes I thought I felt her hand on my shoulder. Finally, we are all merry. For once, we were the family from the Christmas cards, and we would be that family for years to come, with my babies growing up with Nick's babies.

My reverie was broken by the vibration of my cell phone. Michael? Why would he be calling on Christmas day?

"Elizabeth, we have to pick up a body and I need you to come help."

"Michael, it's Christmas."

"Yeah, well, guess the dead lady didn't get the word. I need you to hurry; the police are waiting for us at the house."

"Can't somebody else do it?"

"You're the new guy at Western View, so it's on you."

"But I just got engaged!"

There was a pause, and Michael snapped, "Do you really think it's about you when a family just found their mother dead in her chair on Christmas morning?"

"I'll be there as soon as I can," I said.

Dante looked stormy.

"I'm sorry," I said, "there's been a death. I'll meet you at your mother's as soon as I can."

"I have to drive you back to your place to get your Jeep." His jaw was so tight it was hard to get the words out.

"I'm sorry," I repeated when we got to his car.

"This is not going to work," Dante said.

What wasn't going to work? This marriage? Was he going to break up with me for being forced to work on Christmas because of my job? I didn't have the courage to ask.

"Have fun," he snarled as he dropped me off in front of my house and sped away.

I can fix this, I told myself as I forced a jittery hand to line up the key with the Jeep door lock. I'll make it up to him when I get to his mom's.

☙

Michael didn't look any happier than I was. "It's about time!"

"Get off my back!" I barked back. That ended the conversation for the duration of our ride to Mrs. Morton's bungalow, where two officers and a middle-aged man waited in the driveway.

"You're going to need a mask," one of the officers told us. It turned out Mrs. Morton lived alone and hadn't been discovered until her nephew arrived that morning. He had been dispatched to chauffeur her to the family's Christmas get-together. She was less than fresh.

"Jesus," Michael said, when he saw the corpse. "We're going to need protective gear in case her ankles burst."

After death, blood settles in the lowest region of the body, pulled down by gravity. Over time, as tissue breaks down and becomes more fragile, it becomes difficult to move a body without breaking the skin, which releases a flood of liquid bio-hazard. Since Mrs. Morton had been sitting in her favorite easy chair when she died, her feet and ankles looked like purple water balloons.

Michael saw my lower lip start to tremble at the sight of those ankles and pulled me out of the house. He told me to get myself together as he pulled shoe covers and face shields out of the van. He helped me get into a water-resistant gown and cap and then located two plastic body bags.

"Go really slow and don't try to move the legs. Just let me handle the lower body," he instructed. I nodded, impressed by his calm control over the situation. He didn't seem like the same Jersey thug I was used to, and was I ever glad for that.

Michael told the nephew to wait outside, and we went back to the living room. For forty-five minutes Michael directed the gentle, agonizingly slow and horrifyingly messy removal of poor Mrs. Morton. For once he didn't crack a single inappropriate joke or act disrespectfully in any way, even though the situation was ripe for gallows humor. Even I had thought of the Morton's salt tagline when her ankles broke, but I sensed he wasn't open to any funny business just then.

"You did all right," he said after it was over. "Guess you'll make a mortician yet. Did you nail the exam?" My face must have betrayed me, because his eyebrows shot up.

"My letter hasn't come yet," I said. "Everybody who passed was supposed to get their letter Wednesday. That means I failed."

Michael shrugged. "You'll take it again."

"Glen will probably use it as an excuse to fire me."

Michael shrugged again. "Then I guess that ring on your finger will be your saving grace, after all."

"I don't know about that," I said, thinking of the last time I had seen Dante's face.

"Well, if you're determined to waste your life on him, make him pay for the pleasure," Michael said, opening the van door.

I stomped over to the passenger side and heaved myself into the seat. "That's kind of mean!" I shouted.

He just shrugged—again.

"You can be such an ass," I spat, thinking how nice it would be to deck him square in his shrugging, self-righteous self.

❧

Dante was less pissy when I arrived at his mother's house. If he was still mad he would have had to hide it, because the rest of the family was excited to see me. Everybody wanted to kiss the soon-to-be bride and see the ring and feed me. It was several minutes before I could give Dante a chaste peck on the lips and whisper, "Forgive me?"

"You smell funny," he replied. It was Mrs. Morton. Sometimes there's no way to keep the smell of death out of hair and clothes.

"Sorry," I said again. "It's my job."

"We need to talk about your job," Dante said. "Later."

"That might not be an issue after this week," I confessed, but Dante didn't seem to hear me. Or maybe he just didn't want to talk about it right then. He's right, I thought, looking around. The house was pulsing with joyous children and everybody was talking a mile a minute. One of Dante's nephews came to show me his new fire truck, and that helped put Western View out of my mind. We were supposed to be celebrating!

Dante kept his distance from the smell of Mrs. Morton, but over the course of the evening he relaxed and warmed up. By the time he escorted me to my Jeep he was telling everyone his "wife" needed to get home. All seemed forgiven.

"I love Christmas at your house," I said as we kissed goodnight.

"You could have fooled me earlier."

"I couldn't help that. You know I wouldn't have left if I had a choice, right?"

"So you say, but it's over and I love you anyway. Drive carefully," Dante said, and returned to the house.

He had a funny way of showing it, I thought as I cruised through the twinkling streets and made my way home. Men! Always so righteously touchy. If anyone had a right to be waspish, wasn't it me? I was the one who was about to be unemployed and disgraced. Dread settled in the pit of my stomach. Nurse Nancy and Michael were the only people who knew the letter hadn't arrived. And why hadn't Dante asked about my test yet? It didn't go unnoticed that he really didn't care about it. That upset me as much as having to tell my dad and face Glen on Monday.

I felt nauseous as I parked the Jeep. I thought about Mr. McHenry and the promise I had made to him.

"Oh, Mom," I prayed into the darkness, "what am I going to do?"

Chapter 18

Incinerator Baiter

WHAT HAPPENED TO YOU?" NURSE NANCY ASKED WHEN I dragged myself into the kitchen Friday morning. I frowned and gave her the nutshell story of my adventures since Christmas Eve. By the time I finished, I could tell she hated Dante.

"I don't know if I should be happy for you or annoyed or . . . ?"

"Me, neither. Want to go to Big Bear Bagel?"

"Don't you work today?"

"Why rush to the scene of my demise?"

We jumped in the car. She reminded me I could take the test again. This was just a little bump in the road. I was convinced Glen would use this as an excuse to get rid of me and hire someone who was already licensed.

"So, you'll find another job," Nurse Nancy said. "Life will go on."

"Western View is part of a huge corporate chain. The other available jobs will be with them."

"Maybe one of the independent funeral homes is hiring?"

"They're mostly family owned and not usually hiring," I explained, then told her how guilty I felt about not being able to keep my promise to Mr. McHenry. "Who will take a cup of soup out to him when he's sitting at his wife's grave?"

She looked at me while I navigated morning side-street traffic. "You've had too much drama in too short a time. You'll figure out something soon. And be busy planning your wedding to that guy."

"If Dante still wants to marry someone who scoots from the family dinner table to move decaying bodies," I moaned.

My favorite nurse stared hard and said, "That's life, Luke. He needs to learn to deal."

"Honestly, I don't know how I would have gotten through it without Michael. Is that ironic or what?"

"Sometimes people surprise us."

"I guess. He was so . . . well, *competent*. He knew what he knew and made sure we got through it." I scoffed. "Normally, he's a juvenile delinquent."

"Come on," she said, "we're going to be late." Ignoring my whining, she goaded me into my jacket and out the door of the Jeep.

"Upward and onward," I muttered with a frown as I stepped onto the curb. "At least Glen isn't working today."

On my way in to Western View, I decided to clean out my desk. I would leave immediately after my expected termination on Monday. I could not pack my things with Glen jeering and gloating over my humiliated, poor little self. Too much to bear. I might manage to walk from his office to the door with my head up, but anything more would push my scant reserves of dignity. After turning on the lights and unlocking the doors, I went in search of a cardboard box.

I sifted through the basement store room, looking for an empty carton. A voice behind me asked, "Looking for something?" As was now traditional, I screamed. Wouldn't any normal person? Michael grinned at me.

"That was mean!"

"Sorry," he said, in a tone that indicated he clearly wasn't. "Thought you might be digging around for me. You'll have to take a number, though. I've been helping Santa make the ladies happy this Christmas. There's still a couple in line before you—twins, even."

I frowned and turned back to my search. I was dangerously close to tears and didn't need his crap. Michael didn't move. I growled, "What are you doing here? I thought I was the only one working today and everybody else was on-call."

"Mrs. Morton," he said. "For obvious reasons, the family has decided to cremate."

"Do you have to do that today?" I snapped.

"Do you want her oozing in the cooler any longer?" He had a point there. "What are you looking for?" Michael asked again.

"An empty box about so big," I replied, holding out my hands to indicate the size I needed.

"For what?"

I sighed and explained how I planned to save myself from the post-dismissal walk of shame.

"Are you sure your letter wasn't lost in the mail?" Michael said. "You're smart and you studied hard. I have a hell of a time believing you didn't pass."

"How should I know? It's not like I can call the post office and ask if they have a letter lying around."

"Call the Mortuary Board," Michael suggested, laughing.

Hope dawned. Oh, yes, why hadn't I thought of that? But my mind played out an imagined conversation where some entry-level bureaucrat had been forced to work Friday after Christmas and took it out on me by destroying my career plans. Hope set quickly. Michael rolled his eyes, took my arm, and marched me up the stairs and down the hall to my desk.

"Call!" he said, pointing at the phone.

I dug up the number and dialed up the Mortuary and Cemetery Board. Michael slouched in the visitor's chair across from me. Was he staring at my chest? Such a tool.

After waiting a while, listening to vapid hold music, a young woman came on the line. I gave her my identifying information and heard her keyboard clacking.

"Elizabeth Fournier, f-o-u-r-n-i-e-r?" she finally asked, which made me want to scream.

"Yes," I said, as steadily as I could.

"Your Funeral Services Practitioner license is effective as of this week and expires in two years. Is there anything else I can help you with?"

"Are you sure?"

"Yes, ma'am. But if there's nothing else I can help you with, I have another call coming in." I thanked her, hung up the phone, and burst into tears.

"Whoa! Whoa! Whoa!" Michael said, focused on my face. He looked scared. "Crap! Did you fail?"

I shook my head. "Then why are you crying?" he demanded.

I couldn't speak for sobbing. I just shrugged my shoulders.

"Crazy women!" Michael said. He got up and retrieved a box of tissue from the credenza behind my desk. "Stop that! Stop that," he insisted, but I couldn't. "Aw, Jesus," Michael muttered. He patted my back, which made me hiccup. "C'mon, calm down." Michael pressed, dabbing at my wet face with a handful of tissues. "Why do girls have to cry about everything?"

"I don't know!" I bawled.

"Well, stop it! I hate when women cry," he said, still thrusting tissues at my face.

I tried taking some deep breaths, raggedy feel-sorry-for-myself breaths, accompanied by pitiful, whimpering, sniffling sounds.

"Stop, stop," Michael now whispered. He took my face in his hands and told me to settle down. I took a few more deep breaths, and the worst of the sobbing ended.

Michael inspected my face for signs of further emotional eruption. He continued to make quiet shushing sounds. My hiccups and whimpers really had made him nervous. It was kind of sweet, I thought. Who would have guessed Michael had a soft side? I thought of how respectful he had been in Mrs. Morton's living room and realized he was more complicated than I gave him credit for. As he gazed at me, my next sniffle landed with a wave of emotion and warning bells. I jerked backward in my seat, which caused him to start and jerk backward as well. This was not a good dance.

I scrambled out of the chair. "I have to wash my face."

"I have to start the oven," Michael announced, heading for the door. "Congratulations on passing your test."

Blinking back another round of tears, I watched him retreat. My heart soared. I had done it! I was a licensed funeral director! My dad was going to be so proud of me. I couldn't wait to tell my family.

I did it, Mom! I shouted in my head as I danced toward the ladies room. I couldn't wait to tell Nurse Nancy. Richard! I couldn't wait to tell Richard. Dante! Well . . . he'd forgiven me for Christmas, right? Maybe he would be happy because I was happy.

In the bathroom, I got a good look at my face and was appalled by how puffy I looked. Mascara was all over the place. "I can't believe Michael saw me like this," I moaned at my reflection. Why did I care? He was just the cremator, after all. I shook off my misgivings and set to work reconstructing my face.

☙

When Dad heard the news, he immediately invited everybody out for dinner that night: Dante, Nurse Nancy, Nick and Phoebe, and anybody else I wanted to invite. His treat, at his favorite Italian place. Kevin and Ryan were out of town, but Richard and his wife were pleased to be included, and Dante's parents said they wouldn't miss it. I saw Michael before he left for the afternoon and wondered if I should invite him, but after the crying jag, I decided against it. My reaction with him had been the emotional fallout of tons of stress tangled up in giant relief, but I was afraid Michael saw me as a complete basket case. Nor did I want Dante to think anything peculiar was going on that absolutely was not. Jesus, what if Michael told the story of my nervous breakdown in the office?

I was the last to arrive at the restaurant. When I made my entrance, I heard a hearty, "There she is!" Mr. Bonatello, the owner, proceeded to kiss my cheeks and announce to the entire restaurant that congratulations were in order. I was blushing by the time he seated me next to Dante.

"A bottle of my best wine on the house!" Mr. Bonatello announced, motioning to one of his sons to bring the vino.

"Where did you find the letter?" Nurse Nancy demanded.

"I didn't! I had to call the state to find out." Everybody shook their heads and groused about the government, then the wine was poured and I was toasted and the last of my worries melted away.

"Of course, you know what this means," I said. "Upsell, upsell, upsell!" Everybody laughed and teased me about selling coffins with crazy names like "Majestic Titan Super-Sealed Corpse Preservation System." Richard told the story of my first performance of "Wind Beneath my Wings," and I recounted a few tales from my job as late night crypt keeper.

I could have stayed at that table forever; but eventually Nick and Phoebe had to relieve their babysitter, and my dad was tiring fast.

Dante and I were alone at the table. "You haven't said much tonight," I remarked.

"I'm just watching your happiness," he said, pouring the last of the wine into his glass.

"Are you happy for me?" I asked.

He kissed me and said, "Of course, you know all I want is your happiness." Was the warm glow I felt showing?

"I love you so much," I said, and he kissed me again. "I feel amazing tonight. What do you think about me having my own funeral home one day?"

"I think you're going to have your own home one day soon, *ours*, so I don't know if it's realistic for you to do both. But I can agree you feel amazing," Dante said, running his hand up my thigh. I blushed and pushed his hand away.

"Not here," I whispered. "Mr. Bonatello has known me since I was little girl and goes to our church. I don't want to offend him."

"Oh, all right," Dante conceded. "I'm glad you're a decent girl, I guess, but let's hurry up and make an honest woman out of you so Mr. Bonatello doesn't have to worry."

"I am an honest woman!" I protested with a giggle.

"How about a Valentine's Day wedding?" Dante suggested.

"That's too soon! We'd never get everything ready on time."

"What's to get ready? Buy a dress and we'll go see the priest." I knew the priest would require pre-marital counseling, and we needed to plan a reception if we wanted to celebrate with our families. He threw out some other near-future dates, but none seemed quite right. I felt more overwhelmed than excited.

"I'm tired; let me think about some of these and check my calendar. We don't have to decide tonight." Dante agreed reluctantly, as I made a promise not to keep him waiting too long and sealed it with a kiss.

"Want to go get a room?" Dante asked suggestively, but before I could answer, my phone started vibrating.

"Crap. It's work.

"Of course, it is," he said, scoffing. He stood up and was gone before I could finish the call. It was a family member in a panic. She couldn't remember if she'd faxed the list of pallbearers for her dad's funeral the next day. I assured her all was well; the programs had been printed.

"Oh, thank you!" she gushed. "Now I can sleep well tonight."

"Always glad to help," I said.

I looked at the empty space where Dante's Corvette had been parked. I thought about calling his cell phone but opted to drive to his place. I'll surprise him, I thought, and it will all be forgotten. The surprise was on me—Dante wasn't home.

I parked across the street and waited, but the cold was getting to me. Skirts and stilettos make for lousy winter stake-out attire. I called Dante's mobile phone.

"Yeah!" he said. I could hear loud music in the background.

"It's me. I was wondering where you are."

"Are you checking up on me?"

"No, it's not like that," I protested, but Dante interrupted me before I could explain myself.

"Look, you got stuff to do and I got stuff to do, so don't be that girl." That girl? What girl? But he had hung up.

I looked towards his house and saw the neighbor lady peering out her living room window. Oh geez, I thought, she's going to recognize my vehicle and tell him I sat here all night, stalking him. I took off; I needed a good night's sleep.

I lay in bed for a long while, running tapes of the conversations I'd had with Dante over and over in my brain. It was a frustrating process. I'd recall certain dialogue, knowing Dante had been unfair to me, but then I would doubt myself. What was the beginning of our troubles; how could it have been different? I never found any real answers or sense of resolution. My childhood question and answer, "Why? Just because," was never enough when I was little, and it sure as hell wasn't enough now when I had grown up problems to deal with.

Since I couldn't figure it out, I slipped back into a comfortable habit of magical thinking. After my mother's death, I had lived in a castle in the sky; I thought Mom had become a fairy, or an angel, perhaps floating on a cloud somewhere. Not much had changed. Now I was a grown woman and still making up stories about myself. This time, I wanted to believe I would be rescued by a tall, dark, and handsome man who looked like Dante. But this time, he would be ten times nicer to me.

Somehow Nurse Nancy's cats knew I needed them close to me that night. They planted themselves firmly on my body, making it difficult to move or think about anything besides their soft fur and how good it felt when they stretched out a fuzzy paw and draped it over my arm.

Chapter 19

Winter Wondering

TRUE TO ITS REPUTATION IN THE FUNERAL INDUSTRY, JANUARY WAS insanely busy. I made sure to pull my weight plus a little extra at Western View. Upon hearing the news of my engagement, Glen had predicted I'd slack off during the months I was planning my wedding.

I woke up dreading work, as it was my day of coffin sitting. According to Islamic tradition, the corpse of a Muslim is not to be left alone between death and burial. All staff were on a rotation system to sit with Jameela. My shift would begin as soon as I arrived to the parlour and end not a minute sooner than four. No checking e-mail, answering my cell, or socializing. And eating in the slumber room was a big no-no.

I relaxed into the sofa, straightaway accepting Dante would be pissed I wouldn't be calling him for all these hours. I found if I called Dante a couple of times a day and then met him straight after work, making sure to attend to his bruised ego, I could keep his petulance at bay. I got good at it, actually, and Dante went back to calling me his soul mate and his angel. Honestly though, it was beginning to feel like I were babysitting this grown man.

Tears welled as I sat in the silence of the room and the plush comfort of the sofa. I was so alone in my walk through this world, even though I had my sexy brown sugar, a large and sparkly engagement ring, and a wonderful extended family eager to include me and my children-to-come.

"That's the complete package, right?" I looked over at Jameela and asked. She looked quite dignified, and I could feel her spirit looking at this silly, pathetic girl breaking down next to her feet. I thought of her as my mother laying there, trying in vain to break out of the confining box and shake me to my senses.

Six hours later, I emerged from the slumber room resolute, and not "just because." I had been reminded that life is a gift; and I have a gift and a dream, and I cannot let a man stand in the way of it.

ℰℑ

By February, my late hours were showing on me. Even Dad mentioned it. Didn't matter, I pressed on, I had no choice. My sales numbers were up to the required benchmarks, but Glen was still pressuring me for more.

"Flu season is funeral season," he lectured. "If you're only meeting benchmark in the winter, you won't come summer. Right now, you should be making the money that will see you through the slow months."

Blah, blah, blah, I chanted in my head to block out his nagging. More than ever I entertained the dream of having my own funeral parlour, where I could focus on the bereaved instead of Glen's bonus issues. Richard reminded me, though, that it would be about impossible to succeed all by myself in a large metropolitan area.

"Think about the competition you'd be facing," he said. "Established homes with teams of funeral directors. I don't see a single woman being able to pull that off. Maybe if you were marrying into one of the family operations. Is your fiancé set on staying in construction?"

"I'm pretty sure he wouldn't be called to the funeral industry."

"Then forget it," Richard advised. "Just consider sales quotas the dues you have to pay for the privilege of working heinous hours with miserable people at a job that will never be properly compensated."

Well put; he made his point. What was I doing in the funeral industry, anyway? The checks were feeble, and everybody said the work would destroy my body before its time. I didn't feel like I was helping anyone.

Maybe I should find a job as an event planner, I thought one day, after hanging up with the caterer and dashing to meet the rental company delivering an extra tent. But there, across the sodden grass, sat Mr. McHenry, silently grieving his Helen. I'm sure he hoped exposure to the lousy weather would result in pneumonia. Michael had made sure there was a chair for the old man's use next to the grave. He no longer needed to lug his own lawn chair from the trunk of his Pontiac. Mr. McHenry looked so pitiful.

I waded through the grass in my accursed black pumps and asked him to come in for a cup of coffee. I could smell Scotch on his breath, and he looked jaundiced. "You have to stop doing this to yourself," I said.

"Why?"

"Well, because."

"Just because?" Mr. McHenry asked. Were his bleary eyes accusing me of being a bullshitter? Or was that me, admitting I was?

"I feel like I'm letting him down," I told Dante one night.

"For what?"

"For not, I don't know, helping him cope better, I guess."

"Do you get paid to help him cope better months after the funeral?"

"Well, no."

"Right, so leave that to the shrinks. Your job is to get dead people looking good for the service, give everybody a chance to cry, and then get the hole covered as soon as the family pulls out of the cemetery."

"That doesn't seem like enough, somehow. Charging outrageous prices and then standing around in my pretty black suit."

"Geez, Elizabeth," Dante said. "How come you spend so much time worrying about everybody else and never have the time to worry about what I need?"

"That's not fair," I protested. "You know I spend as much time with you as I can. I'm neglecting everything else in my life except you and my job."

"Oh, really? You come up with a wedding date yet?"

I sighed.

"I figured," Dante growled. I moved the conversation to less dangerous waters. But looming larger for me was Mr. McHenry. I couldn't get him out of my head.

I considered asking Michael what he thought about the situation, but he had been especially crude since my Christmas Day engagement announcement. He was on a mission to make sure I knew all about his success as a player. His crack about "the twins" had been just the beginning. If I had to hear one more suggestive remark about a random party girl, I was going to vomit.

The good news was I'd heard from Willow. She was coming home for a few weeks of furlough. She'd be couch surfing at Kevin's and Ryan's, and there was an intimate *Welcome Back, Kotter* theme dinner planned for her first Friday night in town. I couldn't wait to see her and was proud of the Sweathogs costumes I had put together. I had to whine at Dante to get him into his Barbarino outfit, but I insisted that if he couldn't get in touch with his inner Travolta, I was going without him. He acquiesced, begrudgingly.

"I don't know why you can't have normal friends,"

"My friends are perfectly normal; they just like a little wacky fun."

"Oh, is that what we're calling it these days."

"*Dante!*" I warned him, as the door flew open. Ryan was utterly charming as Horshack.

"Oh! Oh! Oh!" he shouted as he reached out to hug me and take my casserole dish with the blue cornflower motif. In the kitchen, Willow appeared as Gabe Kotter and Kevin was decked out as Rosalie "Hotsie" Totsie, the girl rumored to have put the "sweat" in Sweathog. I laughed my head off, but Dante seemed to be missing the joke.

Dinner was '70s trash-style cuisine: Hamburger Helper, Banquet Salisbury steak with mashed potatoes TV dinners, even Tang and quiche, which Kevin explained was okay to be eaten by real men prior to the '80s.

Dante headed straight for the giant bowl of high-octane fruit punch, while I showered Willow with questions about her trip and Ryan set the table. Somewhere, the boys had scored a set of Corningware embossed with harvest gold flowers and found Melmac tumblers. With the four of us back together at the kitchen table, it felt as if I had come back home again after a long trip. I couldn't wait to have Willow get to know Dante, and I truly hoped my three favorite guys would hit it off a little better than they had at the "Come as Your Favorite Shipwreck Victim" party.

In hindsight, I should have steered Dante towards non-alcoholic beverage choices if I wanted him to make a good impression. The Melmac tumblers were on the large side, and to be fair, he had a right to be nervous about meeting his fiancée's friends for the first time. Well, not completely the first time, but you can pick up what I'm laying down.

Willow shared sweet stories of helping downtrodden South Americans, pleased she could make a difference in their lives. She said she was certain they would never forget meeting her. It led to Dante accusing her of having a "white savior complex," thinking she was the "great white hope" for all the "pathetic brown people."

The whole discussion was so embarrassing that I went back the next day to apologize to my loving friends. They were gracious but refused to let me leave until I confessed how often Dante got drunk and obnoxious.

"I'm not exactly sure," I said. "He usually has a drink or two when we're together, but so do I."

"Au contraire!" said Kevin. "You sipped on one and a half. He had something like five and probably would have had more if we hadn't insisted the party was over when Willow started crying."

"And where is he today?" Willow asked. "Why are you here alone? Shouldn't he be making the apologies?"

For a minute, I thought the humiliation would make me cry. Ryan saw my mood nosedive and scooted closer to wrap an arm around me. He nestled in close. "Honey, we love you. We will always love you and we will back your play, no matter what, but you should probably take a hard look at this guy before you get to the altar."

"When is the wedding, Hon?" Willow asked.

"I don't know," I said. "We haven't set a date yet. I can't find one that seems right."

Everybody stared at me until I started to fidget. Ryan let me loose, and I sat up feeling utterly dejected.

Willow broke the silence. "I think you need to search your soul about this." Kevin nodded.

"But I love him," I said, pathetically. "And I love his family, and they love me." They all looked at me with heartbreaking sympathy. Feeling self-conscious, I made an excuse about work and left.

❦

The next day was Sunday. I had promised to accompany Dante's grandmother to Mass, even though I was on the verge of ending our relationship. Mrs. Perez was a sweet, tiny thing who almost always wore pink. She had a gentle vibrancy I hoped to achieve when I was the revered matriarch of my own family.

The sermon was on Mark 8:36: "For how does it benefit a man, if he gains the whole world, and yet causes harm to his soul?" Given the conversation I'd had the previous day, I found it a squirm-inducing choice. How did the priest know?

On the way home, I asked Mrs. Perez about her husband. She boasted of what a hard worker and good provider he was. She had been orphaned as a little girl and married young. They were together more than fifty years and raised eight sons who helped their father establish the construction business.

"How did you know he was the right one?" I asked.

"Oh, you don't," the little old lady replied. "You pick a man from a decent family and then you make him the right one."

"How do you do that?"

"You make up your mind when you go into it that 'this is it' and you'll do what you have to so it sticks."

"What if he has serious problems? Like, what if he runs around on you or drinks and gets into fights?"

"Oh, you can't worry about that. It's how men act. They have to be strong and provide for the family, and after that, sometimes they need to blow off a little steam. That's all. It doesn't mean much."

"It sounds terrible."

"Is Dante acting up with you, Elizabeth? Never mind. When you get married, you can fix that. Men get into all kinds of trouble until they have a strong woman and a baby on the way to make them behave."

"Shouldn't they take responsibility for their own behavior?" I suggested as we pulled into the driveway. Mrs. Perez scoffed.

"Come have some ceviche, *flaca*."

I walked her in, but pled work so I didn't have to stay. Dante was disappointed but seemed more interested in something his brothers were fooling with in the garage. He let me go with a reminder about our Valentine's Day date.

"Wouldn't miss it," I assured him and got out of there.

With careful planning, I managed to avoid Dante until our date. It didn't hurt that four souls had lost their lives on Sunday and showed up at Western View first thing Monday morning. I felt guilty about being grateful for the loss of so many people, but I needed time to think.

I loved Dante, I truly did. I loved how he was with his family, and how he sometimes made me feel like I was the only person he set his gaze upon. I thought of our summer together. He hadn't been drinking so much back then, had he?

Chapter 20

Valentine's Day Massacre

I WENT UPSTAIRS TO GIVE MY CLOTHES A THOROUGH LOOK-SEE. IF I didn't have anything, I would borrow a dress from a friend. I was too boringly responsible to put an outfit on credit in my cash-strapped state even if it was Valentine's dinner. I'd only use my charge card when a pair of black heels had to be freshly replaced because of turf ruination. My shoes aerated the cemetery lawn more than I cared for.

My closet was small but consistent: On every hanger there hung a black, gray or navy blue garment. These were the official dress code colors of my employer. I hadn't bothered to unpack or hang the ballroom gowns and dancing dresses from my Arthur Murray days. No room for bygone memories and clothes of that era in my main closet. Instead, I pushed the door open to the crawlspace and spotted the big box I was hunting for. It was dank and smelly back there, and it made me feel lousy that all my lovely, floating-on-air gowns were crumpled in a box in that stinky domicile. I lugged the box out to my main sitting area and silently asked my mother to help me know what I needed to wear.

Under a few dresses was a red silk number I had worn during a Foxtrot routine with my dance partner, Scotty "the Body" Qazzaz. We had twirled and drifted across the gorgeous wood floor in the ballroom at the Hotel Vancouver in British Columbia during my Portland ballroom dancer days.

I sat amidst my beautiful dresses, relishing grand memories of dances past. It was time to bring that slinky red number back out of the past.

❧

Dante was due to pick me up at work. As soon as I was officially off, I ran to the bathroom to change clothes and refresh my make-up and hair. For the final touch, I bent my head to my knees and gave my full mane a good dose of spray. Flipped it back like a pro and watched every hair fall into place.

"Damn!" I heard someone say as I emerged. It was Michael, of course. I felt so good I couldn't muster up my usual annoyance. I gave him a quick spin and a thank you before I pranced outside to look for my knight in Corvette armor.

"Guess you got a big night planned," Michael said, following me out the door and looking me up and down.

"I do."

"Me, too," he smirked. "It's on me to make sure the single ladies don't feel too lonely this evening." I rolled my eyes and told him to have fun as I spotted Dante in the parking lot.

My dress was very well received. "I feel like the luckiest *hombre* in the world," Dante said, and his gaze told me he truly did.

"Because you are," I teased.

"Who's that guy?" Dante asked, looking back toward the funeral parlour. Michael was standing outside the building watching us.

"Oh nobody, just the guy who watches over the cremations."

"Well, he needs to stop watching your ass."

"Isn't that sweet? You're jealous."

Dante leaned over for a scorching hot kiss. After I melted he sat up and professed, "I don't need to be jealous." Yikes, he got that right.

We left Michael in a cloud of manly exhaust and cruised downtown to El Gaucho. Ever thoughtful, Dante had made reservations, allowing us to parade past the folks shivering in line outside. I thanked him for scheduling ahead and he queried, "Who takes care of you?"

"You do," I replied, "and I have so much to tell you."

We sat, and he indicated a bottle of wine he wanted to a waiter, who appeared quickly to his side.

"Actually, I was thinking maybe we could skip wine with dinner," I said.

"What? Why?" Dante asked.

"Because I want to talk to you about our future, that's all."

Dante shook his head like I was out of my gourd and told the waiter to bring the wine. He said, "What's with you tonight?"

"Nothing is with me. I want to talk to you to about some things, is all."

He looked for our waiter, and suddenly the heavy realization that Dante had a drinking problem landed on me like a grand piano falling from the sky. My mind flashed on the moments that should have given me a clue. When had he ever been without a drink in his hand? His lateness or not showing up at all, picking fights at the end of the night. It pointed in one terrible direction. The wine arrived, and as the waiter poured, I felt as if I was across the room—completely disconnected from the scene. Dante raised his glass and made a toast, but I couldn't concentrate on what he was saying.

"Elizabeth?" he finally prompted. I raised my glass.

What if he does have a problem? I asked myself as I took a sip of smoky Cabernet Sauvignon. I loved him. Wasn't the essence of "for better or worse" standing by your beloved to help them? I *could* help him. I was strong enough. We could get through this together.

"Elizabeth, where did you go?" Dante asked.

"Do you think you drink too much?" I blurted out.

"What?" Dante's face hardened instantly, and I cursed myself. *Have I no diplomacy?*

"I meant for your health, is all," I said. "Isn't it supposed to lower fertility?" I had no idea, but my brain had been overtaken by a particularly virulent strain of stupidity. It was the best I could come up with.

"There's nothing wrong with my fertility," he snarled, "and there's nothing wrong with having a drink with dinner." The waiter chose that moment to stop by our table. Dante viciously waved him off. My heart was pounding so hard my ears hurt.

"You have a lot of nerve criticizing me for having a drink after a hard day's work," he continued. "But what would you know about it? You can barely support yourself with your so-called 'career' so obviously, you never have a day where you give it your all."

My jaw dropped open. I started to tremble but couldn't reply. Dante, on the other hand, was having zero trouble finding his words.

"Do you know what I think about all day? Do you?" he asked. I shook my head. "I think about making money," he said. "For *us*, for the family we're going to have. I don't whine about hating sales or how unfair my boss is, I *perform*. For us. And, at the end of the day, if I want a drink to relax, I've earned it, because I'm the man. That's the difference between you and me."

Dante sat back and poured himself another glass of wine and drank the whole thing without taking his eyes off me.

"I work hard," I whimpered.

"You put make-up on dead people and pass out tissue and have ridiculous dreams of burying people in banana leaves and other dumb hippie nature stuff."

The waiter reappeared. Dante asked for the bill and made a point of explaining that we wouldn't be eating, because I needed to learn the value of what he provided for me. The kind waiter gave me a look of such undeniable pity he might as well have been officiating at my own funeral. All I wanted to do was crawl in a tire swing and die.

I got to my feet and ran—at least rushed as fast as one can in high heels on trembling legs. I dashed out the door, aware the entire restaurant was staring at me, and took the first right down an alley where no one could see me. Fortunately, it was clean and mostly empty. A few smokers were gathered several feet away. I tucked myself into a shadow where I could pant and shake in privacy.

It took me a long time to settle down and realize I was miles away from where my Jeep was parked at Western View. Shit, shit, shit, I thought, kicking the brick wall I leaned against. How would I get home? I scrolled through the address book in my phone. Nick and Phoebe had gone out, and Dad would already be in bed. Besides, did I want to have to explain myself to one of them? I thought not. Kevin and Ryan had gone out of town for a romantic weekend, but maybe Willow was around. Her phone went straight to voicemail. Nurse Nancy was working that night. Richard, maybe? It would be embarrassing, but I figured I could make up some lie. I dialed his number and learned he was way out in the southeastern corner of Clackamas County, picking up a body. Didn't he ever get a day off? Feeling increasingly cold and desperate, I kept scrolling and made more unsuccessful calls.

I heard a voice say, "Call Michael." I looked around. Was somebody playing a joke on me? There was nobody there.

"Mom?" I whispered, but all I could hear were the smokers laughing. There was no way I was calling Michael—I'd had enough humiliation for one night. Then I remembered Tri-Met. I didn't need rescuing. Perfectly sensible people took the Max train or bus every day when they didn't have a car. I squared my shoulders, took a deep breath, and marched out of that alley prepared to take charge of my own destiny. I was a professional woman, for the love of God.

I made it all the way over to the Max station before I realized I didn't have my purse with me. For all I knew, it was still hanging on the back of my chair in the restaurant. Probably Dante had taken it with him, I hoped. Before I totally lost it, I sat down on the bus stop bench and took some deep breaths. Then I noticed somebody watching me. A creepy guy lifted himself off a wall he'd been glued to and sauntered over.

"You got any spare change?" he asked.

"I don't even have money for the bus," I said, before I realized how unwise it was to tell a stranger I was stranded downtown. The guy leered over me until I stood up and walked away. I made a beeline to another bench where a young couple sat. I scrolled through my phone aimlessly. Finally, I gave up and dialed Michael's number.

"Miss me already?" he said when he answered. I would have hung up but Scary Bus Guy was circling closer.

"I need a ride," I admitted.

"Where's Prince *Ecantador*?"

"It's a long story. Would you be willing to pick me up and take me back to work so I can get my Jeep?"

"I don't know, I'm in the middle of some pretty hot action over here," Michael said.

"Please, I'll pay for your gas when I get my purse back."

"You're downtown with no money on a dark night?"

"Yes," I confessed. "I know, idiotic."

"I'll be right there," Michael said and the line went dead.

For the next ten minutes, I eased my way from bus bench to bus bench, so I wasn't standing alone. Scary Guy lurked around the shadows but kept his distance. After what seemed an hour, Michael pulled up in the bus lane, and I jumped in his big blue Ford truck like a mountain lion was after me.

To his credit, Michael didn't say anything about how I'd landed in such a ridiculous position. He simply asked me if I was all right. When we reached Western View, he parked next to my Jeep and a new realization dawned.

"Oh hell," I said. "I don't have my keys. My purse is in the restaurant."

Michael's brows furrowed. "How did you have your phone?"

"I always keep it in my bra so I can feel it vibrate without disturbing anyone when I'm in meetings with families."

"Good trick," he said, looking impressed. "So, back to the restaurant?"

"I seriously cannot go back in there tonight," I said. "Just drop me off at my house and I'll see if I can break in through a window or something."

"Look, I don't know what happened, but I don't think being arrested for breaking and entering is going to be an improvement on your night."

I giggled. "At least jail is warm."

"Why don't we go back to the restaurant? I'll go inside and get your purse."

"That's sweet of you, but we don't even know if it's there."

"Geez, Elizabeth, so call them. Do I have to think of everything?" Sheepishly, I dialed information for the number and had the operator connect me. It was there. Dante never bothered to grab it for me!

"Good, then I'll go in and get it for you," Michael said.

"They're not going to give it to a strange man who just shows up. Or at least I hope they wouldn't."

"Okay, call back and tell them a guy named Michael is coming to get it. I have a driver's license if they need to see it."

"How do you always know what to do?" I asked.

He smiled a genuine smile; it was nice. He started up the truck. "Let's go back, and I will walk in there with you." And he did. It reminded me of picking up Mrs. Morton's body. Michael took charge and eased my anxiety-ridden self through the process of entering the restaurant, claiming my purse, and walking back out like it was all in a day's work.

"Thank you," I said on our way up the hill to Western View. "Sometimes you can be, so . . . well, not what I expect."

"What do you expect?" he probed.

"You're sort of a punk sometimes."

Michael laughed out loud and threw his head back. "You're a gutsy lady, you know that?" He into the parking lot of Western View. Headlights fell on the shape of a black Corvette, and he stopped laughing. "Uh, oh."

"Oh, my God," I whispered. Dante was leaning against the rear panel of his car. He didn't look happy. My heart thudded in my chest.

"Don't get out if it's not safe," Michael instructed. He pulled into a parking space on the far side, away from Dante.

"I can't believe this is happening," I whispered as I watched Dante walk toward the truck.

"Just be calm," Michael cautioned. He rolled down his window and said good evening to my obviously furious fiancé.

"Oh, I see how it is," Dante said. "Is this why you spend so much time at work, Elizabeth?" He was so drunk I could smell the liquor on his breath from my seat.

"Look, buddy," said Michael. "All I'm doing is making sure she gets home safely."

"I'm not your buddy," growled Dante. "But that's my fiancée, and you're trespassing."

Michael raised his hands like he was trying to avoid being shot by a cop. "I'm just chauffeuring. I don't know what happened tonight, but it seems like a good idea for both of you to go home. You can talk it out in the morning, when you're sober."

"You think you can tell me what to do with my woman?"

"Dante, please," I begged.

"Shut up, Elizabeth!" he yelled. "If you weren't running around behind my back, this wouldn't be happening."

"I'm not . . . !"

"Shut! Up!" Dante barked and then headed around to the passenger side of the truck. Michael quickly jabbed the door locks so they were all engaged. Then he manually unlocked his side, got out and relocked, then followed Dante to my side of the truck.

"Look, you need to go home and sleep it off," Michael said.

Dante made all kinds of threats. "I'll kick your ass, you Pollack. Hear me, you bitch? I will get you fired for screwing around with my girl. You will pay, you bitch. I'm gonna kill you."

He pushed Michael in the chest. That was it. I screamed, "Stop it, Dante! Stop it, or I'll call the police!" He gave me a look to break my heart,

but I held up my cell phone with complete confidence. He had to understand I was ready to have him arrested if need be.

"Fine!" Dante shouted. "You want this dumb bitch, she's yours! I'm
done!" He stormed to his car and peeled out of the parking lot. I wondered
if I should call the police anyway, to see if they could catch him before he
killed himself or someone else.

Michael rapped on the window and motioned for me to unlock the
truck doors. "Are you doing okay over there?" he asked, climbing back into
the driver's seat.

"I guess so." I was too embarrassed to look at him. "Thank you. Okay?
Thank you. Once again."

"Why don't you go home and get a good night's sleep. This will probably
look better in the morning."

I went home but certainly didn't sleep. "Mom?" I whispered tear-
fully, not long before the sun peeped over the horizon. "I'm sorry, but you
shouldn't have told me to call Michael. You might have really messed up
this time."

Chapter 21

Love Bites

MY PLAN WAS TO CALL IN SICK THE NEXT DAY. I WAS ASHAMED TO face Michael for one thing, and too heartbroken to guarantee I wouldn't start bawling at the least provocation. Before I got around to leaving Glen a message, he called to say Mr. McHenry had passed earlier that morning. The son wanted to meet with me at nine o'clock. For months, I had anticipated Mr. McHenry's death as a sorrowful occasion—one of the times when there would be no way to keep much emotional distance—but strangely, I found I couldn't feel much after all. Mr. McHenry's death had been added to the heap of grief I was already carrying; it wasn't possible to feel any sadder.

I pulled on a suit and drove numbly to Western View. I was ready to go through the motions as if everything was normal.

Well, not totally normal: I was in complete supersonic evasion mode. Dante called a few times, which I let vibrate to voice mail. Michael was harder to avoid, since he seemed to be trying to catch me alone. I nearly walked into a wall twice in my efforts to elude him.

By end of the day I saw him headed toward my office. I ducked into the conference room without looking to see if it was already in use.

Glen was in there with a family. *Crap!* In babbling my way out of that situation, I managed to make my boss even more convinced of my incompetence.

I sneaked up the hall and peeked into my office before fully committing myself to entry. No Michael. Relieved, I dashed in and sat down, looking as if I had a very important phone call to make. What I saw stopped me short. In the middle of my desk lay the bloom of a white lily—symbol of peace and innocence.

He stole that! I thought. The only place it could have come from was a funeral bouquet. How cheesy!

I heard a rustle outside my door and looked up to see Michael watching me. He turned away and headed toward the back stairs. My God, why did he have to be so immature about everything? Couldn't he guess I was having a hard day?

I caught him downstairs, where he pretended to be engrossed with some aspect of an oven control panel.

"Did you steal this?" I asked, holding up the lily bloom in my outstretched hand.

"The other guy didn't need it," he replied, still not looking at me.

"I'm really not up to playing games today," I said, petulantly.

"I get it. It's not like you make a big secret of how you feel about me, but don't treat me like somehow this is my fault. I just wanted to make sure you're all right. I'm funny that way."

How I felt about him? What was that supposed to mean? How did he think I felt about him? What did I feel?

"Look," Michael said. "You gotta know I like you, right?"

"Well, yeah, I guess," I said. "But . . ." But—he was too young, and what do I know about Jersey boys?

". . . But I don't meet whatever standard you set, I get it," said Michael. "That doesn't mean you can't treat me with a little respect, even when you don't need me to do your dirty work."

"I don't . . . !"

"Yeah," Michael interrupted. "You do."

"That's not fair," I said, blinking hard to avoid a tear cascade. I didn't want a showdown today of all days.

Michael did. "You don't owe me anything, but if you could see your way to treating me like the kind of friend who gets out of a truck to face down your drunk, pissed off boyfriend, that would be great."

I blinked faster. "I can do that."

"Super," Michael replied, flatly. "What time are you leaving?"

"I don't know, why?"

"Because if you haven't noticed, I don't have anything to do here, but I didn't know if you felt comfortable walking to your car alone tonight."

I looked around at the perfectly clean room—ovens off, everything in its place. A hot tear made its way down my face. "I didn't think of that," I said.

"That I would look out for you, or that Prince Charmless might be back after work tonight?"

"Neither! I've been planning Mr. McHenry's funeral." My body did one of those weird spasms that happen right before the flood gates open and the real bawling begins.

"Don't do that!" Michael said. Reflexively, I started taking deep breaths and got myself under control. He wanted to know if Dante was still raging over our date gone bad.

"I haven't talked to him, but he left some voice mails earlier," I said.

"Better listen to them," Michael advised.

There were seven messages. Dante began his day by deriding me for my supposed affair with Michael: *"I can't believe you would cheat on me with that loser you work with!"*

By mid-day, he sounded worried and conciliatory, but made it clear I would have to earn his forgiveness: *"You need to call me. I need to hear your voice. I'm still totally pissed at you and you need to be punished for what you did, but you need to call me back as soon as you get this."*

By afternoon, my lack of response wasn't setting well with him. His scorn for me was fully present. The last message was mean and scary: *"Look, you stupid bitch, I'll be waiting for you outside, and you will never forget what I have to say to you. You are going to be sorry for who you are."*

"You're right," I told Michael. "I don't think I want to walk to my car alone."

"Is your roommate home tonight?" he asked.

I shook my head.

"Then I'll follow you back to your place and make sure you're inside safely."

I was delivered safely and watched his big truck pull away from the living room window. I made a solemn oath to myself to start treating Michael better. Maybe he was too young and too Jersey to be a boyfriend, but he was a good guy.

"No more rolling my eyes at him," I said to the empty house as my phone started vibrating. Dante, of course. I threw it in the bottom of my bag and left it on the couch with the cats. I turned off all the lights and ran upstairs to hide under my covers.

Lack of sleep plus the emotions of the day took over. I was asleep and dreaming immediately. I dreamed I was pregnant with Dante's child but he insisted the baby was Michael's. My eyes shot open. Every cell in my body was instantly alert and terrified at the sound of someone on the stairs. I felt around for a weapon and came up with a pink slipper. Oh no, not much of a deterrent! Why didn't I have mace or something? This was the pathetic weaponry I came up with: a tube of lip balm, a day-old glass of Diet Coke, and a notepad on the chair next to the futon. The somebody came closer. I considered breaking the drinking glass when I heard, "Elizabeth? Are you up?"

I screamed like I was the star of a shower scene in a horror movie, then the lights popped on. Being of sound mind, sort of, I did what any sensible person would do and threw myself under the covers to await death with a complete lack of dignity. Somebody else screamed and then I heard Nurse Nancy saying, "Are you all right?"

"Oh, my God, Nurse Nancy!" I yelled from underneath the duvet.

"Luke?" she called back.

I sprang out of the bed and tripped my way over my covers onto her feet. "What the hell is going on?" she shrieked. "Your Jeep doors are wide open."

"Was the house door locked?" I demanded. She assured me it was, but I made her go downstairs with me and double check anyway. I explained, chaotically as possible, what had happened over the past twenty-four hours. Nurse Nancy was astounded but not entirely shocked.

"You knew he had a drinking problem?" I asked. "Why didn't you say anything?"

"I didn't know, but I was seeing a pattern that bugged me."

"Why didn't you say anything?" I repeated.

"Would you have listened?"

She had me there. I played Dante's phone messages for her—two more had arrived—and asked if she thought I should be scared.

"I think you should be cautious," she replied. "The way he's acting, there will probably be some drama."

We talked over my better-safe-than-sorry options. I did not want my family involved any more than necessary, so I refused to discuss staying at my father's or brother's houses. Finally, I came up with the idea of asking Kevin and Ryan if I could hang out at their place in the evenings while Nurse Nancy worked swing shift. It meant an embarrassing conversation, but it would be better than cowering under the covers until my brave roomie got home.

"Call them first thing in the morning," Nurse Nancy said, and then ordered me upstairs to bed.

Again, it took me no time at all to fall asleep. But not for long. Sometime after the bars closed, Dante showed up pounding at our door and slurring my name at the top of his voice. Adrenaline got me down the stairs, but Nurse Nancy beat me to the door. She stood in front of the porch window and, in her most no-nonsense-nurse voice, let Dante know he'd better leave or she was calling the police.

I panicked. "No!" I shouted. "I don't want him arrested!" Dante heard my voice and started rattling the door handle.

"Elizabeth, unlock the door," he whined.

"Elizabeth," Nancy said, all authority, "stay away from the door." She stopped me dead in my tracks and whispered, "Get out of sight." I fled to the kitchen.

Dante begged to come in again, then switched to shouting, but Nurse Nancy was resolute. She told him one more time to go away. As he started screaming "Dumb bitch!" she began to dial.

From my vantage point in the kitchen, I saw her lift the phone to her ear. My anxiety nearly got the best of me, but Nurse Nancy looked up in time to see me take a step forward. She shot me a no-holds-barred look that sent me scurrying back around the corner of the kitchen wall. She assured the emergency operator she would stay on the line then calmly yelled to Dante the police were on their way.

No, no, no! I was thinking. I considered going out there to see if I could get Dante to leave before the police arrived. I could go out the back door! Fortunately, my pounding heart had paralyzed the rest of my body. Before I could kick start my physical capacities, Dante realized Nurse Nancy was serious and stormed off. I heard her give a description of his Corvette and the direction he was driving, and then she hung up the phone.

She found me in the kitchen. "Are you hanging in there?" she asked.

My mouth wasn't working, but I shook my head no. She flipped the light on and told me everything would be fine. I didn't believe her, but it felt good to hear that confident, determined, protective voice of hers.

"I don't want to tell my dad," I whimpered, a slumping heap.

"Believe me, your dad will forgive you for not marrying a drunken douche bag."

"But he's a really nice guy," I continued to whine.

"No, he's really not," Nurse Nancy said. She pushed a stool towards me from the kitchen island and professionally advised me that I needed a stiff drink, or at least she did. My nurse set about preparing hot toddies with plenty of bourbon. This was an excellent idea because before long, there was a policeman at our door who needed to take a statement. I made it through the police report, then she swiftly tucked me into blankets on the couch. I watched her make sure every inch of the windows were covered by tightly shut blinds.

"The efficiency of nurses is a wonder to behold," I said, sleepily. My resolute protector just smiled and set herself up for the rest of the night in an easy chair with a view of the door.

The next thing I knew, the sun was shining through opened window blinds, and I could smell eggs cooking in the kitchen. I followed my nose and found the brave nurse looking little worse for her evening's wear.

"How do you do it?" I asked her. "I look like an authentic zombie and you're flying around here like nothing happened."

Nurse Nancy shrugged. "That's my crisis mode; I suspend falling apart until I've managed what has to be managed."

"That seems like a good technique. I'll have to try it."

"You might want to start right away, because I doubt that's the last we'll be seeing of your newly-minted ex, Señor Douche."

I frowned. "Isn't there something I could do? Maybe change the wedding date until he gets counseling and stops drinking?"

Nancy set a plate of eggs and toast in front of me. "If that's the way you're going to play this, he'll definitely be screaming on our porch more often, so you'll want to start practicing your crisis mode skills today."

"Are you being serious?"

"I am serious," she said and sure enough, her face was set in the same expression she held while telling Dante to get off the porch. "Finding out before the wedding that the person you plan to spend your life with is a drunk who scares the hell out of you is a gift, Elizabeth."

"But I love him."

"No, you love the sweet, sexy, family guy you thought he was. Turns out he's not that guy."

"What if I got him to go to A.A.?" I asked.

Nancy didn't even dignify that with an answer.

Chapter 22

Spiritus Eruptius

THE NEXT SEVERAL WEEKS WERE A WOEFUL TALE OF HOW DESIRE AND denial team up to make a girl play the fool. I thrashed through the break up until my friends started cringing every time I mentioned the subject. Eventually, I was completely embarrassed in front of everyone I knew and plenty of strangers besides.

On a day off, I walked to the little bar at the end of my street, looking for a quick escape from my life. I had a hell of a time getting out of bed, and I literally had nothing to do all day but play the reels of fights with my ex in my head. How dare he always be so damn selfish.

The place was dead. I made my way to the bar and waited to be served.

"You don't look like a mortician," the bartender declared. I smiled the smile I smile every time I hear this observation. He follows that up with, "Did you know a sheriff's dispatcher sounds the same when calling a funeral home about a death call that he does calling a tow truck driver about a flat tire? Not everything is so sacred anymore. Death is a weird career choice."

I glumly retorted, "I have no regrets being a mortician; some of my greatest moments are those shared with the dead."

He shares that he was raised in a funeral home and sometimes he was sent downstairs to the basement to bring supper to dad. That would really freak him out to interrupt his father, hard at work repairing a body. He said that one time he walked in and a head was sitting on the table *next* to the body. He was still freaked over it. His first job was helping dress the bodies with his older brother. They were just kids, and all they could think about was if they'd hurry up, supper won't be cold. "Why did that room always remind me of supper?" he asked the air as he handed me a Rolling Rock.

Michael found me planting roses the following afternoon on the McHenrys' graves and asked if I always gardened in my funeral shoes.

"Baby, I've washed hearses in my funeral shoes," I bragged. He took the small spade out of my hand and started digging. I unwrapped and positioned the cuttings, double checking that I had the colors placed correctly. Michael covered the roots and gently tamped down the dirt with his boots. I took in his permanently bemused expression, the mop of curly hair, and the bit of mischief in his dark eyes. He looked good to me.

"Why are we doing this?' Michael asked. "You on some sort of beautification campaign?"

"No, just keeping a promise to two people who stayed in love," I said. Michael stood uncomfortably close, looking at me somewhat devotedly with his big eyes.

"You have a soft heart," he observed.

"Is that good?"

"I guess it depends on who you give it to." He had me there.

"You probably think I'm pretty stupid."

"I think you can do better," said Michael.

"You mean with you?" I replied, trying to sound light-lighthearted.

"Compared to a mean drunk? Yeah, I do, actually, but we're not going there."

What? Suddenly, surprisingly, I felt anxious. "What do you mean?" I asked.

"I guess you think I'm pretty stupid," Michael replied.

"I don't think you're being fair. This is a hard time for me."

"Yeah," Michael said, looking deeply into my eyes. "It ain't easy being what you think you're supposed to be instead of what you are, is it?"

"What the hell does that mean?"

"It means you have all this . . . I don't know, *spirit,* I guess, but you're so busy worrying about what other people think of you that you keep pulling yourself up short."

"I do not!"

"No? Then if you're the sassy, independent woman you pretend to be, what are you doing trying to repair things with a loser?"

I didn't really want to work on fixing everything with Dante, but there was no way I was going to admit any failure. I stared angrily across the rolling hills of Western View.

"I thought you liked me," I barked, wondering why I cared.

"I do," Michael said. He drove the spade into the ground forcefully and walked away. I couldn't watch him go, so I busied myself collecting and folding the plastic bags I had taken off the roses. By the time I stood up, Michael was nowhere to be seen. There was just the spade standing where he had stood. I pulled it out of the ground and returned it to the equipment shed, thinking about how Michael looked at me. He saw something in me I didn't, and I wondered what it was.

It didn't matter. After all, I sure as hell wasn't going to take up with the likes of Jersey Boy. This was my life and I wanted the whole enchilada: the handsome husband who wore oxford shirts and dress shoes to work, the successful career, the perfectly groomed home and the beautiful children who would be a credit to us at their private school. I needed someone a little more *Forbes*, a little less *Hot Rod Magazine*. I was worth it!

I strode back to the funeral home, head high, and cleaned the mud off my pumps. One look in the ladies room mirror restored my confidence. Screw Michael and his opinions. I had what it took to attract someone who could give me the lifestyle I deserved. I'd show him; I'd show everybody. I scrubbed dirt out from underneath my fingernails, repaired my make-up, and got ready to take back my life. The scene with Michael at the McHenrys' grave would be my last humiliation, thank you very much.

I drove straight to my father's home after work to let him know there would be no wedding.

"What happened?" Dad asked.

"Turns out he's a mean drunk," I said simply.

"Then you're better off without him," Dad said.

"I'm old and single without him," I groused, digging around in the refrigerator for any possible can of soda.

"Your day is coming," Dad replied. "I don't worry about you."

"You don't?"

"No," Dad said. "I knew from the time you were little you had the moxie to come out all right."

"You did?"

"Yeah. You're like your mother that way. Don't settle for any man who doesn't appreciate it."

"Did you appreciate that about Mom?" I asked.

"Oh, yeah," Dad said with a telling smile. "She was spirited. I didn't always know what to do with it, but I had to rise to the occasion to keep up with her."

I loved that and asked him to explain.

"Oh, I don't know, I was just a better version of myself with her. I had more courage."

Maybe it was just Dad's use of the word "spirited," but it put Michael back in my mind, which seemed totally crazy. On the other hand, the guy from Jersey had given me the impetus to stand up and give Dante's ring back. That's crazy, I thought, popping open a Diet Pepsi.

❧

My friends were continually remarkable as my heart healed. Kevin and Ryan offered to throw me a "Come as Your Favorite Character from a Breakup Movie" party. They marked the occasion by making a mix CD of heartbreak songs that I was eventually forced to throw under the seat of my Jeep. There are only so many days a girl can cry during her work commute to a Rascal Flatts song about the lost one and only.

If I had a late-night first call, which means a body is ready to be transported from the place of death, Willow was always game to accompany me across town to pick up a deceased loved one and bring them into the care of the funeral home. I was only sent on calls where a hospital morgue was involved—did this mean Glen didn't feel he could trust me in a mourning family's home? My only interaction was meeting security in the loading dock area and wheeling my gurney inside the morgue.

Willow wanted to assist. She didn't want pay; she claimed to really dig the experience of it all. I was thankful; it served as my only form of social life, plus the nightshift was unsettling. In unison, we transferred the body onto the cot using a bedsheet as a sling, wrapped the body in plastic, tightened the belts around torso and legs, folded the sides of the cot to cover the body, and silently wheeled the decedent into the mortuary van.

Once securely in the van, Willow noted, "Is every morgue located in a non-descript, out-of-the-way location in the hospital?"

"More times than not they're in the basement across from food services."

"What's the smelliest one you've had to deal with?"

"Multnomah County Medical Examiner's Office used to be in Northeast Portland, and it was horrible. You'd walk in and see a bunch of those metal rolling drawers like in the movies, and some would be marked 'Male Torso #1' and spooky crap like that. Then you would have to wade through a sea of bodies on tables in the walk-in cooler to fetch who you needed to pluck out of there."

We both hated the plastic. We understood the sanitary precautions but knew there had to be a better way. She suggested using old flour sacks sewn together or covering the person with a beautiful quilt, rather than zipping them up in a zippered bag.

Once home after a pleasant ride with my good friend and my bed pillows fluffed, I was ready to drift off to dreamland. But sometimes I missed the ferryboat. I would stay in the same position for what seemed like an hour, contemplating the concept of time.

I want more time. I am trapped by the active, intelligent person's ongoing dilemma, which is the lack of time. Life simultaneously seems too precious to waste in front of the television, and too precious to let slip by without enjoying leisure time and purposeful contemplation. I want time to reflect. I want time to nap. I want time to pursue and develop a great relationship with someone. I want time to explore my fascination with canned foods. I want time to visit my father and niece. I want time to bake cookies for a deserving guy, and learn how to cook a great steak. I want time to get in my Jeep, drive somewhere pretty, and snap a roll of pictures. I want so much time that I might, just might, find myself lying on my bed staring at the ceiling, so bored that I wish I could die, like I did once when I was seven.

I finally turned my head to see what time it was, and I was quite surprised to find 5:37 a.m. staring back at me from the digital display. I would hear my alarm ring in twenty minutes, so I decided to spring the coup early and get in a smidge longer morning workout.

ლ

Michael's reaction was confusing. After trying to get me to go out with him when I was unavailable I thought he would jump at this new opportunity, but he didn't. Day after day went by; he was friendly enough but no further. No invitations to happy hour at 52nd Ave Sports Bar, no lurking around awaiting a chance to start up a conversation. He didn't even try to make me jealous with tales of his weekend exploits. Weeks went by and finally, on a slow Friday that gave me way too much time to think, I went looking for him.

He was shelving cremains downstairs. "What gives?" I asked.

"Ashes get stored here until the families come to collect them," he replied.

"No, I mean with us."

Michael stopped filing dead people and looked at me. "What us?"

"That's what I'm asking. Don't you like me anymore?"

"Are you kidding? I'm totally into you. You're all I talk about to my friends," he said.

"Then why don't you act like it anymore?" I asked.

"You never liked that before."

Seriously? He was going to make me beg for his attention? I thought, though, about all the times I rolled my eyes at him and realized I was getting a deserved bit of pushback. I took a deep breath and admitted I would like it if he liked me. A huge, goofy grin spread across Michael's face and for a moment I reconsidered, but there was no going back at this point. I don't know what tricks my newly configured mind was playing on me, but he was also looking *really cute* and taller than I remembered.

"Does this mean you'll go out with me?" he asked.

I nodded.

"Tonight?"

I thought a moment, then agreed. Michael started shelving cremains as fast as he could. "I'll pick you up in an hour," he said. "Wear comfortable clothes; there is something I've been dying to show you."

"An hour? I'll hardly be home by then."

"That's okay, just go home and put on some jeans and shoes without heels."

"You'd better not be taking me to a race track!"

"You'll love it. Please, Elizabeth. Just trust me."

"Famous last words," I said, but I left promptly and by the time he arrived at my house I was in jeans and sensible shoes as instructed.

"You have a date?" Nurse Nancy asked when I came back down from my room with a sweater over my shoulder and an apprehensive look on my face.

How would I explain to friends that I was going on an actual date with the guy I had been calling the "Incinerator Baiter" for so long? Oh well, there would be time enough for that after our second date—if there was a second date—so I fibbed. "I'm going to hang out with a friend from work."

"Rock on, Luke!" she called in my direction as I raced to meet Michael before he came to the door. I stood behind a tree to make sure Darth couldn't see me from the dining room windows and jumped in his truck.

"On the lam from the law or just happy to see me?" he asked, which made me giggle despite myself.

"Where are we going?" I asked as we pulled away.

"My place," he said.

"Michael!" I protested.

"No, it's not what you think. Trust me!" he insisted.

Oh crap, I thought. What the hell had I gotten myself into?

Chapter 23

Unearthing Mr. Right

MICHAEL TOOK ME TO A FUNERAL HOME ON OUR FIRST DATE. NO kidding. He lived in an old, yet elegant, funeral parlour that had been stately in its heyday. It stood on a brick foundation nearly three feet above ground level with capacious steps approaching the entrances and verandahs. An early sixteenth century wooden icon of a little boy hung on one wall inside, and three pencil drawings by Old Masters hung on another. A seventeenth century Flemish chest with ebony and inlaid red tortoiseshell stood in the corner of the room. Red velvet paper covered the walls.

Michael led me through the building and up a set of stairs. He showed me how to cross the roof and traverse a thin attic space, which suddenly dropped us onto the balcony of the chapel.

"How cool!" I exclaimed. Michael told me it was just the beginning and encouraged me to explore further, letting me lead the way so I would have the thrill of discovery. The place was full of bizarre hidden doors and passages. I hadn't been so intrigued since I poked around the oldest sections of cemeteries as a girl, only this time I had a companion who laughed with me when I made up silly stories about the place.

When I thought I'd found the last architectural surprise, Michael grabbed a grocery bag of picnic supplies he'd stowed when we first arrived and steered me to a set of pull down stairs in the attic. These accessed a small damp platform on the roof, but Michael had a tarp and sleeping bag stashed up there and spread them out for a dry place to sit.

"Come here often?" I joked, wondering if I was about to be the latest in a long series of women he tried to seduce in this private corner of the city.

"It's a good place to get away from it all," he said, doing nothing to ease my suspicions.

"Don't your dates get cold?" I asked, not subtly.

"I don't bring them here."

"Why not?" I asked, as he shook out a blanket and spread it over my lap.

"People are strange about funeral homes. You know, either they're weirded out about mortuaries or they have a weird interest." I nodded. I did know.

"Plus I kind of like having this place to myself," Michael added.

"Then why am I here?"

Michael busied himself unpacking the picnic he'd brought and opened a bottle of wine. He poured a pretty good pinot noir into a plastic glass.

"You're not like the women I usually date."

Personally, I thought that required some clarification but didn't know how to ask for it without coming off as if I were fishing for compliments. I assembled cheese and salami on crusty bread as if it were the most fascinating activity in the world.

Side-by-side, leaning against the wall of one of the more interesting buildings in the city, we speculated over why the mortuary Michael lived in was full of secret chambers. We got to know each other without any of the attitude of the past. Michael came from a Catholic Italian-American family, and he loved them dearly. He was also a fisherman, which I found surprising for some reason. He wanted to know absolutely everything about me, so I told him about my family, my mother's death, and how I had been an odd and lonely girl. I told him about my life before the funeral trade, as a ballroom dance instructor and DJ Liza James. It sort of surprised him.

We reached the subject of our work and what a horse's ass Glen was, and whether or not we had any future career ambitions.

"I have a dream of running my own place," I confided, "but everybody tells me it's out of the question, since I am a girl with no capital or family business to take over."

"Why would you want to?" Michael asked. "The big corporates are buying up all the little guys, anyway. It would be a constant fight just to stay afloat." Like most people I talked to, he thought it made more sense to put my time in until I could get a management position with some parlour lorded over by the almighty funeral corporation.

"You're probably right," I admitted, glumly. I confessed how much I hated the focus on upselling and my thoughts about the industry falling short of what it could be. He heard, and sat patiently, as I further expounded about how embalming fluid and concrete and metal caskets and casket hardware were doing nothing good for the environment.

"You get kind of deep about this," Michael observed.

I blushed. "Sorry."

"No, don't be. I like it," he said. Several brownie points got added to Michael's growing tally.

We talked about funeral customs in faraway places and the strange things we'd seen on the job and stories we'd heard, like Wang from China. Wang was attending a wake in his home when an explosion from a weather rocket took off half his roof and left him dead in the wreckage. Because it had been a stormy day, it was assumed that lightning had killed Wang and left half his home in ruins. However, as Wang was being placed into the cremation chamber at his own funeral, his body exploded, causing the chamber's oven doors to fly off their hinges. Only then was it discovered that a small weather rocket filled with silver iodide, shot into the sky to break up hail into rain, failed to explode in the atmosphere and instead had fallen through Wang's roof and acted like a bullet, instantly killing Wang as it lodged into his body.

The night was easy, companionable, and, eventually, the sun did rise.

"Want to go to breakfast?" Michael asked.

At a local pancake house, we stuffed our gleeful faces with fat cheese omelets and talked until the early birds had trickled out and families with young kids started filling the booths. Across the aisle from us, a curly-haired little girl started flirting with Michael, which made us laugh. He seemed good with kids; I asked him if he wanted a big family or small.

Michael shrugged. "I don't know. I'm not really the marrying kind."

My heart sank and anxiety rose up, but I did my best to avoid showing it. *For Pete's sake,* I chided myself, *you're not serious about this guy, settle down.*

"You want kids?" Michael asked.

"Just one. Just one healthy son."

"You probably want the whole thing, huh? Husband, white picket fence, a kid, little dog, and the SUV."

"I don't care for little dogs, and I don't think a white fence is necessary."

Michael nodded his head a few times, seriously, as if it was just what he had expected. Subjects got changed, and before long he suggested we leave and drove me home.

"Thank you for trusting me enough to come see my special place," he said as I left his truck. "I've wanted to show it to you for a long time."

He looked so earnest and sweet, I couldn't help but forgive him for not wanting a wife or kids. Okay then, he wasn't the marrying type; all it meant was I'd have to be careful of my heart. He was still a nice guy, and I wanted him as my friend. I gave him a hug and watched him pull away from the curb. I saw him watching me in his rear view mirror, and it was hard not to run dramatically down the street to stop him.

☙

For the next few weeks, I spent all my free time getting to know Michael and avoiding my friends. Like it or not, my heart was involved, which seemed crazy—I didn't want this now. How would I break it off if I did meet someone interested in marriage and a family?

Being with Michael was so carefree; I had never been treated better by a man. Reviewing all the drama with Dante, a man who did want marriage and children, I wondered if I should just accept the goodness that entered my life with Michael and not worry about the rest. Then, I'd spend time with my little niece and a baby craving swelled up inside me until I couldn't contain it. One of my own to hold and love! The whole situation was confusing, so I put my mind to pretending it didn't exist—the time I spent with Michael was set apart from the rest of life, my separate, calm, easy-going space. I told myself it was what I needed *for right now.*

We spent a lot of our dates processing cremains and doing funerary things. Or, we hung out on the roof of the mortuary where he lived and played board games. Michael was a Scrabble champ, but I could beat him at Dominoes. We didn't need any particular "date" activity; we enjoyed whatever we were doing because we were together—off to the gym, cooking, lazing about. Sometimes I couldn't believe he was the same guy who used to try to scare me by breathing on my shoulder in the basement of Western View. Then he would do something nutty like hide a rubber finger in our meal, but now I considered his irreverent pranks part of his charm. Who was this new, accepting Elizabeth?

Three weeks after we started dating, Michael said, "I've never wanted to get married before, but I'll tell you something: If our relationship is this good a year from now, I'm asking you to marry me."

If our relationship is this good a year from now, I thought, I will say yes.

Obviously, it was time to tell my friends about Michael. I organized a "casual" get-together. At first I thought I might invite Kevin and Ryan to a "Come as Your Favorite Stereotypical Italian" party, but thought how easily it might backfire and let that brilliant idea go.

A lower-key party commenced. "The 'Incinerator Baiter'?" Kevin asked, sampling Nurse Nancy's illustrious baba ghanoush.

"Please don't say that after he arrives," I begged. "I'm sorry I ever called him that. It would really hurt his feelings if he knew. Well, maybe not, but I don't want to look like a jerk."

"Mr. McCreeper McCreeperson is coming here tonight?" Ryan squealed. Willow chastened him with a dark look. I announced that Michael would be along as soon as he finished the cremation he was working on. The guys continued to joke and carry on until I was so nervous I almost called Michael and told him the party was a no-go.

When he arrived, I could hardly manage the introductions.

"We've heard a lot about you," Kevin said mischievously, as he shook Michael's hand.

"Oh yeah?" Michael said. "Tell me one thing you've heard." I about fainted, which made him laugh out loud. Everybody got the joke and started laughing, so I joined in and took beer orders immediately.

It was one of those excellent nights where folks relaxed and one-upped each other with stories, and the world seemed like a friendly, tender place. A perfect cocktail party with my favorite people and I hated to see it end.

"He's a keeper," Kevin said, as he hugged me goodbye.

"I'm so happy for you," Ryan chimed in.

Willow whispered, "I've never seen you so comfortable in your own skin. Go with it."

I shut the door behind them and looked back at Nurse Nancy and Michael. They were clearing the dishes from the table and chatting away and laughing together. It seemed my mother's voice had been right after all.

☙

Our courtship made work a lot more fun. A trip downstairs to hunt for a file might lead to a surprising, warm hug from behind. A message via the building's intercom system could contain playful, sweet double *entendres*, that were even more satisfactory when Glen heard them and had no idea what they were about. It burnt Glen's toast to see me enjoying myself at work; his snotty little comments rolled off me and hardly registered. Happiness is amazing emotional armor.

Michael and I spent lots of time in the haunted bowels of the building, keeping company as he ran the ovens, or together on the road picking up bodies. Working together over the months gave us lots of time to talk, and we slipped into a cooperative relationship quite naturally. To my surprise, Michael became open to serious conversations about owning our own mortuary one day. He was also more pragmatic about the situation than I was.

"It's not whether you can or can't, so much. It's really more about how you would make it happen. What have you got in savings?"

I retrieved my checkbook from my bag and peered at the figures—my finger moving down the columns as I calculated.

"What is that?" Michael asked.

"My accounting system," I said, holding it up.

"Where's your ledger?"

"I don't use one. I record the check numbers and amount here."

"And then what?"

"When I'm out of checks, I throw it away."

Michael was horrified and amused. "You won't be able to get away with that when you're running a business," he advised.

"Why not? It's working just fine." I had only been overdrawn once, my credit score was impeccable, and I was saving a big chunk of my income. I thought he should be impressed, but that wasn't the case. He also insinuated the Internal Revenue Service wouldn't be impressed either.

"Do you know how to use spreadsheets?" he asked.

"I hate spreadsheets!"

"If we pull this off, maybe I should keep the books."

I scowled and insisted I could handle it.

"We'll see," he said, stifling a chuckle as he reached for my pad of checks. He did get more respectful when he saw my balances, which he added to the business plan he was already working up. "Between your savings and mine, we have a start, but realistically, we need several more years of additional savings to put together the down payment."

I frowned. "That long? Are you sure?"

He showed me the estimated costs of the fixed assets—a gigantic number.

"Ugh! My life is passing before me while I waste my time pushing people into buying premium caskets."

"Your life is not passing before you, Drama Queen," Michael teased, pulling me toward him and kissing away my disappointment. "We just have to figure this out, together."

Together. Damn, I thought. What a sweet word.

With our eyes on the prize of our own funeral home, we worked harder than ever. Weeks flew by. Before I knew it, I was taking Michael to meet my family at a 4th of July barbecue. Then in the blink of an eye, autumn arrived, and presto, the rainy days of winter. Michael took me home to meet his parents at Christmas. They acted like it was a foregone conclusion our engagement would be announced soon. On our way to Midnight Mass downtown at St. Mary's Cathedral, I asked Michael if his family knew something I didn't.

"They know I've never brought a woman home to meet them before," he said. Ironic, I thought, flushing in his praise, how the man I had originally brushed off turned out to be The One. The One who always thought I was awesome.

Perhaps ours wasn't the most traditionally romantic relationship. That's to be expected when so many of our dates included a corpse.

He asked me to marry him at the funeral parlour. Valentine's Day had arrived, and we were headed out for sushi. Michael had the ring in his pocket and a speech at the ready, but we were unexpectedly called back to the mortuary to intake a body. So, in the visitation room, next to a lady who had been laid to rest in a top-of-the-line mahogany casket, he asked me to share my life with him.

I spent the following week phoning friends and hearing the same comments about how they knew all along this was the guy for me; how Anthony and Dante were such douche bags (boy, did my friends love that word!) and they had had to hold their tongues and wait out our courtships; how someone finally came along to exhume me from the graveyard of lame relationships.

I organized a cross-country wedding in five months—funeral directors have mad event planning skills—and we were married in New Jersey at the Palace at Somerset Park.

I know all brides say their big day was magical, but mine truly was. Friends from far reaches of San Francisco and rural Wyoming hopped planes to the East Coast and donned periwinkle gowns to serve as my bridesmaids, as little girls walked in bare feet and sprinkled rose petals. Michael's eldest cousin planted pungent and flowing herbs in white-painted terra cotta pots and set them on the tables as D-I-Y centerpieces. Two nights prior to the wedding, his mother presented me with an exquisite blue rosary all the women in Michael's family had carried on their wedding day—I had the family florist weave it through my bouquet so it elegantly draped from my white flowers as I walked the aisle. My bouquet held small frames containing pictures of my mother that only I knew were there. And throughout the whole day, only I knew that she was indeed there.

One month later, I peed on a stick and found out I was going to have a baby.

Chapter 24

Building a Wee Legacy

MICHAEL AND I WERE FINE WITH THE EXPEDIENCY OF THE GETting pregnant part, but as usual, we had two very different approaches. I wanted to pay for every screening test possible. I was concerned about Down's Syndrome and every other possible issue I'd ever read about. Michael, infuriatingly, had no worries at all. He figured every pregnancy was smooth sailing. I began walking an hour every morning and watched myself for any little change or sign of sickness. I was weirdly asymptomatic.

Michael suggested we could make some extra money to pay for the upcoming arrival by doing removals, bringing the deceased loved one back to the funeral home, for five different funeral homes. These were evening jobs, and at the trill of a phone we'd lurch out of bed, step into our shoes and take off in the death van. The looks on people's faces when I navigated the gurney after my stomach got huge were worthy of a coffee table book.

Our social life became a party of two. All his Portland friends were busy studying for their funeral director's licensing tests, and we had to put Kevin and Ryan's costume parties on the back burner while working our so-called graveyard shift.

On these nighttime drives we played games or discussed what life would be like for our future son, "Jack."

I had a boyfriend named Jack who had died. At low points in my life, I would dream of a little boy bearing his resemblance. In the dream, a little guy of five or six would be with me, hanging out in his jeans, denim jacket, and cowboy boots. It was never clear that he was my son, but in this soothing vision he was, and his name was Jack. He was a comfort to me and I wanted to honor him by giving my real baby the name. It also didn't hurt that my first impression of Michael had been, *He looks like Baby Jack in my dreams.*

"Jack?" Michael asked when he heard what I had named our fetus. "I like it, but what about Jack and my last name?"

"Obviously, he'll have your last name," I said, and thought no more about it. I couldn't understand what his problem was; did he object to naming the baby after my dead boyfriend? The third time he questioned me about Jack as a name, he stopped the van so he could face me.

"You don't think this is a problem?"

"Um, no, 'cause you're the father. We are married and it makes sense to me. I never thought he would have my last name. I just figured you are traditional enough this wouldn't even be a discussion."

"Elizabeth, why aren't you getting this? My last name is Potts. The kid will be Jack Potts. Jack Potts! Get it?"

I looked out the window and coincidentally spotted a looming and very lit-up Jackpot Gas Station. My heart sunk and I slumped in my seat. So much for my dreams of a little cowboy named Jack.

Money was our real issue. We didn't want to dig into our nest egg if we could help it—that was for our goal of buying a funeral home one day—so we got creative with the odd-job search. My hard-working agent told me about a casting call for a video spokesperson at a casino on the beach. I had no problem picturing myself as an ambassador of fun, so I headed to the coast. The head of casino marketing decided I certainly had the personality they were looking for and the "gaming look." I nailed it.

What a glorious gig! With the lights primed and hot, I stood on an apple crate and told the Internet gambling world about the latest opportunities to place their bets:

"This Ancient Egyptian-themed game offers twenty pay lines on five reels. The colorful and mystical Pharaohs give you numerous opportunities to win, with two Wilds, four Scatters, and up to twenty retriggering Free Spins and generous Multipliers!"

The only hitch in the plan was my soon-to-be swollen belly. I didn't want to lose such a fabulous job, so I asked the boss man if they would film me close-up once my pregnancy became obvious. Thankfully, the casino prided itself on being a family friendly bastion; a plan was made for my "character" to wear sweater sets that would disguise my growing tummy. Every month I headed to Target or Macy's in search of twinsets in sizes and colors that looked right for the season and were structured for camouflage duty.

In the backstage dressing rooms, I sat in the same makeup chairs as the members of the famous bands who performed on the main stage. I became privy to the musician's demands. Barry Manilow let his promoters bring members of his fan cub into the venue early to decorate his dressing room with signs proclaiming their love for Mr. Manilow. Crazy Marilyn Manson always wanted the air-conditioner on full blast and requested a bald hooker with no teeth—truly.

My perk was having the hair and makeup team transform me into a more glamorous version of myself. I also scored front row seats at the Billy Ray Cyrus concert and all the free soda I could guzzle. Sometimes people recognized me from the videos and I had moments of minor celebrity glory, which was a blast. After years of dressing soberly and acting seriously in my career as a funeral director, my inner glamour puss was free to toss her head, smile radiantly, and glow like a slot sensation. I gave the camera my gaming all.

"Play Ruby of the Nile this month and you will be credited with double points!"

"Fisherman's Friend will certainly be your friend when you Reel 'em In! Dazzle the crowd when you land the Big Whopper!"

"Coming this month in the casino showroom: Sha Na Na!"

Michael and my friends were thoroughly entertained by the idea of me as a casino personality and howled with laughter over my antics.

"While you're playing starlet, are you allowed to haul that everywhere you go?" Kevin asked me once, indicating my precious, super-sized, convenience store soda cup.

"No, I have to use the little glasses the casino provides."

"Those tiny little things?" Ryan asked, "What do you do, run back and forth to the soda bar every minute?"

"Nope, I get a dozen glasses from the kitchen, put 'em on a tray, and fill them all at once. The dishwashers hate me."

The Diva in me made everyone laugh, and the consensus was if I hadn't been called to the funeral industry, I could have had a fine career as a chi chi celebrity famous for being who she is.

"You know, like the Gabor sisters," Ryan explained.

"If the Gabor sisters were birthing a calf," I added, holding my nesting baby belly.

"You might have to position yourself behind a couch all night like sit-com actresses do when they start to show," Michael advised, rubbing my swelling tummy affectionately.

❧

Toward the end of my second trimester, I got a phone call from an old funeral industry friend. A friend of a colleague had a small funeral home out in the country he was going to close, because he had nobody to operate it. With pen and paper out, I got the contact information. Maybe this was our way out of Western View!

I called immediately to see if I could get an interview. We were set for the very next morning.

"Please let this be it," I prayed through the windshield. "Mom, if you can hear me, please see what you can do to pull some strings up there."

I was headed east, along the country highway that meanders by the Clackamas River. The sun was winking through the trees, which got thicker as I climbed towards the forests of Mount Hood. The road sparkled with promise. I imagined what life would be like if Michael and I moved to the country to raise our baby in this fresh air.

I whizzed by a pasture full of miniature goats and hollered, "We could have goats!" A farm house yard where a flock of geese had congregated around a plastic kiddie pool made me giddy: "We could have geese!"

I found my intersection and looked for a sign to the property, "Cornerstone Funeral Services." Easy enough, as there was nothing else around except the funeral home and, directly across the road, a mom-and-pop grocery.

I made my turn, and the guy pumping gas outside the store waved at me. That was all the encouragement I needed, plus I had time, so I stopped for a soda. It was a quaint little shop. As I walked in, the woman behind the counter asked me how I was doing. A few minutes later, fortified with soda and good will, I pulled onto the funeral home property. Yet another person, a woman I would learn was the owner's wife, waved at me. Within five minutes, three people had laid eyes on me and actually seen me. I wasn't just another figment of energy moving past, I was a human being who had been acknowledged. My heart soared.

The funeral home was tiny. George, the owner, explained that it was originally a goat barn he had remodeled to serve as a funeral home, and he needed somebody licensed to run it. He showed me inside where I found paperwork and files all over the place. The mortuary board had just been out to inspect, and it looked like a hurricane had hit.

George invited me to sit down. I expected him to start the interview, but he just stared at me for a while. Then, "So, what do you think, kid?"

What did I think? I didn't have the first clue. What was his offer? Not very much, it turned out.

George couldn't pay me much per hour. The previous manager had racked up lots of bills that had to be paid off before the place was back in the black. I explained I'd have to talk to my husband before any decision. George said he could certainly understand that, but he hoped I'd give the place serious thought.

As I drove away, the gas station attendant waved again and I waved back. I cruised toward the city, past geese at their mid-morning ablutions, past the grazing goats, back to the thinner scrim of trees, thinking the whole way about whether this was an opportunity in the rough or the next worst idea of my life. I was pretty sure I knew what Michael was going to say, and he didn't disappoint.

"What the hell? No, Elizabeth, that's crazy."

"I'm not making much more than that now," I reasoned, "and I hate taking families into that arrangement room! I hate selling them crap they don't need just to keep management off my back."

"You think there won't be any sales at the new place? They have to keep the lights on in the goat barn somehow."

"I know, but the overhead is much lower and it's in Clackamas County. They can do backyard burials there."

"We have a baby coming," he pointed out, as if I didn't know.

"I could see about getting more voice over work," I suggested. Michael rolled his eyes and said he couldn't talk about it anymore; he was due at work in the basement.

Maybe Richard could give me reasons why this wasn't a totally lost cause. I called him but then lost heart and felt weird. I talked about it as if it were a hypothetical goal for "someday"—me, running a small town mortuary.

Exasperated with my mincing around, Richard finally asked, "Are you talking about that guy's goat barn out back of beyond, where the lady he had running it just got in trouble with the mortuary board?"

"Damn, do you know everything that happens in this business?"

"Pretty much, darlin'," said Richard. "You can stop beating around the bush. I wouldn't touch it with a ten-foot pole."

"Why not?"

"For one thing, there is no way I'm going to muck around out in the country. The air smells funny out there. Besides, I'm about to be promoted. The old relic who has been running this place since God was in short pants is finally retiring."

"What do you think about it as an opportunity for me?"

"Professional suicide," Richard said. "If he loses the business or decides to fire you, you are screwed, because the big corporates won't hire you back."

"It's just that I have a gut feeling about this."

Richard sighed, as in: Such a dear idiot. "Then I won't waste my breath trying to talk you out of your romantic notions. But if you're going to jump off this bridge, at least get your contract in writing and insist on some sort of severance package. You will need something to live on when you come limping back into town."

I thanked him gloomily and hung up, then called Nick. After all, he was a business smartie. He listened to the details but agreed with Michael and Richard that it was a bad move.

"There will be other opportunities, Elizabeth. Keep your ear to the ground," Nick said. It didn't feel as comforting as he intended.

The rest of the evening I moped about and prayed and thought about that cold little goat barn and how much I wanted out of Western View. Michael read my mood when he stepped in the door. He kissed my forehead gently.

"Your chance is coming," he said. "You don't have to jump at the first thing. Give yourself time to find something really great."

We didn't talk more about it. We hadn't been getting enough sleep between our day jobs and running around all night after bodies, so we went to bed. Despite my tiredness I couldn't drift off. I prayed some more; and by morning I knew Cornerstone was the right choice, even with all its problems and risk.

A half hour before the alarm was set to ring, I shook Michael awake. He looked so sweet and boyish, eyes all bleary and hair standing on end, but I couldn't hold back and confessed—I wanted to take my chances on Cornerstone, come what may.

"What will we do if it doesn't work?"

"I don't know," I admitted. "But honestly, I know it's the right choice, and I'm asking you to have faith in it."

Michael did not look satisfied with this answer. He looked a bit angry and put upon, actually. After a long silence he let out a deep breath and said, "I don't have faith in it. I think it's a crazy decision. But if you really believe in what you're doing, I won't stand in your way, and I'll do whatever I can to help you."

"Really!"

"But!" he said, sternly. "If this fails, it's on you."

Excited, I started to throw my arms around him, but he hopped out of bed. As I watched him stalk away, I told myself failure would not be an option, anyway, anyhow.

Chapter 25

The Patron Saint of
Widows and Widowers

GEORGE WAS PLEASED I ACCEPTED HIS OFFER, AND GLEN SEEMED stoked to receive my letter of resignation, so at least two people were happy with my news. Everybody else was kind but skeptical. Kevin offered to throw me a "Come as Your Favorite Dead Pioneer" bash.

"I think the five of us would be exceptional as the Donner Party," he said. I laughed but reminded him I was facing an extremely uncertain time, right before Baby Not-Jack was due to arrive.

"If I make a go of this, we can have a party to celebrate my success," I promised.

I hated having everyone worry about me, especially Michael. "I can do this," I told Baby Not-Jack, who gave me a cheerful kick. I had no idea how I would pull it off, but I had a dream of turning Cornerstone into something special. If I was in it, I was in it to win it.

My first month at the little funeral home in Boring, Oregon can only be described as bleak. The phone hardly rang. When it did, it was most likely a salesperson or bill collector on the line. I only served two families the whole month. I kept telling Baby Not-Jack I could do it, and Baby Not-Jack kept kicking me cheerfully. But something would have to change if I were to be known as the town undertaker.

To relieve my loneliness and refill my extremely large soda cup with pregnancy-friendly lemonade, I'd walk across the road to the Barton Store a few times a day. Stuffed, dusty heads of hunting trophies watched me come in from high on the walls. The cashier always gave a friendly greeting; the locals had gossip to share and current affairs to debate, and they hardly noticed me.

"Well," I told Baby Not-Jack one morning, "if we're going to be part of community life, we'll just have to introduce ourselves."

I grabbed my cup and walked across the road, my warmest smile affixed. When I reached the store, the old timers were chatting away over coffee and donuts across scruffy wagon wheel tables. I understood that a simple handshake and my status as the new kid in town was not going to result in any quick intimacy. Besides, what would I say? "Hi, I'm Elizabeth, here to serve all your burial needs!"

I stifled a giggle at the thought, filled my soda cup, exchanged "good mornings" with the cashier, and went back across the road. "We need an excuse to introduce ourselves," I told Baby Not-Jack.

Try as I might, I couldn't think of one.

Every night, I locked the door on the re-purposed goat barn and drove back to Portland to face Michael with the news that, no, I hadn't managed to schedule another funeral. Every night, he received the news in his take-no-prisoners Jersey style and suggested I might still be able to get re-hired at Western View, if I pled temporary insanity from pregnancy hormones.

"I'm not quitting!" I insisted. "I'll make this work. You'll see." Unfortunately, Michael was pretty sure I was leading us straight to the poor house.

The second month didn't start out much better. At least, by then I had all the files put away properly and the dust shoveled out of the place. Cornerstone was ready to receive company. All I had to do was figure out how to get mourners through the door. Sales reps kept ringing the phone with plenty of advertising opportunities, but I had no money to take them up on it. Since my predecessor had bought copious amounts of ad space and all kinds of ridiculous inventory, Cornerstone was in the red for the foreseeable future. I used my own credit card to print business cards.

"Now we're paying for you to work there?" Michael shouted the morning he saw the charges from the printer.

"It was only forty dollars. I can reimburse myself after I bring in a few funerals." I tried sounding as level-headed as possible, but it didn't take a genius to see I hadn't impressed him with my business savvy.

"Never mind," I whispered to Baby Not-Jack as I drove to work. "He'll see."

I pulled into the Barton Store and heaved myself out of the car, my signature giant red cup in hand. Despite lackluster results in meeting the locals, I always looked forward to my morning pregnancy lemonade refill. It was a chance to soak in human noise and bustle, before retiring into the silence of the tiny funeral home across the lane.

I smiled and nodded as I passed the folks seated at tables. I received a few smiles and nods back, which was progress, at least.

"Hey!" I heard a voice call from behind me. "Hey you, lady!"

Was he talking to me? I turned to find a white-haired gentleman gesturing towards me.

"Are you the lady on the videos at the casino?" he asked. This got everybody's attention. "My wife said she thought you were," the man said, motioning toward an older woman in a purple sweatshirt with kittens printed on it.

I seized my chance and explained I only did the casino videos as a fun side job. "I'm actually a funeral director. I've been hired to take over at Cornerstone Funeral Services across the road."

Heads began to nod knowingly. A man asked, "You think you can make a go of that?"

"I will," I said, plainly. "I like it here, and I want Cornerstone to become a place people trust as a neighbor."

"You got your work cut out for you," the man replied.

"Oh, leave her alone, Gene," an elderly lady scolded.

"I'm just being realistic is all!" he replied.

The elderly lady put her purse over her arm and pulled herself out of her seat. "I'm Emma Ross, honey," she said, patting the hand I had resting on my belly. "When my time comes, you can bury me. I think it's nice to have somebody local to take care of these things."

"Thank you," I said, giving Emma a grateful smile. "I would be honored."

Somebody muttered, "If she's still here." I kept my smile and shook some hands. Everybody was nice, but I could see they would wait to see if I "stuck" before they invested much confidence in me.

"Well, that was a start," I told Baby Not-Jack when we got back to the Jeep. "Now to earn our place here." Baby Not-Jack, who was in cramped quarters by that time, fluttered and danced with excitement.

I felt more hopeful than I had for weeks. I set to work arranging a tabletop display of urn choices. At Western View, we'd had a room full of actual samples, but Cornerstone didn't have the space or the budget for that kind of inventory. The fact was, if I wanted to establish Cornerstone as *the* choice for green funerals and natural burial, a fabulous urn display was beside the point. What I really wanted was a willow casket for my tiny display area, but even the wholesale price was beyond my means until we started making a profit.

While I tried to make the most of a meager marketing situation, word got around that the new mortician was the Chinook Winds Casino Resort video lady. By my next visit to the Barton Store, it seemed there were extra folks around. A few spoke with me.

"Maybe you should host BINGO nights at the funeral parlour," Michael suggested that night as we carefully negotiated potholes in a gravel road to pick up a body.

"I already thought of that, but Oregon will only give a BINGO license to charitable and fraternal organizations."

"Well, you are non-profit at this point," my husband pointed out. Okay, I had made myself an easy target. I asked him not to remind me.

"Have you thought about joining the local Chamber of Commerce?" he said. "Most of the funeral directors I know are always glad handing at Chamber events or Rotary, stuff like that."

I sighed. "I can't afford the membership, but I appreciate your suggestions. It feels like old times."

"Well, I don't want you to fail," Michael said.

I reached across the center console and lay my hand on his arm. "That means a lot to me," I said.

"What do you take me for?" Michael asked. "Shit, we got bills to pay."

I was offended at first but ended up laughing, which made Michael laugh, too. Soon Baby Not-Jack was squirming and jumping with what I was sure must be glee. Michael reached toward me and we held hands the rest of the way to the crematory.

෴

I worked a full day on the day I gave birth. I was suspicious I might be in the early stages of labor, but couldn't afford to miss what might be the only job for Cornerstone that month. Early in the evening, I met with a large

Brazilian family at their home on Wildcat Mountain to make funeral plans for their patriarch, Rocky.

"What are you doing after this?" one of Rocky's sisters asked during the visit.

"Probably driving myself to the hospital to have a baby," I replied.

Rocky's family thought this was hysterically funny. Two of his daughters whipped open my sweater to have a closer look. They'd thought I was making a joke.

No joke, for when we finished I drove myself to the hospital, knowing it was time. My birthing supplies had been packed and stowed in the back of the van for days. At the hospital, wondering why I wasn't more nervous, I unloaded bottles of wine for the nurses, my family pictures for my room, a long-cherished Tony Bennett CD, and my birth plan. On the examining table, a nurse announced I was dilated three centimeters and really needed to get in bed already. Before long, Michael and Willow arrived.

They told me jokes and fed me ice chips. Willow brushed my hair so I would look great in my pictures. After a while, Almost-Daddy alerted me the baby's head was hanging out, and we figured we should get someone medical in the room.

Then, and at last, our perfect baby girl was born with hardly any trouble at all.

"A girl," Michael crooned, playing with her teensy weensy fingers. "We have to get serious about a name, you know."

"What about Sofia, with the Italian spelling, s-o-f-i-a?" I asked. "Since she's going to be raised in a funeral home."

"What does that have to do with it?"

"Sofia is the Catholic Patron Saint of Widows and Widowers."

"That sounds nice," Michael said, dreamily. He was so smitten I could have named our daughter Twinkie and he'd have been thrilled.

"Look at them, Mom," I prayed, silently. "You were so right about Michael." My dad arrived, interrupting my prayer, but I didn't mind a bit—his face and smile illuminated the room. He had a bouquet of flowers in one hand and a ridiculously over-sized stuffed bear in the other.

"So much beauty in one room!" he declared. "Elizabeth! You remind me of your mother the day you were born."

"Worn out and sweaty?" I joked.

"No. Elegant and all lit up, like an angel in a painting."

I felt like a champion, strong and ready to take on the ecosphere. All my dreams were coming true.

On Sofia's second morning in the world, I rose at the crack of dawn and practiced yoga stretches on the hospital floor. I couldn't afford to lie in bed. I had a funeral home to run and needed to work out my postpartum stiffness and cramping.

A nurse walked in and asked, "Where's the mother?"

"I'm the mother," I said, working my hips toward downward dog position.

She turned on her heels. In a moment, she was back with the doctor. They watched me ease my way into bridge pose, and the doctor deduced I could go home early. I didn't waste a minute packing up my stuff and my baby. After wheeling me to where the funeral van was parked, the transport guy said, "You are the first mom I know of who drove herself to and from the hospital."

"No time to sit still," I said, brightly. If he only knew what was next on my list!

I drove Sofia directly to the crematory to pick up Rocky's cremains, then drove back up Wildcat Mountain. Although I had an urn of ashes in one hand and a newborn in the other, the family still wouldn't have believed my story if I hadn't had the hospital band on my arm.

After they got over their shock, Rocky's wife asked to hold Sofia. I lay my infant daughter in the heartbroken widow's arms and watched her tension and grief ease a bit. Sofia made a tiny squeak and settled in, as if she had been born for the job of comforting the bereaved.

Chapter 26

Grave Business

SOFIA PROVED TO BE AN EXCELLENT ICEBREAKER WITH THE LOCALS. The first time I showed up at the Barton Store carrying my newly minted daughter, the love warmed my heart. Gossip, speculation, and debate stopped while the baby was inspected and cooed over. Jeannie, the owner, declared Sofia the official Barton Store Baby.

"Can I take her picture?" Jeannie wanted to know.

"Sure, why not?"

Jeannie produced a camera and recorded Sofia's sweet infant face for posterity—and for the wall near the register where it was proudly hung.

"You're a hit, kid!" I told Sofia on our way back to the parlour. Sofia gave me a sleepy look and returned to her favorite newborn pastime of napping.

It was easy to have her with me at work; she inherently knew what to do. She was in the midst of bawling only a few times when a call came in. I could latch her onto me for a nice, warm drink of milk to quickly quiet any noise or fuss. The people on the phone had no idea I was breastfeeding my baby while quoting them cremation costs.

One day, I situated Sofia in her baby lounger next to my desk. There, I could keep an eye on her while typing up a death certificate for an elderly woman who had died the day before. The woman's family had to come from out of state, so I had delivered Mrs. Buell to an embalmer. Now it was time to tackle the paperwork.

I was powering up my computer when I heard a loud noise. It sounded like an angry squirrel, coming the direction of the chapel. I went to check it out; there was nothing outside the windows. What the heck? Once more the sound: "tsik tsik tsik, chrrrrrrr . . . siew, siew, siew, siew." It seemed to be coming from the back wall.

"He'd better be outside!" I told the rows of precisely aligned chairs where mourners sat during funerals. Carefully, I explored a bit farther. The closer I got to the fireplace, the louder the scolding.

Concerned this beast might actually be inside the building, I retreated and closed the door to my office. No way would this squirrel run across my baby. With a flashlight from the supply closet, I returned to the chapel fireplace.

Little Rodent was chirping up a storm. When I ran the flashlight around the right edge of the fireplace insert, he about had a noisy stroke. Peering into the narrow gap between the insert and the surround, I saw two furious little eyes glaring back at me.

We contemplated each other anxiously for a long moment when suddenly, he twitched forward. I shrieked operatically and lunged backward, knocking a couple of chairs out of their soldierly lines in the process. Alarmed, the phantom rodent retreated as fast as he could wriggle his compressed carcass in reverse. I watched until he beat a hasty retreat toward the roof, then went to the office to comfort Sofia, who had been wakened by the commotion.

"Don't worry," I told her. "Mommy will get this fixed." I dialed the parlour owner, George, but his wife said he was gone for the day.

"Can I help?" she asked. I told her about the squirrel, leaving out the parts where I had been in fear for my life.

"He must have come down the vent pipe," Linda said. "I'll have George put screen over it when he gets back." I thanked her and hung up.

Sofia went back to sleep, and again I heard skittering noises coming from the fireplace.

Quietly, I shut sleeping Sofia in the office, blocking the crack under the door with some casket catalogues. I marched out to the pump house where George kept miscellaneous tools and materials for the constant repairs required to maintain a forty-acre property. I rummaged around and came up with a few items I thought showed promise.

After a great deal of experimentation, I constructed and installed a wire mesh barrier to fit over the vent pipe. As I installed, my tenant squirrel came up and complained about these efforts to contain him. Little Rodent climbed around the chimney and came within inches of my hands, loudly unhappy. A persistent little bugger, he followed me down to ground level when I went to check on Sofia and latched himself to the screen door so he could scream in my face.

Hours later, I sat back down and typed up Mrs. Buell's death certificate. My suit looked as if I'd been rolling around on the gravel drive. My pantyhose were a lost cause. "I can totally do country life!" I told Sofia during her four o'clock feeding.

When I got home, Michael took in my disheveled appearance and asked if I'd been in a car wreck. "D-I-Y squirrel containment system," I said simply, handing him Baby Sofia. "I have to go take a bath."

"Are you all right?"

"Eye of the Tiger!" I called back before shutting the bathroom door. Michael didn't reply. I think I frightened him, actually.

❧

Over the next couple of months, I spent more time shaking hands than arranging funerals. I coughed up the membership fee for the Estacada Chamber of Commerce and started popping into coffee shops at three nearby towns. My card was stapled to every community bulletin board in a thirty-five-mile radius. I regularly volunteered with the local Meals on Wheels program. On the days Michael had Sofia, I'd stop at Carver Hanger five miles down the river in Carver and sit at the bar for a while to watch football. Somebody would always strike up a conversation with me, asking who I was and what was I doing there.

"I'm the local undertaker," I would say.

They'd stare and say, unfailingly, "You don't look like an undertaker."

"And thank goodness for that, right?" I would reply, giving them my sunniest smile. At the laugh, I knew the ice had been broken. I'd tell them a few amusing funeral stories, then hand out my business cards. Slowly, slowly, I was becoming known. There was a little bit more business every month, but nowhere near what Cornerstone needed to become solvent.

George was understanding, but when the coffins are bare, so are the coffers. One day, he came by the office and explained he couldn't cover my meager salary any more.

"I don't want to lose you, kid," he said. "I think you're the best chance this place has had. Any way you'd stay on for a percentage of the income?"

I said I would, and we shook on it. Once again, we didn't bother with a formal contract. I took it on faith that when families came and paid their bills, I would take some of that money home. George wasn't looking to take any of the profits for himself until I earned a reasonable salary. My job was to make sure the bills were paid, and I'd receive any leftover money.

"So, now you're working for nothing?" Michael said, turning this latest development over in his head. "No, wait, not even nothing, because there are a bunch of work expenses on our credit card. So basically, this is worse than working for free, honey."

I knew this conversation was coming. Exhausted from nights up with the baby and running all over the county trying to drum up business while I worried and snuck charges onto the credit card, I just nodded miserably.

"Elizabeth!" Michael said. "What are you doing? Please explain this to me."

"I don't know. All I can tell you is I know I am in the right place and everything will be all right. Eventually."

Michael shook his head like he was dealing with an idiot.

In response, I put my head on his chest and wrapped my arms around him. He put his arms around me too, and things didn't seem so hard.

"Michael?"

"Yes?"

"I need to spend twenty-five bucks to sponsor a trophy for the car show in Estacada."

"Aw, Jesus, seriously?"

"And I need more business cards. I've gone through the first five hundred."

"You're killing me."

"But you do love me." The coy approach was working.

"All right, come on," he said, with a push towards the bedroom. "We'll take it out in trade. And let's hurry it up. I have a body to pick up, and we can't afford to lose the job."

"Am I going to have to do this every time I want to sponsor a community event?"

"If I say yes, what are you going to do about it?"

"I'll sponsor more community events, of course!"

❧

Pouring rain pounding my office window created a dismal day. The phone rang, and a woman asked if I could meet her and some friends at their favorite pub to discuss funeral arrangements for someone named Wanda. I agreed and said I'd be there in the time it took to make the drive.

Wanda's friends were a close-knit group of gentle people. While filling out the death certificate, they were stumped as to why they weren't allowed to list Wanda's occupation as "Wanderer," and "The Earth" as the accompanying industry. After all, that is what Wanda had been. Her friends felt they could only truly honor Wanda the Wanderer by laying her to rest on the fifteen country acres where she lived.

"This is new territory for me," I said. "Let me make some calls and get back to you."

Clackamas County's Land Planning and Zoning Department confirmed that home burials were allowed and explained the regulations to me. So, I lined up a backhoe, and we were good to go the next day.

The service was top-drawer. Wanda's friends and family played drums, chanted, and spoke of her kindness. We held hands to form a circle around her newly dug resting place and stood in silence as her three sons lowered her gently into the earth. Her tiny frame was cloaked with a quilt she had made as a teenager. Soon, the plain grave was covered with soil, a knoll of dirt on top to compensate for the settling that would happen over time. There was no marker, just native foliage. After a closing prayer, we feasted on fish caught down the way in the Clackamas River.

"It was beautiful," I told Michael that night. "I wish you had been there. It made so much sense."

"How do you mean?" he asked.

"Well, they got to do it in their own way. You could see how much comfort it gave them to be able to stay with her and take care of her body."

"Nobody was grossed out?"

"Nah, they were . . . I don't know . . . They didn't have to go through that weird, disconnected feeling people have when they arrive at the funeral home and first see the body lying in the coffin."

"They were with her the whole time from the time she died until the time she was buried?"

"Right," I said. "Like in the old days, but I felt like I'd discovered something. For once, I didn't have that nagging feeling the whole experience was falling short. I was able to help those people get what they needed from this funeral."

Michael groaned. "I knew it. This is just going to make you more determined to stay."

"I'm not giving this up! Natural burial, green burial—people want these options."

He sighed. "Yeah, yeah, it's the new trend in funerals, yada, yada, but seriously, you have to make the money, right?"

"I wouldn't say it's a trend. Most funeral homes with sales quotas don't promote burying people in their yards. But, I know the rules now, and I don't think anyone else is offering this."

"You'll be popular at parties—a new-age grim reaper—a green reaper!"

"I can't believe you just said that! They were calling me that all day. I'll be the Green Reaper!"

Michael laughed so hard I thought he'd fall over. "We'll get you a dark green robe made out of hemp, and a scythe with a bamboo handle. You can wear it to Kevin and Ryan's next party."

Chapter 27

Pre-Need Planning to Be Green

ANOTHER FAMILY I SERVED FOUND BACKYARD BURIAL TO BE THEIR choice solely based on cost. Their daughter had passed away unexpectedly and money was extremely tight. They chose to place her in a hand-dug hole in front of her favorite cedar tree, inside a sleeping bag. The family hashed out practical matters for a week. Her body had to be buried at least eighteen inches underground, the legal limit, so it wouldn't be at risk of being dug up by bears or dogs.

The regulars at the Barton Store asked me about the burial the following day. Apparently, there's nothing more welcome in a rural cafe or post office lobby than something unusual or juicy to visit about. So, I put the rhododendron bush telegraph to work, spreading the word that I'd just directed my first backyard burial.

Very quickly, I was fielding all kinds of questions. One woman stopped by the parlour to see exactly what kind of operation I was running out of the old goat barn. A fellow named Harry, in his mid-eighties, invited me over for his birthday to talk about death. Specifically, his death.

Harry's wife, Mildred, had told him they would do anything he wanted for his birthday. I don't think she'd expected him to say he wanted the town undertaker to come by, but she was true to her word. Mildred put on the coffee pot and welcomed me in. They were a delightful couple. Harry called me the "Beauty Queen Belle of Boring" when I arrived.

"So, in the most customary sense," Harry asked me, "a green burial means a person is buried in a container that can decompose, along with the remains, and return to the earth's soil. You're saying this can be achieved by being laid to rest in my favorite comforter or sheet? Do I need a specific type of casket?"

"Yes, birthday boy! You got it. Do you have a favorite blanket or comforter?"

Harry got up and walked to the back bedroom to look. Five, maybe ten minutes passed. Mildred and I looked at each other, concerned. She was pushing up from her sunken spot in the couch when Harry reappeared around the corner. He told us to hang on and shuffled down the hall as Old Man Harry, but a few minutes later a rather youthful, proud Harry returned, holding a kitchen cleaver and a bushel of bamboo.

"Can your people make me a big enough box out of this stuff?"

"Oh, Harry," Mildred piped in. "That is so foolhardy." But Harry was on the right track.

"Actually," I said, "earth-friendly caskets are crafted out of a variety of materials: wood, willow, banana leaves, even bamboo branches. Absolutely no metals, plastics, stains, varnishes, or oils are used; bamboo is just perfect."

Harry knew a thing or two about this already, had read about it in *Mother Jones* of all places, and was well versed in the world of eco-coffins.

He said, "They're made from recycled paper, cardboard, even a wicker that looks like a pea pod and comes in lots of colors. There are lots of people who want something handmade and biodegradable—no chemical glues or other toxic components."

Mildred had a priceless look of confusion. "Is that so?" She really wanted to know.

Harry nodded. "There's also a lot more praise for holding the ceremony somewhere dear to the deceased. Simple, stay-at-home burials are becoming quite vogue."

Quite vogue. Wow, I wanted to slip trendy *Mother Jones* quoting Harry in my pocket and take him home.

He continued: "Now explain me this, please. Burial places will often have rules as to what is, or is not, permitted on their property that can clash with having a green burial, is that correct?"

I nodded. "Yes. Some cemeteries require concrete grave liners everywhere on their grounds, but there are others in the area just for green burials. More and more are setting aside space for natural burial."

"Well, that's what I want. I want to get back to the Earth. I want a tree planted on top of me so my body will fertilize it. I want to be free and growing as part of that tree, not all balled up in some metal box inside a concrete bunker."

"That does sound nice," Mildred agreed.

Harry gave her a wink and told her he was hoping she'd choose to be there with him. They could spend eternity "romancing" each other under that tree.

"Oh, you!" Mildred swatted playfully at her husband and blushed with a smile that said she was pleased to be asked.

"Before your time, young lady," Harry explained to me, "the body was always kept at home."

"I love that concept," I replied

"Is that what you want, Harry?" Mildred asked.

"Yeah."

This worried her. "I won't know what to do. My mother used to talk about sitting with the dead, way back when, but I've never done it. By the time I was old enough to remember, there was a mortician to handle all that."

"I would be honored to take care of Harry's body right here at home if you trust me to do that," I said.

"You would come here and handle everything?" Mildred asked. I promised I would.

"Then if that's what my Harry wants, that is what we will do," she declared.

"That's settled then," said Harry, standing up. "Let's eat my birthday pie."

"Whatever it is, Harry does things his own way," Mildred said. "He read a couple of weeks ago about people in Australia being buried standing up. I'm surprised he didn't insist on that."

"I'm going to be buried face down," Harry said, "so people can kiss . . ."

"Harry!" Mildred shrieked. Her husband just laughed and cut us each a huge piece of pie.

❧

Melanie was another local who'd heard about some weird undertaker and had questions. The first time I met her, I was outside filling my bird feeder with black oil sunflower seeds. A rickety old truck pulled up and parked by the funeral home. A very short woman with black spiked hair and about thirty arm bangles got out and announced she wanted to talk to me about death and assorted topics.

"Tell me stuff about cremation. It's the 'envio' way to check out, right? I mean, I don't need to take up any space."

"Well, kind of," I said, "but it has an environmental impact and carbon footprint."

"Okay, wait," Melanie said. "So, what are you saying? You want me to pay you to plug me with chemicals?"

"No, not exactly." I offered her a Diet Coke as we walked into the funeral parlour. Her purple fingernails clawed at the tab like she was on a soda jag.

"Cremation is a great choice," I said. "But it's not the most eco-friendly."

Melanie listened respectfully as I explained the not-so-green aspects to cremation that many people don't consider. For instance, cremation burns fossil fuel, and older cremation facilities can use significantly more energy for this compared to modernized ones. Mercury is also emitted when a person with dental amalgam fillings is cremated, although just how much mercury is widely debated.

"But what else can I do?" Melanie asked. "I really don't want to be put in the ground."

"There is a method, little known in the U.S., but on the rise, called water resomation."

Melanie sat up straighter. "What the hell is that?"

"Rather than cremating with fire, water dissolves the body through alkaline hydrolysis."

"How?"

"A combination of water pressure, heat, and alkalinity. This is the most eco-friendly, sustainable method we have so far."

"Okay, wait. Would that be like putting grandma in a washing machine?"

"Kind of," I said, laughing. "Water resomation accelerates the natural disintegration process, sympathetically returning the body to ash." I could see wheels turning in Melanie's mind. "Hard to wrap your head around, huh?"

"What would they do with my body after the spin cycle?" Melanie asked.

"They'll gently place you in water within a pressurized stainless steel chamber. After a few hours, all that remains is your skeleton, which will be so soft the technician can grind it into ash by hand."

"But what about the dirty wash water?"

"There isn't any. Just a sterile, contaminant-free liquid that can be safely disposed of at a water treatment plant."

"I'll be damned," Melanie said. "How long does this take—a week?"

"A few hours, just like fire-based cremation. And no one has to cut out your pacemaker."

"How come pacemakers can't be left in place for a fire-based cremation?"

"The batteries inside them can explode when heated."

"That'd be a wakeup call," Melanie allowed. "It kind of makes sense, doesn't it? Water cremation—since we're mostly made of water anyway."

"I think it does," I agreed. "I think it will become widespread here once people know it's an option. What about you? Would you prefer alkaline hydrolysis to fire cremation?"

"I wouldn't hesitate for a second." Melanie declared. "Water sounds nicer than fire—gentler." I agreed, enthusiastically. "Too much land is used up to bury people," she continued. "It doesn't sit right with me."

"If you lived in Australia, we could give you a vertical burial."

Melanie grinned and slurped down her Diet Coke. "Okay, wait. Isn't that totally, like, disrespectful?"

"I don't see how. People who choose a vertical burial are placed in biodegradable shrouds and buried in cylindrical holes, feet first. It's different, but there are people who really dig the idea. It uses less land."

"How do they dig the hole? Use one of those rotary auger drills they set utility poles with?"

I nodded while smiling at her gusto.

"Whatever gave the Australians that idea? Can I get another one of these?"

I retrieved another Diet Coke for the fascinated Melanie. "I researched it about a year ago. There was a guy with cancer named Allan, whose dying wish was to be buried upright in a biodegradable body bag. There's no marker or headstone and the location of his grave is identified only by coordinates and a grid reference on the cemetery gate. Apparently, for each body that goes in the ground like this, a tree is planted on a nearby hill."

Melanie cracked the second can, and a bottomless belch came out of her skinny self. It was so loud I almost blushed, but Melanie was way too into our conversation to notice anything.

"Cheaper, right?" she asked.

"Yep."

"So, only in Australia? Why not here?"

"It hasn't made it this far, probably. The Jewish faith is becoming cozy with the idea. Vertical burials take place in Jerusalem and are carried out in accordance with Jewish law. You know Malaysia?"

She nodded.

"Malaysia's Muslim majority doesn't accept cremation. They're considering burying people vertically since that country is running out of cemetery space."

"Kind of puts a crimp in our image of eternal rest, don't it?" Melanie remarked.

I laughed. "I like to think being buried upright makes one more aerodynamic, resulting in a quicker, easier launch up to Heaven."

Melanie chuckled. "Well, when it's my time, put me in the washing machine."

I promised I would, and I felt like I had a new friend.

☙

Throughout the summer and fall, the pace of work picked up. If I wasn't exactly setting the world on fire, I was at least able to take a bit of money home, and this demonstrated great progress. During a late autumn barbecue at our house, I told my friends and family quite truthfully that business had tripled—at least a couple of times—since I'd taken over at Cornerstone.

"How much business did you have the first month?" Nick asked.

"Never you mind about that," I spat. "Who wants more bean dip?"

"Doesn't it get lonely out there?" Ryan asked, reaching for the dip.

"It was pretty lonely at first," I admitted. "It was weird to be at work all day and never have anyone, dead or alive, in the building except unnerving rodents coming down the chimney. But it's not so bad now." I told them about Melanie, who had taken to stopping in fairly regularly, and the country folks I saw at the Barton Store every day. "I even get high schoolers cruising past occasionally to catch a glimpse of the lady undertaker."

"Oh, my God, I have the greatest idea!" Kevin blurted out.

"No!" we all shouted.

"You don't even know what it is," he protested.

"We can guess," I said, "but it's too soon. Let's let people get to know me before we scare them away with a 'Come as Your Favorite Car Accident' party."

"I was thinking 'Teenaged Lovers Who Died in a Crash,'" Kevin confessed. We all howled, except my dad, who looked confused.

"You really do this?" Dad asked Kevin.

"I do, sir," Kevin said matter-of-factly.

"Why?"

"I . . ." For once Kevin's tongue failed him. Finally, he said, "I don't know. The whole concept just got started and I forgot to stop." We started giggling again. Even Sofia, who was bouncing on Willow's lap, squealed and laughed at him.

We ate and told stories and passed Sofia around until the hour grew late. As our guests left, they said how happy they were for me. Of course, they didn't know what my bank book liked like.

"Cold out here," Michael said, as the last car pulled away. "Feels like winter will be early."

"Doesn't it, though." I thought of the drafty goat barn I called a funeral home. I'd been cold all week but hated to bring that up when things had been going so well at Cornerstone. Michael seemed less tense about the whole deal, and I didn't need to burden him with my discomforts.

I figured I was perfectly capable of winterizing the tiny country parlour.

Chapter 28

Stone Cold

WINTERIZING THE OLD GOAT BARN WAS FAIRLY SIMPLE. WITH-out a basement, all I had to do was shut the vents to the crawl space and plug holes to prevent squirrels, mice, and rats from making their own parlours in my parlour walls. I was proud of myself, until I realized how little cold my putty knife had managed to keep out.

The place was poorly insulated, and single-paned windows let in the wind and cold. One windy day, I was on the phone with Nurse Nancy who asked, "Are you in the Jeep?" The thin windows in my office rattled away like beads in a gourd. Concerned the office was too cold for my baby, I made excuses for why Sofia should stay with Michael more often; it meant lots more lonely days for me, though.

My moody pal Melanie came by on one of those lonely, frigid after-noons. I heard her slam her truck door super loud and curse her way up the walk. Eager for company, I rushed out of my office and met her at the front door with a Diet Coke and big, welcoming smile.

"Men are horseshit!" she shouted, pushing past me. "Why do we bother with them?"

She ranted on about her man doing her wrong and other familiar cho-ruses as I trailed along behind her, shutting doors to keep the heat in. When she finally stopped for a breath of air, she looked around and said, "Damn, you could store meat in here. Turn up the heat!"

"All the heat I have is turned up as far as it goes," I lamented.

"What's that on your hands?"

"Mittens. I cut the fingertips out of them so I can type."

"Girl, this is crazy!" Melanie said. "There's a storm expected. The tem-perature is supposed to drop real low tonight."

"I know, but I don't have money for building upgrades right now. I'll just have to make do."

"Where's your baby? You don't have her in here, do you?"

I told her Michael was taking care of Sofia most days when not working, and Willow was babysitting lots, too.

"That's kind of too bad," Melanie mused. "It's nice having a little curtain jerker around."

"I know. I had a family stop in the other day—a lady who lost her daughter to cancer a couple of weeks ago. She wanted to hold Sofia, and it was sad to tell her the baby wasn't with me."

"That kid's a real fixture around here," Melanie said, getting up to inspect the clattering window frames. "Speaking of fixtures, are your pipes winterized?"

"There is heat tape on the main water feed into the building," I assured her, leaving out the part where the thermostat wasn't adjustable.

"It looks like you got a leak in this roof," Melanie shouted from the chapel. "There's a stain on the ceiling."

"I know, I just haven't been able to pinpoint where it's coming from, but when I do I'll seal it up. It doesn't drip."

"Huh," my troubleshooter said doubtfully. "I know a local guy who is pretty good at fixing this kind of stuff."

"Sorry, but I'm as broke as a joke."

"Okay," said Melanie. "It's probably for the best anyway. I used to be with him, and I don't know if we're talking to each other yet or not."

Then she left because she was "freakin' freezing." I remained to shiver on my own.

☙

The next day an ice storm knocked out the power for three days. Worried the pipes would burst and flood the funeral parlour, George hustled off to the hardware store for spray foam insulation to inject into the vents and openings. He discovered mice had been using the water pipe as a runway into the insulation under the floor.

A few hours and more than a few buckets of rodent poison and insulating sealant later, I was freezing, weary, and close to tears. I cranked the heat up as best I could to thaw out. Then I dialed Roxy Montana, my uncle's lady friend I used to spend lots of time with while living in California. She would impart the handywoman knowledge I needed with her soft, auntie/mom delivery. That's what I was truly looking for. No answer on the phone. She was probably out with her horses or down to the ranch.

I muttered and cursed and fretted with frustration until I'd worked myself into a decent crying jag. Finally, I called my husband.

"What have I done?" I bawled when Michael answered his phone.

"Honey? What? What did you do? Were you in a wreck?"

"Yes," I said, sadly. "I am in a wreck." Then I explained how cold it had been at the parlour and told him about the mice and confessed I was afraid I had made a mistake taking the job at Cornerstone.

I braced myself for an "I told you so," but Michael just said, "Hold tight. I'll be there as soon as I can."

A couple of hours later, my wonderful darling arrived on the scene with Philly cheesesteaks for both of us and a Super Big Gulp for me, plus boxes of plastic window insulation. "Damn," he said, walking into the parlour. "Guess it saves on paying for cooler space for the bodies."

"I wish I'd thought of that," I said ruefully. "I could have used the savings to buy more long underwear."

Michael gave me a look I couldn't decipher and told me to come give him a hand. After we finished installing the weather stripping and plastic film, we pulled a couple of chairs up to the office wall heater and unwrapped the cheesesteaks. After a huge bite, Michael asked, "Why are you so quiet?"

It felt crappy to admit I was embarrassed about my situation, but I shrugged and apologized for getting us into it anyway.

"You don't have anything to apologize for."

"Michael, I can barely pay the basic bills let alone bring home a decent paycheck. I'm on the verge of hypothermia in here while dead mice litter the floor—more deadbeat customers."

"Did you put poison on the carpet?"

"Yes."

"The little waxy sticks, or the other kind?"

"What difference does it make? Cornerstone is a joke, and everybody says I won't be able to go back to a corporate job. I have worse problems than dead mice and poisonous carpet."

"Nah," my husband said. "You'll be all right if you went with the name-brand mouse poison."

"Are you listening to me?"

"Yeah. I've been listening to you. Baby, it sounds like you're making progress."

"Not enough. This place needs major repairs."

"Why isn't your landlord doing that?"

"There's forty acres and something always needs fixing, and this place isn't paying for itself."

"Well, you'll have to make it pull its weight."

"I'm trying!"

"Well, hell, Elizabeth, don't give up now."

"Are you serious?" I couldn't believe we had traded positions on this. "It was stupid. I thought it could work for a minute last summer, but obviously, it's not."

"Maybe you need help," Michael suggested.

"There's not enough work here to keep me busy, and anyway, how would I pay anyone?"

Michael glanced at the floor and shuffled his feet before saying, "I meant me."

"How do you mean?"

"I think you should stay, and I think if you need help with something, you should ask me," he said.

"But you thought this was a dumb move."

"Yeah, but it was pretty ballsy of you to do it. I want to see you make it here." There was pride in his voice. I was flabbergasted.

"You're serious."

"Yeah," he said, flashing his trademark goofy grin.

Before I could tell him how much I loved him, the phone rang. I picked it up and said, "Cornerstone Funeral Services," in my best professional voice. There had been an accident. When I hung up, I asked Michael if he had time to go to the Medical Examiner's office with me. We headed out the door, a team.

☙

Having Michael's reinforcement made the rest of the winter a lot easier, at least mentally. I felt surrounded in adoration, wrapped in a warm electric blanket of support, knowing I could call him whenever something came up. No more facing these headaches alone and worrying about how to break bad news to him at the end of the day. I was safe and loved.

The parlour was still colder than a well-digger's britches, except for the days there was a funeral or visitation. I didn't have the funds to spend on electricity to heat the entire building when only my office was in use. Fortunately, most of my drop-ins were country people well-educated about zonal heating. George was generous and helpful, but an old building is an old building.

One bright spot was the lack of rodent activity, sadly offset by the growing leak in the parlour roof. Mourning families had to endure chapel services or visitations while looking at a small garbage can between the chairs. I winced whenever I heard little drops of water plinking and splashing into my make-shift bucket while guests paid their last respects. If it were possible to die of humiliation, I would have been one ashamed mortician lying in a casket, but what could I do?

Was there a program to provide repair grants for well-meaning, hardworking, small businesses that recycle smart? Funds for rural funeral home directors similar to the medical scholarships that pay for your schooling if you agree to work in Alaska for a few years? A magical roofing fairy?

Michael set up a spreadsheet that helped me estimate and track cash flow. It indicated I might be able to hire a cost-friendly roofing contractor just as Sofia entered college. Alternatively, I came up with a stream of excuses just in case my parlour guests inquired about the roof situation.

The leak just cropped up but the repair guy didn't have an opening on his schedule for weeks! They must have known I was fibbing. It's doubtful the busy season for roofers is smack in the middle of Oregon's rainy winters. But nobody called me on it, and I made it through winter with shreds of my dignity intact.

By the time the rainy season begrudgingly gave way to a sunny day now and again, the parlour was doing enough business to break even on the basic bills.

George now offered to sell it to me. "My health's not so good anymore, kid," he explained, "and I think it's time to turn this place loose to you."

He presented his offer while I tried to imagine what Michael would say about it. I hadn't had a substantial paycheck for a very long time, and the business couldn't pay for itself. The only way to purchase it would be to dip into our private funds. Still, I had to think this through. There was no way I could buy a funeral parlour of my own using conventional means, and I wasn't likely to find another chance like the one George was offering. I decided to accept.

Michael, to his credit, cursed just a wee bit when I told him my news. He did acknowledge this was probably the only way I would be able to afford a funeral home of my own before I keeled over myself. But, the tense look on his face returned and stayed there all night and through the next few days.

Fortunately, I was busy with a couple of cremations and one really big green burial that week. This gave me something to talk about besides the new debt I'd acquired and the on-going issue of leaky roofs.

Chapter 29

Buying the Farm

Next Sunday afternoon I was soaking in the bath during Sofia's nap when Michael burst in and announced, "I think I've got it."

"It?" I removed the warm washcloth from my eyes. He was holding a sheaf of printed spreadsheets and notebook pages with rows of penciled figures. I wasn't sure if that boded ill or well. I cautiously asked if he could be more specific.

"We need to move to the country," he said.

"Come again?"

"We've been saving for a house in the city. If we buy near where you work, we can save a bundle and, if we are careful, make ends meet."

"Are you sure?" He was and had the figures to prove it.

"That's our new housing budget?" I asked. "Are we buying a family home or a chicken coop?"

"Elizabeth, you gotta give somewhere," Michael said with a hint of warning in his voice.

"I know, but I always thought maybe Sofia would grow up in Tigard and go to Saint Anthony School like I did."

"Here's a better idea—she'll grow up in the country and go to school with the kids that belong to the people at the Barton Store."

"It's really nice out that way, just so peaceful," I said, smiling. "And you can see the stars at night."

"See? You can teach her the constellations."

"Oh, my God!" I said, sitting up so fast water slopped over the edge of the tub.

"What?"

"We can have goats!"

The look on Michael's face was priceless and nearly worth our months of conflict.

❧

I called my friend Connie, a realtor, for a sit-down about what we were seeking:

"Adobe. No, Mediterranean. A big garden with a maze of sunflowers. It needs to feel safe, and warm. A dramatic ocean view, with maybe some fly-by toucans and big trees with those nests that look like upside-down baskets the Montezuma Oropendola birds make. I think it would be really cool to have a water slide outside my bedroom window into the pool. I guess maybe not a beach house because it would be too far away from our work, but maybe just a huge deck, even though we could only really enjoy it from mid-July to the end of September. On the days it doesn't rain."

Realtor Connie clicked off her pen. "I have no idea what to do with that," she said. I understood her confusion since I had created it in my lunatic fashion.

Michael rolled his eyes. "We need a fantastic bargain, hopefully a place we can turn into a funeral home. Something where we're getting a lot for our money. Maybe a nice place, but somebody died in there and now nobody wants to buy it?"

This also did not clarify things for Connie. "You do realize that is not anything that will be disclosed on the RMLS, right?"

"Maybe we could look online to find houses that meet our approval and tiny budget," I volunteered, "so you don't waste all your gas driving around."

"Good idea," she agreed, relieved.

Michael and I looked at sassy houses only—homes for odd birds, homes that were short-sales, foreclosures, or serious fixer-uppers. I wouldn't even get out of the car for bland or anything that resembled a straight line. I was very drawn to the idea of a Storybook house. I had seen two in my life: one from inside a hearse on the Grave Line Tour that carried tourists to death locations in Beverly Hills; the other at the Montclair Firehouse in Oakland. Harry Oliver's Spadena House in Beverly Hills, also known as the *Witch's*

House, was perfect for me. Imagine how much fun it would be for Sofia to grow up in a Hansel and Gretel setting that was also a mortuary!

Unfortunately, there's not a lot of architecture inspired by 1920s Hollywood set design—or anything offbeat at all, for that matter—in small town Oregon. Realtor Connie encouraged us to expand our search to the surrounding countryside.

We looked at a five bedroom, six bath, 4,000 square-foot-plus sprawling monster on a grass airstrip. The pool was flanked by an extra-tall pink slide built circa 1970, and it emptied into stagnant, green water. The house interior was uncomfortably large and funky. A big rumpus room bloomed with wall-to-wall red shag carpet. Mirrors covered every available wall and some of the ceiling as well.

We commented on the eerie feeling of the property. "If you feel like someone is watching you," Connie said, "that's because the cemetery next door and the surrounding woods are wired with cameras and recording devices. A local bird watcher spotted them a few months ago and tipped off the authorities. They ended up busting five Chinese men who were running a cocaine business out of the rumpus room."

Next up was a 1946 Cape Cod Snout house: charming and uncommon and painted white with bright blue shutters. It was a home that had been meticulously cared for. An unfortunate widow, who had lived there her whole life, was having it short sold out from under her. The open floor plan, ideal for entertaining, featured a cathedral ceiling and sun-splashed living room with a marble-surround gas fireplace open to the dining room. A large sundeck overlooked private, professionally landscaped grounds, including an Olympic-size pool and masonry-walled garden. It looked like a 1940s hotel with all the neoclassical built-ins and moldings. It was ridiculous. I loved it.

Unfortunately, closer inspection revealed the carriage house and Doric columns were crumbling, the pool was not aging gracefully, and something bubbling up through a grate in the basement laundry room spelled trouble. I was looking past all of that, because when you really want something the reality of future costs don't resonate. The final kibosh on the deal though was the worst possible factor for slobs like us with a toddler—every single room had white carpet. Not off-white: snow white. There weren't enough plastic runners in the world to protect this pristine fleece from our spill-prone tribe.

We looked at a slew of similarly eccentric places. We liked the small ranch on a few acres and thought of turning it into a green burial ground, but lost interest when county zoning wouldn't hear of it. There was an old farmhouse with a big ballroom dance floor. We saw a miniature castle that featured a spiral staircase to a tower bedroom, perfect for Princess Sofia, not so great for us.

A few months into our search, we found a new listing of a log home high in the hills. Our car got stuck mid-ascent going up the driveway since it was comprised of unrolled gravel. There was no garage, just an open carport filled with junk. Once inside the house, the bottom floor was an unfinished area containing a large wooden bar. Fluorescent lighting blinked in foreboding fashion.

This mid-1970s cedar plank house was left in its original state, complete with harvest gold refrigerator, range, and tub. Even the five-gallon toilets were gold. Plaid-patterned sofas with wooden arms grouped and defined the sitting areas, and wood paneling was brightened up by a hanging macramé planter and owl. The place was dank, cold, and as depressing as an abandoned disco fern bar. There was no heating source except loud, clicking baseboard heaters. Window seals were broken and black-winged insects fluttered down from the ceiling, a major termite infestation.

Bob, the son of the deceased owners, was working on the home as we looked around. He couldn't believe his realtor had listed it, because there was plenty of work due to bring it up to code. It had sat vacant for years. Bob's parents and their six children built it the summer their youngest graduated high school. With all offspring grown and gone, his parents had built their dream cabin in the woods. They had lived there for thirty-five years and died in the house. Bob was the unfortunate son stuck with unloading it; none of his siblings wanted anything to do with it. They were too haunted by the love their parents had for it.

After hearing all that, the new suckers in town were sure their funky, unrealistic dream home was right before their eyes! We made an offer on the spot. Bob was so shocked he dropped the 2x4s he had been carrying. Then, he took an entire week to get back to us. He had to work through his excitement, grief and depression, to get back to his earlier ecstasy before accepting our offer. We got the place for a name-your-price steal of a deal.

We asked for a lot of reasonable fixes before forking over the cash. Dutiful Bob got them done on his days off from operating a ski lift on Mount Hood. In the meantime, my husband and I started renovating. With the repairs going on, all kinds of characters showed up in our driveway, gunning their 4x4s, to claim our discards. My job was to choose which walls would go and which would stay. I obviously had no great plan or preference because they are all still standing to this day.

Heavy equipment was utilized to spread gravel and roll blacktop over the driveway. A large crane carried in the hot tub and we watched it swing through the thick trees; three men had to grab it to ensure safe placement on the lower deck. Fourteen-foot slabs of re-purposed maple were unloaded, carried haphazardly up a narrow staircase, and out to the deck. The truck carrying appliances couldn't make it anywhere near the house, so makeshift roller skates were strapped onto the fridge and stove for the last leg of their trip to the house. It was insane to see major appliances rolled up our ridiculously steep driveway. I took video every day, adding my out-of-breath narration as I ran up and down many flights of stairs, hoping to catch the action from every angle.

Still, the potential we had assessed on our initial tour of the house outweighed the craziness of renovation. The previous owners were Swedish and the place was full of delights from the Land of the Midnight Sun, including a sauna and an adobe-like fireplace. A rune stone at the edge of the driveway bore the ex-owner's names and the establishing date of the home. We kept all this in their honor, as well as the wooden sign painted with the original owner's name, which was nailed to a tree at the property entrance. We named our new home El Aprisco, "The Sheepfold," after we saw a sign with that named etched on it above the red sheep shed on the property.

We busted ass as our self-imposed deadline—Sofia's third birthday party—loomed. The Rapunzel cake had been ordered and princess invitations handed out. We were determined not to move the festivities to a McDonald's just because the house wasn't ready. Our thought was to turn the party into a house warming soiree as well. Why not? This way we would only have to do one big pre-party cleaning. So, invitations had gone out to all our adult friends, too.

Setbacks made us flexible and fantasy plans were abandoned. Then, our prized stove shattered. My darling husband was reworking the electric current, moving the stove, and fitting cabinets one jumbled afternoon, and something was bound to give. That something was our "such-a-deal," underpriced and refurbished Jenn Air unit. Smashed glass was everywhere.

The party went on as planned. However, as proud a cook as I am, without my stove I had to resort to take-out. I was mortified on behalf of my guests.

"Did all this come with a handsome Asian delivery boy?" Kevin asked as he perused the make-shift Chinese food buffet.

"It came with me in the take-out mortuary van," I replied. Noting his horrified look, I specified, "Up front."

A few days after the party our farm animals arrived. My dear friend Martha Grace needed a new home for her babies, and here we were. We suddenly owned goats, sheep, lambs, a ram, and a calf named Ruby. They were adorable. Sofia and I spent time every day hanging out in their pasture. I loved how the little lambs rubbed their heads against me while I fed them hay and blackberries.

The purpose of our livestock was to clear the land and mow the grass. As a bonus, they entertained the slightly standoffish neighbors who walked their dogs past our fence line a few times a day. This was their excuse to see what the brand new neighbors were up to. Eventually, folks who lived down the way started dropping by to meet the new proprietors of this out-of-place "ski chalet." We were not what they expected, but we did not fail to thrill. The news that a family of morticians had moved in spread like wildfire.

გ

That first year as full-time country folk brought a lot of changes. Everything we did required much more driving. Events we had weathered easily in town—like storms—necessitated a new set of skills. But, the move also made us real members of our community. In the city we could be invisible, cogs in a massive wheel. It didn't matter to the folks at the 7-11 one or three blocks over if someone had broken your heart or you were coming down with the flu. Nobody really knew or cared and this wasn't all a bad thing. There's something very safe in being just one of the crowd; a tiny grain of sand on a large beach.

In a small town, you are somebody. Even if you feel like you haven't done anything with your life or haven't lived farther than a ten-mile radius from where you now stand. Even if you have no education, career, or even direction—you are still somebody. You have a name and an identity to those around you in your small community. It means giving up a lot of privacy, but I feel appreciated in a place where everybody knows my name.

Most importantly, our move demonstrated I was there for the long haul. The townies now knew that the new undertaker was "going to stick." People could count on me to take care of them when there was a death in the family.

One night, after a long day at work, I lowered my sore bag of bones into our steamy hot tub when the cell phone rang. This isn't an uncommon or surprising event in my world, even at eleven-thirty p.m. on a Friday. Morticians always say they retire early because of the strain on their backs from lifting dead bodies. Respiratory issues from harsh chemicals in the prep room also play a negative role. But, I think the super long hours and never-ending pressure of being on call for so many years are the prime cause of gray hairs and an excess of stress.

This late-night call was from a gruff-spoken man who wanted to know where to get a permit.

"A permit for what?" I asked.

"Like to bury someone in the backyard."

"Has someone passed away?" I inquired. It seemed like a logical question, but my caller sounded violated with my asking it.

"Why do you need to know?" the caller asked in a snarky tone.

"You are calling a funeral home and speaking to a funeral director."

He hung up.

About an hour later, the phone rang again. It was the same man.

"I want to put Hal on the side of the house," he said. "I just want you to tell me where I get the paperwork or whatever, because I don't want that thing to happen that the guy had to go through in the South."

"Are you referring to the situation in Alabama where a man buried his wife in their yard next to the house he built for her?"

"Yeah. It was the last promise the guy could keep to her, but then they made him dig her up. I ain't gonna dig Hal up. It ain't going down like that."

"I understand your concern, sir. It's uncommon for private-land burials to be allowed in urban and suburban areas. Are you in rural Clackamas County?"

Silence. Crickets.

I pressed on. "If you are in rural Clackamas County and have at least one acre of land, there probably aren't many restrictions. You don't have to go to the county for an inspection or get any special paperwork. The burial permit gets typed up with the death certificate at the funeral home. If you give me the address, I will come check it out in the morning."

This guy was trying to surrender a loved one into the embrace of the earth, obviously, but he had trust issues. He hung up again.

Fifteen minutes later, another call and it turned out my mystery caller lived down the road. What he really wanted, even though he didn't say it, was help from someone who saw life the way he and Hal did, a neighbor who probably had an understanding of how someone might not want to be separated from their home, even after death. Because I literally had bought the farm, I passed a critical litmus test in his mind.

"What was that all about?" Michael asked when he found me giving the cans a once over in the pantry, as I sometimes did after midnight or whenever I had lots to mentally process. "It sounded like you were running a call center out there on the deck."

"I think I just officially became a real local." I said.

Chapter 30

Filial Piety

I WAS BUSY SWABBING MY HARD-WATER-STAINED TOILET WHEN THE phone rang. I flung off my pink rubber gloves in seconds and ran to the office to grab it.

"Are you that funeral home that has the woman that does the green burials?" asked the caller on the other end.

"You found me," I replied. "My name is Elizabeth. How can I help?"

"I have questions. Is this something you can help my family with?"

The Korean Tran family wanted to meet at seven p.m. I agreed and called Michael to let him know I'd be late. I quick-stepped through scrubbing the rest of the bathroom so I could bake some brownies to offer my guests.

Geoffrey was the eldest in this family of three sons. He was in charge: he drove the car, walked ahead of everyone as they entered the building, was seated first, and was the sibling who pretty much did all the speaking. Geoffrey also pulled out his credit card to pay for my services.

Their father, Mr. Tran, was near the end of his life, and they were most interested in discussing the Forrester Cemetery. They heard it was a hybrid cemetery and wanted to know exactly what the heck that meant.

I explained, "Forrester Cemetery actually isn't considered a hybrid cemetery. That's when a conventional cemetery offers green burial throughout the entire park and allows an option to bury without the use of a vault or outer burial container of any type. You can use a shroud or something homemade instead of a casket. Forrester has an acre set aside specifically for natural burials, but it can't be classified as a hybrid since there is a specific green burial section, rather than allowing green burials anywhere in the park."

Someone's pants started ringing. Geoffrey stopped mid-sentence to shoot his brother, the phone offender, a nasty look. This was Patrick, who shyly slipped off the wicker bench he shared with his younger brother, Lyle. Geoffrey started to talk, but the chatter of Patrick's conversation in the other room seemed deafening in our tiny space.

"I see beauty in all women and don't think there is any standard we have to live up to, and you know that," Patrick was saying.

Geoffrey sighed. "You will need to please excuse Patrick. He is a fashion photographer in Seattle and he deals with, how do you say, very temperamental women."

A fashion photographer, how glamorous, I thought. I quickly wiped the chocolate crumbs off my shirt before Patrick returned. I wondered if he considered me attractive.

Patrick was still chatting away. "True beauty comes from the inside, in a woman's passions, creativity, success, her true essence; it shines out through her eyes and smile. When a woman loves herself, she gives off this air of confidence like a magnet; people are drawn to that—not just her nice rack."

I half-smiled. Lyle horse-laughed while Geoffrey was annoyed beyond belief. I had the feeling Patrick was going to get quite a spanking later.

He returned and absorbed Geoffrey's contempt. "What? There's no such thing as an ugly woman. Ugly behavior, yeah, but there's something beautiful about every woman."

Geoffrey regrouped. "We want to honor our father with a dignified burial. Our culture dictates a few traditions we would like. You are not of our culture, so I need to make sure you and your staff can satisfy this. First, my father will need to be dressed in customary burial clothes. My mother is gathering these now, and we will have them for you when you arrive to our home. Tan and linen is what he will wear. We also would like to spend some time in visitation with him, preferably a half day. Is this acceptable to you, and do you have space here to do something like this?"

"Anything you need, Geoffrey," I said. "I appreciate you entrusting me with your father. I don't have Asian staff members, so I hope this will not be any sort of discomfort for you."

Lyle laughed. He was subject to brief bouts of random giggling, charming and off-putting at the same time. "Geoff can be cool with that, I think," he said.

Big brother Geoffrey was a hard nut to crack. His rubber band was stretched a bit too tight and I had the sense it wasn't only because of his father's impending death. Geoffrey drew himself back from the table and pondered the situation.

"I need this to be an honorable passing. I owe it to my father. I am here on his behalf to make sure all things will be in the correct position, and I feel I am dealing with some interference from my brothers." He locked eyes with them both, quite sternly. "I know this doesn't mean that much to you, but this is our father and I want to lay him to rest most dignified. Lyle, I need you to sit up straight and pay attention, and Patrick, you can have these frivolous conversations once we finish with business."

I gave Geoffrey the number for Larry, my friend and cemetery sexton, to show them the available green spaces. Larry would also talk to them about the physical details of what to expect when Mr. Tran arrived at the cemetery. Geoffrey gave me a slight bow and I returned his parting gesture.

I closed up shop, stopped at my favorite neighboring store for a Diet Mountain Dew, and zipped home. Sofia and Michael were both fast asleep so I kissed their heads and tiptoed away to fire up my laptop. I needed to finish an article about natural burials for *Back Home* magazine. I liked how the article was turning out, but might be up until two a.m. finishing it to my standards, especially with the Tran family on my mind.

"Elizabeth, what are you doing?" Michael called sleepily a few hours later.

"Writing."

Michael stumbled in, looking like he'd been working too many hours on top of caring for a toddler. "Why do you bother with that?" he asked.

"I want to help teach people about green burial, and it's free marketing for Cornerstone."

"You already work too much! Your daughter and I miss you." Off he headed, back to bed, as I winced and felt like a crappy mother.

I felt this way sometimes—okay, a lot. I knew the life I was giving Sofia was a far cry from my childhood, at least the real early years when mom stayed at home with Nick and me and Dad went to work. She was a member of the PTA and Den Mother of my brother's Boy Scout Troop.

I was a working mother. I slept in the house every night and Sofia saw me every day, but I didn't read as many books to her or play as many games

228 ❦ Elizabeth Fournier

with her as I should. My mom was trained as an educator but chose to raise us full-time. I was demonstrating to my daughter the validity of a fulfilling career and the value women bring to work. Were one of those choices better? I didn't know. My heart was constantly pulled between two great loves—my work and my family.

I closed the lid on the laptop and went to curl up with Michael.

"Aren't you going to write?" he asked, drowsily.

"Later," I said. "Right now I just want to be near you." We scooted around and nuzzled comfortably into each other as I finally surrendered to sleep, exhausted.

When I awoke the next morning, Sofia was laying crosswise in our bed, her sweaty arm on top of me. For such a petite thing she took up a lot of room. I held her and thought of the Tran family and their culture and what their father's funeral would mean to them.

In many cultures, burial rites are as important as how people are treated in life. Some families pay a steep premium to ensure customs are honored, especially when these traditions are not in line with typical American burial practices. In some cultures, embalming or cremation is taboo. The greater availability of natural burials fills an important need in our nation of immigrants.

Laying there, holding my daughter, I thought about the loss of a father. What would this mean to Geoffrey? How would becoming the patriarch of his family affect life as he knew it? Was the family taking a turn sitting around Mr. Tran's bedside, listening for shallow breathing and watching for signs of his journey to the other side? How did Mrs. Tran feel about acquiring the burial clothes for her husband, the father of her three sons?

Larry's call interrupted my contemplation. He told me the Tran family would be out to the cemetery within the hour. I explained how important it was to Geoffrey and his brothers to know their father would be buried in an honorable space. They'd spent months taking their father to doctors; he'd been poked and prodded in front of them, and they wanted him to truly rest in peace and return to the earth.

"Anything for you, dear," my wonderful Larry said, and I knew the family would be in tender hands. Larry was a gentle soul, the right man for the job. He was an old hippie, a free spirit, a person with a very large heart grounded in love.

The cemetery where Mr. Tran was buried a week later was wooded, quiet and remote. The burial space had been sensitively picked out to quickly and easily return to looking as natural as the life in the surrounding forest of wild ferns, squirrels, and birds. Mr. Tran's burial was soft and kind, beautiful and green, rich and dignified. By the end of the day the great weight on Geoffrey Tran's shoulders sat easier somehow, more balanced.

Home that night, I told Michael about Mr. Tran's funeral. "I feel really good about what I could help make happen for them."

"You should," Michael replied as he put the finishing touches on dinner and delivered Sofia's plate to her. "We spent our day playing princess."

"I was Rappingzul!" Sofia said around a mouthful of pasta and peas.

"You got to be Rapunzel?" Damn, I hated that I missed that. Over dinner, Sofia told me about how funny her daddy had been when he pretended to climb up her princess hair and how they had built a tall castle for her out of the furniture.

"What did you do, Mommy?" Sofia asked.

"I helped a man give his daddy a very sweet funeral."

"Because he loved his daddy?"

"Yes."

"Good Mommy!" Sofia crowed. "Tomorrow you do another funeral and Daddy and I are going to play princess with the goats."

"Good Daddy!" I said, winking at my husband, which made him grin the way he does when he's happy to have pleased his girls.

"Can Mrs. Butler play too, Daddy?" Sofia asked.

"Who is Mrs. Butler?"

"Ghost of the lady who used to live here," Michael explained.

Later, I asked Michael if he thought we should be worried about Sofia chatting up the deceased.

"Nah," he said. "You've been talking to a dead lady for years and you turned out all right."

Had I turned out all right?

Chapter 31

The Summer of Free Advertising

B Y MY THIRD SUMMER AT CORNERSTONE, I KNEW TO EXPECT THEM: the "floaters." As soon as the sun broke through the gloomy winter cloud cover for six hours in a row, everyone in the Portland Metro area would launch their inner tubes, rubber rafts, and floating coolers (stocked with Pabst Blue Ribbon), into the Clackamas River. They'd flood into nearby Barton Park. When it happens, summer days are punctuated with sounds of sirens as first responders speed past the parlour on their way to break up a fight or deal with someone suffering from alcohol poisoning. There's also the regular and ongoing rescue of stranded flotation devices full of people. Our precious two-lane highway to town ends up jammed with cars blaring Taylor Swift or Toby Keith.

I popped up from scrubbing the toilet one morning to a horrible noise out on Highway 224. I ran to see that cars had crashed and melded into a jumbo mess of twisted aluminum and steel. Traffic would be bogged down worse than ever for hours. People were cutting right across our lawn to get to the store for smokes, or to make their way down to the river to swim. Litter blew across the highway and landed on my front stoop. I picked up about ninety-five cents in empties and found a beige hand towel with the word "Breathe" stitched on the lower corner. I sighed; sometimes it's hard to make the best of things.

Then I had an idea. If I had to endure these people throwing beer cans out car windows onto the funeral home property and hearing F-bombs all summer, a little free advertising seemed like fair trade. I put on a tiny sundress, grabbed my rag and spray bottle, marched across the field, and proceeded to give my very large road sign a thorough cleaning. All eyes were on me as I sprayed and wiped and sprayed and wiped. The more honking and yelling that ensued, the more I knew I was getting a free bang for my non-existent marketing buck.

Y'all come on back to the country now, ya hear? And while you're at it, come pull up a chair in my parlour . . . and stay a while.

I noticed cars were veering around an object in the road, so my inner Northwest Nancy Drew investigated. A huge passenger side mirror had fallen off a truck. It was intact, not too scratched up and the glass wasn't shattered. Mine! I sauntered out onto our country thoroughfare and picked it up.

Back at the parlour, I dug a hole outside my office window, jammed the pole I'd attached to the mirror into the soft terrain, and went inside to check my handiwork. I adjusted it just a tad, and voila! I had a new screening system right outside my office. When someone rang the doorbell, I simply leaned toward the window a smidge, looked to the left and my marvelous roadkill mirror let me know who was at the front door. The door knocker couldn't see me check them out, yet I was prepared for whoever arrived unannounced. Well, almost.

"What is the mess out there on your road?"

It was Richard. There was no mistaking that voice. I extracted myself from the archive boxes I was sorting through in the back closet and tried straightening myself up, but it was too late and the parlour was too small. He caught me at mid-smooth.

"You'll want to get the dust bunny out of your hair as well," he advised.

I thanked him and swiped at my head.

"Is there some sort of music festival or a hog calling in your neighborhood today?" asked the ever-so-sardonic Richard.

"It's like this all summer, they go floating on tubes down the river to the Carver Park," I explained. "But why are you out here in it?"

"I was at the casket rollout at Wilbert in Clackamas. I thought since I was in the neighborhood, I'd check out your little funeral home on the prairie."

I pointed out Cornerstone was not on the prairie but in the woods. My little goat barn was a far cry from the large, well-appointed parlour Richard and I had worked at together.

"Let me give you the dollar tour," I offered.

"I saw the whole place on my way in here."

"That's true," I allowed. "I'll get you some water, from a well don't cha know, and we can catch up if you have time." Richard seemed pleased to be asked, so I plated a few cookies I'd baked for a previous funeral while he took a second look around. I thanked the saints it was a sunny day. I didn't think I could stand having Richard see a rain-catching trash can in my chapel.

"Do you only do natural burial?" he asked, looking over my new willow casket display.

"No, I offer standard burials and cremation services too, but I encourage my families to at least consider some old school burial practices." I explained that I found my preferred methods kinder, not just to Earth, but to humans as well.

Richard sniffed in jest, but not too loudly. "Give me an example."

I told him about a funeral I'd directed the previous week. The decedent, Paulie, was in his sixties and died peacefully in his home. His family wanted to honor him in a way they felt suited his life. He was embalmed and laid in a traditional metal casket wearing his best leather shoes. His favorite Elvis songs rang out to family and friends, and his favorite Virginia ham and sourdough rolls were provided for the generous repast. The room was decorated by the florist with lots of fresh flowers in dark-hued bouquets. All pretty, but standard stuff.

Paulie had two college-aged sons who wanted to participate in their father's farewell but weren't sure what to do with themselves—they weren't comfortable with the not-so-eco-friendly service.

"I love him, but we just see—saw—the world differently," one of the sons commented. His tone was respectful but sad.

A thought struck me. Paulie's son had a large trailer hitched behind his mountain bike. "Why don't we load your father's casket into your cart and use pedal power to bring him to the cemetery," I suggested.

The son's eyes lit up. "Can I?"

"I don't see why not. It's only about a quarter of a mile to the cemetery, and the road is smooth."

As I explained to Richard, "He was able to do something for his father that reflected the way that son chose to live his young life. After that, the son seemed more at peace about accepting the service that reflected his father's life."

Richard, who had been listening intently, sat back. "Huh. I thought that was going to be a lot more hippie-dippy than it turned out to be."

I laughed. "I do get some people you would call hippie-dippie, but most of the families I work with are just everyday folks."

"And business is good?"

"Mmm. I can honestly say it's growing."

"Well," Richard said, primly wiping cookie crumb off his chin, "if anybody can do this, I think it's you."

"You do?"

He shrugged. "You got moxie."

Surprised, I practically gushed out my thanks to him.

"And, I have kind of an ulterior motive."

"What's that?" I asked, trying not to sound suspicious.

"We're starting to get people asking for this kind of thing." He swept his arm around as if the interior of my reception area was an icon of oncoming, sweeping change. "I might have the occasional referral for you, now that I've seen the place."

I felt like I just passed a major test. Richard, Mr. We-Will-Stop-Embalming-Over-My-Dead-Body was going to make referrals to me? It got even better.

"I might also have questions from time to time. I've been promoted to managing director and I'm making some proposals to green things up a bit."

"Richard, I'm impressed," I said. "And, I'm always happy to answer your questions. It will give me a chance to return some of the favors you've done for me over the years."

We chatted a bit longer, sharing the latest trade news. As he rose to leave, he paused and reached into the pocket of his suit jacket. "Here," he said, "I picked this up for you on my last vacation." It was a logo pen from a funeral home in the Netherlands.

"Richard, you're the best!" I squealed.

"I don't know," he said, looking around one more time. "I'd better get on it or you're going to lap me. Who would have thought we'd come back to just wrapping folks in a quilt and putting them in a dirt hole?" He shook his head all the way back to his highly-polished Town Car.

That night, as Michael and I mucked out the farm animal lean-to shed together, I told him about Richard's visit. "Funny coincidence," he said, "Because I have a referral for you today, too—a Mr. Stracci—he needs to meet your other Richard. He needs a green burial casket."

❧

"We're Italian-American," Mr. Stracci told me in my office the next day. "When I was growing up, we still had women in the family who wore a black dress every day for an entire year after the funeral. We have traditions in our families, you know?"

He told me about growing up in a big household that lived deep in Italian Harlem, the Italian section of New York City boasting the birthplace of Al Pacino.

"On Sunday, after Mass, everybody came to my grandparents' home with food and instruments. There was eating and dancing and lots of love. My family knew the secret for the happiest days and this is what I want to do for our papa. I want to gather and celebrate at our home."

"I would be honored to help you do that."

"There's one more thing," Mr. Stracci said. "I want to work with someone to build my father a casket like it used to be done in the old days. I need the help of a real master craftsman."

"I know just the person," I said, picking up the phone.

Before long, we were making our way down the rocky drive to the entrance of the property belonging to my friend, Richard Clarke. Renowned for his artistic craftsman-style designs, Richard makes a variety of wooden items, including hand-carved caskets, out of western red cedar from his property. His shop, a serene haven, sits in the midst of soaring trees that tower over the Clackamas River basin.

Mr. Stracci and I got out of my vehicle and walked to the edge of the cliff to take in the view. Large birds peacefully soared across the sky, and the wind quietly rustled the branches of the ancient trees. The air had that sharp, clean smell of forest.

"Mesmerizing," Mr. Stracci said.

"I always think that when I come here, too," I replied.

Richard joined us and introduced himself.

"You are living in God's glorious country, Mr. Clarke," said Mr. Stracci. "I have a good feeling about this. How did you become a coffin maker?"

Unconsciously stroking his bushy beard, Richard explained how, as a younger man, he had been involved in the fine art scene in San Francisco. "A fellow veteran asked me to build a casket, and somehow it just evolved from there."

Richard invited us to his shop, and on the way, Mr. Stracci told us his father had made wine until he grew too feeble. "He kept his equipment in the cellar, which smelled of grapes and wine all year long. Only the men and boys were allowed to touch or go near his wine equipment."

Inside the shop, Richard was putting the finishing touches on a cedar casket.

"What a sight!" Mr. Stracci said, taking in the warm, gleaming wood and elegantly simple lines of the piece. "How long does something like this take?"

"A good three or four days, but I love the process." Richard smiled. "So much so that I sometimes feel a little sad when the job is finished."

"I hope you will let me hire you to work with me," Mr. Stracci said, sincerely.

"I will," Richard said. "I like your stories and I want to pick your brain for cooking tips. Italian is one of my favorites."

"Oh, the food! Every August my older cousins and I would harvest tomatoes under the careful orchestration of our aunt. We had to pick fifty large boxes of fresh tomatoes to make enough tomato paste—and this was just for two families. We'd fill two hundred jars. I remember eating nothing without this gravy on it all winter and into the following summer."

I left the two men happily looking through various cuts of wood to choose just the right pieces for Papa Stracci's casket. Several days later, amid a large gathering of extended family, Mr. Stracci was able to lay his father to rest in a fine homemade coffin. It was a joyful epitaph in wood for the patriarch.

Chapter 32

Gallows Humor

ONE SUNNY DAY I ARRIVED AT WORK TO FIND TOURISTS WANDER-ing outside the parlour. They had stopped by to pose for a pic-ture next to the Boring Funeral Home sign. This happens with surprising frequency.

"There isn't a Boring Funeral Home," I explained. "There's just my place, Cornerstone."

"That's lame," one of the young men said.

"It isn't quite the same funny souvenir, is it?"

"Why's this place named Boring?" a fiercely tattooed young woman asked.

"It was named after an early homesteader, W. H. Boring. The first school was located on his land and the community ended up being named after him."

They agreed among themselves that they were getting bored with the place with every passing minute and took off. If only they knew all the stories. I could hear the phone ringing inside, so I rushed to catch it right in time. It was the daughter of a man I was scheduled to bury.

"I'm still looking for Dad's will and I can't find it. I've checked his office, all his files and his computer. I'm afraid it's lost and don't know what to do."

Joni's father had passed away in the night a couple of days ago, in his high-rise Portland apartment building. It was unexpected and Joni had found him, a very stressful experience. In going over the circumstances, I asked her if she had checked the freezer. She broke out in a laugh, which was nice to hear.

"Well, it wouldn't hurt. People often hide wads of cash or an important document in a zip lock bag in the freezer," I said. "I had a little guy in here last year who kept all his spare money inside a tobacco pouch in his freezer. He hid a bundle of hundreds there whenever he saw his drunken brother walking up the driveway. They stayed as fresh and crisp as his tobacco, so he started stashing all his notes, documents and money there. He said he checks the freezer first thing whenever he misplaces something."

She giggled and told me it reminded her of the Brady Bunch episode where Marcia had such a crush on some groovy boy, she absentmindedly left her schoolbooks in the fridge. I laughed; I hardly knew Joni, but I really liked her—our Brady bond was taking hold.

"If the will isn't there, look for an envelope taped to the bottom of a shelf in the kitchen or behind a picture on a wall. Also, look under the stairs, his mattress, within pairs of socks, and inside books."

I could feel her frowning through the phone.

"Yeah, I don't think my dad was that clever," she said.

I urged her on. "You'll never know unless you look."

"I feel like I don't want to do this at all," she confessed. "Can I just hold off for a couple of weeks?"

"If you're going to hold off on burial, you will need to consider embalming or cremation. Refrigeration only buys you so much time."

"Ah, I hadn't thought of that. Is it really, really bad?"

"Eventually, yes. And anyway, there are important emotional reasons to have the service. It will help you start getting some closure."

"What a job you have," she said. "What's the funniest creepy thing you ever dealt with?"

I smiled, but suggested it might not be the right time for stories like that.

"Please? I'm curious. I swear I won't freak out. I could use a little gallows humor," Joni insisted.

I told her the story of the day many moons back when I was vacuuming a slumber room and backed into the decedent lying there. She wasn't in a casket but on her personal couch—that was how the family wanted it set up. Since they had taken about ten days to decide on arrangements, the body wasn't in the best condition. The funeral directors had tried to help her deteriorated state by strategically positioning her on the couch. I was the unlucky soul who bumped into her at her weakest link. My vacuuming was cut short when part of her arm landed in my path.

Joni, bless her, laughed a great big belly laugh.

"My brother loves that story, too," I told her.

"This is all normal, right?" she asked, more soberly.

"Totally normal. Just a part of life," I said.

"Thanks. I'm really glad we called you," Joni said. "I don't think I could go through this with just anybody."

"Glad I could help. Do you feel ready to schedule the date yet?"

"Yes. Let's do this thing."

We coordinated calendars, and I helped Joni make choices about her dad's service. By the time I hung up, she was rummaging through his freezer, determined to find the will and take care of business.

My friend Melanie arrived next. She came bearing gifts: a mess of black oil sunflower seeds in a cardboard box lined with crushed purple sateen cloth. "The seeds are for your feathered friends. I'm sure you can give the box to someone who doesn't like the water cremation idea."

Melanie's dad had died a couple of weeks before in Iowa. She didn't need my professional services, but she did need a friend. "I feel like shit," she said. "Can I hang out for a bit? Do you have anyone here or anything?"

I believe in divine timing; this was one of those moments when someone showed up and needed my full attention—happily, my date book was blank and the phone silent. These are moments where undertaking is truly my ministry. We settled into my office. I asked Melanie if she wanted to share what she was going through.

"Nah, I just like you and want to hear you talk," Melanie said. "But maybe not about death."

Oh boy, she had opened up a can of random and I'm not exactly shy! I confessed a few of the crazier things about me to my waiting pal.

"What do you mean you rearrange people's cans?"

"I have a talent for it. I save people I love from poor canned food placement," I said. We were both grinning like a couple of fools by this time. "People don't get what a gift they have in all those colorful cans."

"What do you do, creep into their homes at night?"

"No, I'll do something innocent like ask if I can get a glass of water, and then I'm in. I sneak a quick peek into their cabinets and if they are in disarray, I might offer to whip up a snack. That buys me time. While I cook, I can unload a cabinet, wipe it down, and quickly group the cans by product."

Chuckling, Melanie declared me a hoot. "You don't do this during home funerals, do you?"

I laughed. "I will not lie. I have sometimes been tempted, but so far I've restrained myself."

"What do your friends say when they find your handiwork?"

"I've heard that some of them think it's annoying, but no one has ever said that directly to the Queen of Cans."

"I'll bet you have the cleanest cupboards in the world at your house." said Melanie.

"They are glorious," I admitted. "I even arrange my cans by month and year in addition to food type."

"You don't think this is a little OCD?"

"Maybe a little," I allowed, "but it sure is pretty, and I dig reading the labels. That's a Fournier thing. If you set a random can of corn on a Fournier table, one of us will pick it up to find out where it was canned and read aloud the recipe on the back."

"You know what I like about you?" Melanie asked. I shook my head. "You're totally nuts. I thought you might be wackadoodle because you chose this creepy job and hang out with dead people, but now I see your craziness runs deeper than I realized."

"Oh, we've just brushed the surface," I said, and launched into the time I crashed Joe DiMaggio's funeral.

It was San Francisco, 1999, and services for the Yankee Clipper were invite-only. Across the street in Washington Square Park, fans, reporters, TV trucks, and gawkers, including me, were sandwiched between orange cones, grousing that no Yankees had been invited. I surveyed the park crowd looking for George Steinbrenner.

I'd arrived late, so I missed the seven limousines that pulled up to the church that morning, shuttling fifty DiMaggio family members and friends to the service. Word on the grass was the presiding priest had known DiMaggio since the two grew up together, and Joe's surviving sibling, Dominic, would be giving the eulogy.

Even though the blocks of mourners were behind a police barricade, it wasn't just a crowd of lookie-loos. A lot of ballplayers and ballplayers' kids were standing among us in grassy North Beach Park, San Francisco's Italian enclave where DiMaggio spent his childhood. Many people were neighbors with connections to him.

I had to get closer. I wanted to be part of the funeral, not just a gawker drinking Diet Pepsi in the park. I moved closer and resorted to my go-to measures: flirting with a security guard who let me in the parish offices near the cathedral to use the bathroom. He figured once I came out he'd get my number, but I stayed inside, perched on my temporary kneeler of a church toilet as I strained to hear the majesty of "Ave Maria."

My cover was blown when the rejected security fellow narced on me, and a female guard banged on the stall door. Out to the street I went.

I rejoined my park mates in time to shout "Bravo!" and applaud as Joltin' Joe was carried out of the cathedral in a brown casket covered in white flowers.

Melanie laughed uproariously at this story. "You got balls, kid!" she said.

The loony-stories-about-Elizabeth marathon was finally interrupted by the phone. It was Joni.

"You'll never guess where I found Dad's will," she declared.

"Where?"

"He had cleaned out a can of nuts and stashed it in there. It was on the cupboard shelf, lined up alongside the green beans and asparagus tips."

"He had the nuts between green beans and asparagus tips? That's crazy!" I said, giving Melanie a wink. She could barely suppress her laughs as I advised Joni on her next steps.

I hung up with Joni just as Michael arrived with Sofia.

"Mommy!" my daughter called, racing to my chair. "Mrs. Butler won't stop sitting on my bed!"

"Ask her nicely to move," I suggested.

"I already did!"

"Butler?" Melanie said, "As in the people who used to live in your house?"

Sofia, Michael, and I nodded.

"But they're dead," Melanie said.

"Yes," we all agreed.

"Well, I guess they certainly dug their log cabin," Melanie said. "I can see those two spending their afterlife there in the hills. Have you managed to get any solid evidence it's for sure Mr. and Mrs. Butler?"

I explained we had to take Sofia's word for it. Not that I hadn't tried. Once I took a bag of white flour and poured some in a mirror on the floor of Sofia's bedroom. I had Sofia ask the ghost, in a clear but friendly voice, to write her name in the flour and to please stay in the room until we came back.

I returned the next day to learn the ghost's name, but instead of other-worldly writing on the mirror I found flour everywhere. The dog had gotten into the room through the secret door in the closet and rolled in it. I spent the next few hours getting the pound of flour out of the carpet, cursing the ghost at full lung capacity.

Melanie thought that was the best story yet, but I wasn't quite done.

"You know, Sofia announced a new ghost was dropping in on her dreams. According to her, it was a cigarette-smoking ghost. She definitely thinks it's a boy this time 'because it's *stinky.*'"

Chapter 33

Funeral Fidelis

As the business grew, I relied more and more on my husband's help. In addition to doing the lion's share of Sofia's daily care, he did a lot of the transport work and the parlour repairs. Michael kept the books in the kind of pristine condition only a bottom line money sort of guy has the patience for—and boy, he needed major patience sometimes.

With the rainy season once again looming, I began to fret about the leak in the roof. I know, I know, roofs are supposed to be fixed when it's not raining, but my pitiful income had made the situation easy to ignore during summer, when the ceiling wasn't dripping. Michael looked it over but couldn't pinpoint the problem. He finally urged me to hire a contractor.

"I can't afford a repairman, you know that," I replied.

"You're not charging enough!"

"I'm not raising prices!"

"Elizabeth, be reasonable, we're not running a charity."

"I'm aware, but you know I feel strongly about remaining as close to non-profit as possible."

"The profits are how we eat and fix roofs and keep the doors open!"

"Oh, don't be dramatic. We're hardly starving!" Concerned Sofia would overhear, I flicked on my Mother RADAR. She was upstairs in her loft. I could hear her chattering away to Mrs. Butler. Michael lowered his voice.

"I'm not saying you have to start charging some outrageous amount, but if you priced things more fairly, the books would balance a little easier."

"I'm not doing it," I hissed.

Michael threw up his hands. "Why did you get us into this if you're just going to give everything away?"

This was not a new argument for us. I already knew there was nothing I could say that would reconcile our perspectives on the issue. The truth was—and is—we both had a fair point, but high ideals were not getting the roof fixed.

I resolved to spend less time on consulting I didn't charge for, and more time seeking work that would improve my profit and loss statement. I emailed a note to my work account to remind myself that I owed the community I served a healthy business. Then I could be there for them when they needed me.

"I can do this," I whispered, as I hit the send button. "I am resolute!"

That lasted until morning, when a family arrived at the parlour carrying a shoe box. I welcomed them in, assuming the box meant they had taken up a collection in church, or during a football game, to pay for the services of a loved one who had just passed. I hadn't received the usual call from hospice or the medical examiner, although I don't think too much of it when a family shows up without an appointment. We are in the country and it is what you do.

This was a family of four children. They situated themselves in the wicker chairs around my front room table. Everyone looked pensive, even as I offered them a pile of peanut butter cookies. No one moved an inch.

"Take your time and begin sharing whenever you feel moved to speak," I told them.

We sat in silence for a very long three minutes. Finally, the oldest child at the table, a thirteen-year-old, lifted the lid off the Sketchers box to reveal three deceased puppies, angelic little creatures with their paws on each other as if they were only taking a break from playtime. Tears immediately came to my eyes.

After some quiet time, when I could tell they were a bit steadier, the conversation began. I took basic precautions in handling the remains of the deceased. "First, I'm going to dump the cookies. Pronto. Always avoid eating and drinking near, or while handling, remains," I explained.

I asked if I could lay the puppies, Kevin, Nick, and Joe—Jonas Brothers!—in a more suitable, protective environment and they agreed. I brought out a very small fetal casket. The thirteen-year-old immediately snapped pics for her Instagram account.

The story of the puppies' birth, short life, and sudden death came out in bits from the assembled. When I learned the pups had been dead since the previous evening, I checked off one of the questions from my mental spreadsheet. Rigor mortis usually sets in within three hours and lasts for a number of days; the time since death determines whether or not the body will remain in position. Since the family had discovered the bodies immediately after the time of death, they were able to arrange the baby pups in the heartbreaking but natural position I discovered them in.

I felt deeply for these delicate people with sad faces and guided them through funeral plans.

"Some families opt to bury their pets at cemeteries designated specifically for pets. But, there should be no issues if you decide to use your backyard. Animal burial is far shallower than the requirements for human burial." The clan opted for their side yard and I approved. A family grave site would reaffirm the importance of this small but deep loss to the family.

"So, let me give you kids some ideas of some things to do, okay? I really think assembling a memorial display in honor of the little babies might be nice. You can find objects from around the yard to decorate the grave. Each of you can gather a bag of shells, flowers, feathers, bark, acorns, leaves, twigs, stones, berries, and keepsake objects," I said. "This is Oregon, so you will be able to find a lot of neat things. Maybe you could also draw a picture."

The kids got into the funeral groove. They told me their cousin's ferret in another state was super old, and it shouldn't be long before he crosses over to wherever it is those funky things go. I advised them of the wisdom of checking local ordinances before interring anything larger than a hamster, canary, or goldfish.

I instructed them how to guard against any possible disease and warned them to use extreme caution when handling animal remains.

"Be smart. Wear disposable rubber or plastic gloves when handling the little bodies." They assured me they would follow this precaution and set out with the tiny casket to prepare for their first natural burial.

As I waved goodbye I noticed a light rain had started. Grabbing the trash can, I hurried to the chapel. "That's not the kind of rainmaker I need around here!" I shouted at the ceiling.

It drizzled on and off all day. At long intervals, a drop of water would plunk into the trash can. I took it as a complete condemnation every time. Berating myself for my financial shortcomings, I prepared for an upcoming memorial service. It was a cremation, the bread and butter of my little shop, but suddenly I felt guilty for having given the family one of my homemade lint urns instead of selling them an item that would turn a profit. I couldn't help myself—no hedge fund mistress of the universe was I. The cost of even a simple memorial service and cremation was a stretch for them, and lint urns are environmentally friendly, biodegradable, and a natural demonstration of the cycle of life. Wasn't it only right that I lived by my values, despite the sacrifices that entailed?

Plunk. "Shut up," I growled at the trash can. "It's not like I spent anything making the lint urn. It's just my time and a little flour invested."

The lint urns were an Earth Day 40th Anniversary initiative. Out came the beautifully hued lint from the dryer trap when Sofia's pastel clothing was dry. I knew dryer dregs could be turned into something worthy. Willow hooked me up with her new roommate, an artist and Bohemian hipster named Marliese. The urns are created from papier-mâché fluffy lint—it doesn't require an MFA to make one. All you have to do is mix water and lint in a saucepan. Stir continuously, add flour, and keep stirring until the mixture holds together, forming peaks, then pour it out onto several layers of newspaper to cool. Be warned, the smell is rather . . . well, according to Sofia, "like hot old socks." I figure it's a smelly sacrifice for the greater good, but it may not be the best D-I-Y option for the strong of nose and weak of stomach.

When the lint mixture is cool enough to handle, form it around a vase or other container. Over the next four or five days, as it dries, it will harden over the mold. The dried pieces can be assembled with non-toxic glue or biodegradable thread, or adhered to eco-friendly paper. The fun part is to paint, decoupage, or decorate any way you want.

Marliese and I had asked for and received donations of dryer lint from local businesses, and we turned out a whole line of papier-mâché urns. We named the styles after the businesses that donated the lint. For instance, "Final Ride Roadster" was fashioned out of contributions from the local auto-detailing shop. We sold a couple at an Earth Day booth; although, as Michael helpfully pointed out, we didn't come close to earning anything for the time invested. Marliese and I didn't feel that was the point. We saw the project as a creative, educational opportunity.

Michael felt creative education could wait until after our financial problems were solved. Readers may now fill in the blanks regarding the squabble we had over the value of creative time versus the responsibility of individuals to contribute to their community without expectation of recompense. It was a semi-civilized, philosophical squabble!

Anyway, I still owned a lint urn or two, so in a moment of compassion, or weakness . . . I gave one to the Warner family, whose great-aunt I was scheduled to memorialize the next day. No big deal, right?

Plunk. "Shit!"

I considered calling people who owed me for funeral services, but I couldn't see what good that would do. When the families I serve need to make payments, it is because they truly do not have much money. If any of them had won the lottery lately, I was pretty sure they would have stopped in to pay off their account. Since that hadn't happened, I was confident they were still making do on the small income that had prompted the need for a payment plan in the first place. My values confirmed, I hit the highway to pick up the great-aunt's ashes and enshrine them in their linty ossuary.

The next day I woke to a downpour. I might as well have had a cheese grater covering the chapel for all the good the roof was doing me. I rang George and asked if he had a large tarp; he did and volunteered to help me get it over the roof. My early days of retro-fitting the building with squirrel screens had taught me to keep a set of work clothes around. I changed quickly and met George in the back of the building.

Twenty minutes of cursing and flailing later, we tied down the tarp. George mentioned he'd known the roofing was shot and had always planned to replace it, but with forty acres there had always been something more pressing to fix.

"You're sure it needs replacement? I was hoping it just needed a patch job."

"Naw, the whole thing needs to be replaced," he said. "No question about that."

I thanked him and swore I would not start weeping. That turned out to be harder than expected as the soaking rain continued for the next two days. I reminded myself I was perfectly capable of finding a solution, and I would find a solution. For good measure, I also begged my mother and St. Joseph of Arimathea to kindly do whatever they could on behalf of my ailing little mortuary.

Later that week, I was at the Barton Store for soda refills and an afternoon chat with the regulars when somebody asked me why my roof was tarped.

"It leaks."

I meant to paste my everything-is-hunky-dory smile on and cook up a story about how the contractor couldn't get out for a few weeks, but I was so discouraged I admitted I couldn't afford the repairs.

"You want us to check it out?" a guy named Brad asked.

"That's a kind offer," I said, "but I honestly don't have money to pay you."

"There's no charge for looking," Brad said, and motioned to a couple of his friends.

They followed me over to the parlour in their construction truck and set to work. They removed a few boards to check the underside of the roof sheathing and looked for water stains to pinpoint the leak's location. They spread a drop cloth on the floor below the leak, placed a stepladder on the cloth, and put on manly safety glasses. Positioned on top of the ladder, they worked to cut out a section of drywall right at the stained ceiling. There was some cringing when they saw sheets of rotted plaster.

It was getting dark, but my hometown heroes stayed to save the day. Brad climbed the extension ladder to the roof. After he made it past the eagle weather vane, he gave his buddy the thumbs up to join him. The roofing mastic was carefully inspected for cracks and holes at the upper rim of the flashing; the lower edges of the roof shingles were lifted to expose the outer portion of the pipe flashing.

"There's water under these shingles," Brad called down to me. "That means you have a problem with your shingles and flashing installation." The men descended, and Brad explained that whoever had flashed the roof had botched the job, badly.

"Damn, so I really do have to replace the entire roof."

"And you have some water damage to repair."

Silently I chanted, *I will not cry, I will not cry, I will not cry.* But it didn't help.

"Aw, don't take it so hard," Brad said. "We'll figure something out."

We? Who was "we"?

I guess my face registered that question because Brad clapped his hand on my shoulder and said, "We're neighbors; we'll figure out something."

"Okay," I said, smiling as if I believed something could be figured out. "Can I offer you guys some cookies?" There was a general agreement that cookies were welcome. I passed around the batch I had baked earlier and thanked them profusely.

After they left, I realized my little funeral home in the big woods now had, besides a leak, a big hole cut out of the chapel ceiling. I began to chant my new mantra: I will not cry, I will not cry, I will not cry, but it didn't help. I whimpered all the way home.

"What's wrong?" Michael asked when he saw my red eyes.

"Nothing," I lied. "The service today just kind of got to me. It was very sweet and sad."

He was suspicious but didn't pursue the matter. I spent the rest of the night sending out e-mails to see if I could rustle up extra voiceover work, although I wasn't sure when I'd find time to do it.

The next morning I almost called in sick. They only thing that got me up and into my clothes was my concern that Michael would insist on driving over to the parlour to tack a sign to the door. I wasn't ready to tell him the roof repairs needed to be done immediately. Why rush into these things?

When I reached Cornerstone, Brad was waiting in the parking lot with a stack of labeled boxes on the edge of my lawn.

"What's all this?" I asked.

"Roofing supplies," he said. "I bought them wholesale for you. I also talked to some folks last night. Vernon Clark says he owes you money for his mom's funeral, so if you'd be willing to work out a trade, he'll take care of your roof right away. Bud Leonard is mostly retired these days, but he said he'd come help, too. He's the grandfather of that little girl who died last year. His family was real pleased with the funeral you put on. Anyway, if your husband can help with the labor, too, you should be all set."

My mouth fell right open. "Are you serious?" I asked. There was no mistaking my disbelief.

Brad laughed and clapped me on the shoulder again. "I told you, Elizabeth, we're neighbors now. You're our funeral person. Of course folks are going to help out where they can. And we all know George from way back. You people are kind folks."

Chapter 34

Family Rituals

I JUST CAN'T GET OVER IT," I TOLD JEANNIE DURING MY MIDDAY catchup at the Barton Store. "I'm so touched that people would help me like this."

She smiled as she beat a smoke from her crumpled pack. "We take care of our own out here, and you're one of us now."

"But, I haven't even lived here very long."

"No, but most people know at least one person you've laid to rest. Folks know when their time comes you'll be there for them. Think of it like them having a way to be there for you in your hour of need." She smiled at her quickness momentarily before she flicked her Bic.

"It's just amazing," I said, blinking back another round of tears.

"Country places have to be kind of like big families. We bicker with each other, but we also look out for each other." With a chuckle and shake of her head, Jeannie added, "Just surrender and accept it, 'cause you can't get out of it alive!"

I smiled and looked across the road. Old shingles were flying off the roof of my little parlour. "I guess I'd be crazy to want to," I told Jeannie.

Ruth Leonard, wife of one of the men who was working on my roof, walked in and greeted us both cheerfully. "Looks like the men are making progress over there!"

"Yes, they are," I said, "and I very much appreciate you giving up your husband's time so he can do this."

"Oh, don't worry about that," Ruth said. "He's been a little underfoot since he retired anyway. I'm glad he has something to do."

"Well, I'm still grateful." Understatement!

She looked thoughtfully at me for a long moment and then said, "He wanted to. You know, when we lost our grandbaby that was the hardest thing we've ever lived through." A tear slid down her face. She didn't need to continue.

I nodded and put my arm around her, feeling emotional myself. It had been the hardest funeral I had ever directed—a baby girl, just a year old, beaten to death by her mother's punk-ass boyfriend. For nights afterward, I could barely sleep for thinking of that beautiful baby in her tiny white casket deep in the earth. Whenever I visited that cemetery, on official business or just for a walk with Sofia in her stroller, I stopped at the baby girl's grave, haunted by the terrible loss of her life.

"You don't know," Ruth said, wrapping her arms around me and speaking low into my ear, "how much it means to people—the work you do. We didn't want a stranger to take care of our baby girl."

We hugged each other for a long moment, then separated, looking and feeling self-conscious. Jeannie stood up and hugged us both. "You see?" Jeannie said to me, her arm still over my shoulder. "Like a big family."

"I always wanted a big family," I warbled as I dabbed at the tears soaking my face.

Jeannie grinned and said, "Well be more specific about your family wish next time, 'cause this one has more than its fair share of oddballs, and now you're stuck with us, until death do we part."

I had to get going. My afternoon appointment was about to arrive at the store to pick me up.

☙

Jamie lived her life with respect for the environment and she wanted to demonstrate that same respect while planning her death. She was near the end stages of her time in this world so her life partner, Eric, had contacted me that morning for help.

"I know she has always spoken of being buried under the oak tree in our backyard, and I really didn't take her too seriously," he told me over the phone. "But you helped the homestead down the street and they said we can actually do this. Is that right?"

"We can if your property meets the guidelines," I said. "Unfortunately, I'm having roof repairs done and I can hardly hear over the construction noise. Could we meet in person? I can look over the site at your place, if you want me to meet you there."

Eric agreed and offered to pick me up since it was easy to get lost on the way. We decided to meet at the Barton Store to steer clear of the construction. Eric pulled up as Ruth was leaving with her pastries. After officially introducing ourselves, Eric asked for a minute to pick up Jamie's favorite Tiparillo cigars.

"She's got cancer and gonna die anyway, so why not let her enjoy herself any way she wants?" he explained.

We hopped in his truck. On the way, I ran through the county's requirements, establishing that he owned the land, the property was at least an acre, and there was a suitable spot at least thirty feet from a public right of way. Ten questions later, I got his permission to call the county zoning and planning commission for due diligence.

"And you must know that you cannot deem this a 'cemetery,' nor can you ever charge anyone for a burial space. You can bury everyone you know back there if you have room, but it cannot officially have a name, and you can't take any cash. Got it?"

The way Eric was beaming as he said, "Got it!" told me he'd joined the "backyard burial club."

Their house was way, way out in the country on a forested stretch of property. We passed through Estacada and drove many more miles east, to finally make our way up a long, dusty hill. I had a great feeling about this place. We stopped for a moment so he could introduce me as "the town mortician lady" to his neighbor, Natasha—a lovely lady, with a pleasant smile and aged face.

As we turned into his property, Eric told me Natasha and Jamie had been best friends for thirty years. "I got 'em these dumb t-shirts that say BFF on 'em for Christmas last year. They were in 'em all the time gardening."

Birds chirped from the trees, and there was a heady fragrance in the air from the rows of lilacs Jamie had cultivated. "Pretty damn nice, right?" Eric said. "We finally got this place to stop looking like such a ghetto, and she has to up and get sick on me. I'm just glad our kids are grown so they can show up when it happens. I need her to leave this Earth in a good way."

I promised him a send-off befitting a woman who I learned collected cans before it was the cool thing to do and never took a drink from a Styrofoam cup. It turned out I wouldn't have much time to prepare.

Jamie died of complications from her cancer before sunrise the next day. Eric telephoned me right away. He was blindsided by how quickly she went. He'd hoped to have her burial space pre-dug and a casket fashioned by an old carpenter buddy of his. He wanted to paint their tiny home lavender in her honor. He grieved over his Jamie being gone. He was inconsolable about the things he had wanted to do before his beloved died and now couldn't make happen.

I told Eric to stay with Jamie, to talk with her about all the beautiful things they had done in this lifetime, to tell her about the even more amazing things the two of them would experience when they met again. I asked him to put Natasha on the line; she was in the kitchen steeping oolong tea for him. Natasha stepped out on the porch with her phone for privacy. She lit up one of the little cigars she and Jamie favored.

"Natasha," I said, "we can do this. I need some help from you, but we can honor Jamie and have her burial by sundown. I need you to phone their kids and have them get in their cars now. They aren't that far away and should have time to get it together and make it here. Eric's got a little utility tractor. I'll call my friend John to come over now and start digging. Do you think Eric would be good with that, or do we need John to load up his backhoe and trek it out there?"

Natasha understood. "He is immobilized. I can guarantee he'll stay in there and not come out until he takes her out with him."

"That's fine. I've already talked to her hospice team; they can get a death certificate and permit taken care of right away. We really just need the space prepared, and John is a pro. Stay by the phone and I'll have John call when he's on his way out. All you have to do is meet him outside and show him the space Eric showed me yesterday. How are you doing with all this?"

"I guess as well as can be expected. I feel odd that she isn't here to tell this to. Well, I guess she sort of is."

I paused long enough to make sure she'd completed all her thoughts. "You are doing very well, Natasha, and you're really helping your friend. When you feel ready, maybe in a few hours or so, you might want to help Eric decide on what blanket or quilt or shrouding you want to use, okay? Or we can use a natural casket I have with me. Anything he wants is perfect."

I promised I was only a phone call away. I would keep my cell with me if I was away from the office. Natasha was ready to phone their tribe and instruct people to show up for a seven p.m. ceremony. I would arrive at four p.m. to bathe Jamie and get her ready for her final farewell.

Michael was up, preparing for an early morning start on the roofing project and bagging lunches in the kitchen while the coffee perked. I told him what was going on. "I know I was supposed to take Sofia all day, but is there any way you could take her mid-afternoon?" I asked.

"I'll make it happen," he said. "You do what you need to do."

"Thank you, honey. You always come through when I need you."

My husband kissed me on the forehead. "That's what family does."

"Well, I don't know how I managed before you."

"I believe you said you spent a lot of time crying in tire swings," replied Michael. He popped a yogurt and some carrot sticks in a bag and handed it to me with a wink. "Go be the Green Reaper."

I settled in at my home office and asked John to go to the property. While dressing Sofia and preparing her breakfast, I visited with a few of Eric and Jamie's friends who had phoned to coordinate their thoughts about what the service should look like.

Done with that, Sofia and I curled up in a chair to watch a video she'd checked out at the library—an episode compilation called *Sesame Street: 40 Years of Sunny Days*. Halfway into the video, the scene opened on Big Bird walking over to his friends to hand out the sketches he made for them. I froze. This was the scene where Mr. Hooper had died. "Just because" still haunted me and explained nothing, even as a seasoned mortician.

I watched my child with great interest during the segment. I waited for tears since she is sensitive and would feel bad for her yellow bird friend. But instead, after Gordon's famous final words, she looked at me and said, "Mom, tell Gordon that Mr. Pooper died because he was old. Old people get sick and die. Tell Gordon, okay? Because Big Bird needs to know that Mr. Pooper is at the funeral home because he is dead."

Hugging my daughter close, I relayed sadly, "I can't talk to Big Bird. I don't know him personally. Mr. Hooper went to a different funeral home."

"Oh!" said Sofia, wrinkling her tiny brow. "Poor Big Bird."

I hugged and kissed her darling self until she protested. Lightness came over my being. Maybe "just because" was the perfect answer for those who didn't have an answer. Maybe the adults on Sesame Street were trying their best to make it make sense. Just like the nuns at my school and my grandfather and even my father had tried when my mother died.

I was ready to let go and no longer allow myself to feel haunted. Just because.

☙

Just before four p.m., I drove slowly up the path to the house. Jamie's brother, Phil, was walking to the shed and saw me pull in. He ambled over, waving and carrying a small tree. "Will this be okay?" he asked. "I wasn't sure what would be best for the top of the grave, since I don't think we want any headstone."

I was touched at how delicate the little tree looked in his burly hands. "It will be picture-perfect," I said. "It's exquisite."

"I want her to have something nice, and for Eric to be able to come out here in the evenings and know she is with her lilacs and this tree. When she finally goes, she'll give nutrients for a new life and provide food and shelter for these birds out here."

"Phil, I think you're one heck of a guy and a great brother to her," I said. "I'm going to head into the house and see how everyone is doing. Is there anything I should know or be aware of before I go in? Are you doing all right?"

Phil shook his head. "My aunt brought a big pot of gumbo over, so if you want some, it's on the stove."

Inside the house, friends and family were in a flurry of activity. I was introduced around. Auntie Rita was washing dishes. Angela, a family friend, braided flowers together so Jamie would have a lovely crown. Florence, Jamie's cousin, tuned her guitar for the celebration's acoustical accompaniment. Natasha was painting Jamie's toenails a delicious shade of purple, and Eric sat beside his beloved, holding her hand and singing softly.

I cried; the love in that two-room home overflowed into the universe. I stood in silence, knowing my still presence was all they needed, for they were being divinely guided.

An hour later we filled a large basin of water and carried it to the bed. I'd brought lavender-colored and scented loofah sponges for the bathing ritual. Eric grabbed a camera and snapped pictures of the female tribe that surrounded his beautiful bride as they gently, lovingly applied oils to Jamie's skin.

"The sun is getting low in the sky," Eric finally said. "I'm ready."

For her shroud, he chose Jamie's favorite lilac-colored, hand-woven rug that hung on the wall of their bedroom. We were wrapping Jamie in her gorgeous tapestry when Phil arrived with a long cart, ready to take his sister out of the house on her last ride. Friends had been gathering outside; Phil helped direct them toward the open meadow near the lilacs. I watched through the window as guests flowed methodically to where they needed to be.

We placed Jamie carefully in her humble chariot. As the sun began to set, Phil wheeled his sister across the property. His steps were measured and sure. Florence strummed Cat Stevens' "Where Do the Children Play?" on her black-faced guitar. Eric walked behind deep in thought, while Auntie Rita and Natasha, arms held high, half-walked and half-swayed to the music.

We arrived at the burial site. Jamie was lowered into the ground right away. Often, the deceased is placed beside the grave, or on a lowering device above, but Eric preferred his wife be lowered immediately so we could sing along with Florence as we tossed cut lilacs onto the purple shroud.

Near the end of our graveside vigil, Jamie's shovel-bearing son, Garth, finally broke down in tears. All arms held him, forming a perfect chain of bodies. It was hard to tell where one person stopped and the next started. When he was able, Garth primed the area right next to the grave and we planted the tree, watching its sweet leaves stir in the slight breeze.

Later, over a scrumptious potluck dinner, I asked Garth how he was feeling in the moment.

"Is it weird if I think this was kind of nice?" he asked. "I don't mean Mom being dead, but doing it this way with all of us here together."

"I don't think that's the least bit weird. I think it's how it should be when we lose someone we love. It's easier to bear when we do it together."

"Yeah," he said. "That sounds right."

Chapter 35

Nearest and Dearest

NOBODY KNOWS LIKE AN UNDERTAKER THAT, DESPITE AMAZING advances in medicine and technology, the mortality rate for human beings still remains 100%. It's a fact: all of us are going to die someday. But as much as a person knows that and is reminded of it every day as she goes about her work burying the dead, the day one of her own dies it will come as a bone-rattling shock.

"Kevin is dead, Elizabeth."

I almost dropped the phone. "What? Ryan, are you sure? No, that was dumb. Dead? I don't understand."

In a tortured voice, Ryan tried to explain. "He's been really bad the last couple of months, but he swore me to secrecy. He, he . . ." Ryan's voice broke around ragged sobs.

I searched desperately through my brain for what I was supposed to do. The information was in there, I was a funeral director for Christ's sake, but I couldn't get my mind around it.

Ryan got himself together before I did and said, "He asked to have you do the funeral."

Inside my head a little blonde girl was shrieking, "I cannot do this! No! I cannot do this."

"Of course," my mouth croaked, which somehow had the effect of releasing a tiny thread of funeral director know-how. "Is anyone with you?"

"No."

More of my brain cells rose to the occasion. "Where are you?"

"In the hospital room with Kevin. They said I could have some time."

I asked a few more questions, jotted down the hospital room number, and told him to hang on. I'd be there as soon as traffic allowed. I called

Willow as I dashed about locking doors. She could be at the hospital within fifteen minutes; she was a few blocks away at an environmental non-profit she founded. While I dug my wallet out from under my desk and retrieved an intake packet from the file cabinet, I hit the speed dial for Michael.

"Hey, babe," he answered, the sound of his voice nearly making me lose it again. *What if I lost him? Wait, I will. I will lose him some day. I can't. I can't do this.*

"Honey?"

I shook my head to clear my thoughts.

"Elizabeth, what's wrong?"

"Kevin is dead."

"What? When?"

"Just now. I'm going to the hospital to be with Ryan. He wants me to do the funeral. I don't know if I can do this."

"Take a couple of breaths; you can do this. You want me to come with you?"

I sniffed and said, "Yes, but I need to go right away."

"Sofia and I will be right behind you," my husband said and then called to Sofia to put on her shoes.

"Stay on the line with me until we lose signal, please," I asked, as I turned the van engine over. "I just want to be able to hear your voice."

He agreed, with the caveat I would put the phone on speaker and keep it in my lap so I could attend to the wheel. I pulled out of my driveway, turned in front of the Barton Store without even looking to see whose vehicles were in the parking lot, and got onto the highway. I listened to my precious husband and daughter go through the ritual of getting ready to leave the house. Deep inside me, there was a claw squeezing my heart so hard each breath hurt. Their voices became garbled as I steered around corners and the signal lost strength. Soon enough, I reached a cell dead zone and they were gone.

"I can't do this," I said to my neighbor's goats as I passed by.

"I can't do this," I said to the gaggle of geese that lived a mile or two farther down the road.

"I have to do this," I told a pair of alpacas someone had recently pastured in their side yard.

"I have to!" I shouted at an Australian shepherd who ran along his fence line barking at my van.

"I can't let him down. Mom, please help me do this. I can't let Kevin down. Please don't let me screw this up."

Somehow, I arrived safely at the hospital and stumbled to the correct floor and hall, to the room where Willow cradled Ryan in her arms as if he were a toddler. Kevin's body lay still and silent before them. Illness had done so much damage I hardly recognized my dear friend. With reserves of strength, I lurched across what seemed like miles of linoleum to join Ryan and Willow in their embrace. As one, we rocked and crooned until our sorrow swirled around us, shrouding us from the rest of the world.

When I could speak, I said, "I'm sorry we didn't know. We would have been here for you this whole time."

"He didn't want that," Ryan said. "He couldn't stand to have anybody see him like this." Ryan took a deep, ragged breath. "He wants his ashes buried in our yard under the tree outside our bedroom window, and no funeral. He wants a 'Bring Your Favorite '50s Funeral Food in Vintage Crockery' potluck wake."

Despite myself, I started to giggle. "That's our Kevin."

A chuckle bubbled out of Ryan and mixed itself together with the misery in his voice. "He just wants us to be happy. That's his legacy."

Willow grinned and volunteered a tuna casserole with potato chip topping. "My mom has an avocado-green baking dish that will be perfect for the occasion," she said.

Ryan nodded and asked me if I could make a Jell-O mold.

"The disgusting one with mayonnaise or the kind someone would actually eat?" I asked, wondering if Dad still had Mom's old '70s copper mold.

"Mayo would be funnier and more retro, but I'll leave it to your judgment. It's probably not nice to make people gag at a wake." That set us to tittering again, so we were in pretty good shape when my daughter and husband arrived.

"Mommy!" Sofia called, running toward me. Suddenly, she caught sight of Kevin and froze. Michael and I watched her closely. Sofia had seen dead bodies before but never someone she knew well. Her eyes widened. "Uh, oh. Uncle Kevin is dead like Mr. Pooper."

We all nodded.

"That's what Daddy said, but I thought he meant somebody else."

I held out my arms and Sofia came over to snuggle with me. "Are you all right?" I asked her.

"Yes, but I'm sad."

"I'm sad too, honey. We're all sad." We each took our time to hold and be held and finally say goodbye to Kevin's body. Michael volunteered to do the removal, but I wanted to see Kevin through his last ride.

"Can I go?" Ryan asked.

I started to ask if he was sure, but I could see by his face he was. Well, why not? I had seen many times how people who helped prepare their loved ones' bodies for natural burial experienced greater connection and solace. Why not make that happen for Ryan and Kevin? I asked if anyone else wanted to go. In the end, we were a tiny procession of two vehicles: Ryan and I in the van carrying Kevin's body, and Michael chauffeuring Willow and Sofia in our Jeep. I had stepped out to the nursing station to get verbal authorization from an attending physician to sign the death certificate. Ryan signed the cremation authorization on the way to the crematory so Kevin's body could be cremated immediately, with us there. We took one last look at our dear friend, kissed his head, and sat down to be next to him through the process.

It was a sad and nearly silent vigil. Sofia, a born comforter, crawled in Ryan's lap and snuggled with him until she fell asleep in his arms. The rest of us held hands and thought of our friend. When the main burner ignited, I almost choked and Michael put his arm around me. In my head, I prayed to my mother and all the saints of the dead to watch over Kevin as he made his way through whatever comes next.

A few hours later, when Kevin's cremains were cool enough to handle, the cremator moved them to a work table. There were surgical pins among the bone fragments, which had to be picked out by hand before the last step.

"He was hit by a car once when he was riding his bicycle," Ryan said, quietly. "He had to have pins in his back. There should be twelve."

Bobby, the technician and an old friend of Michael's, nodded and carefully, respectfully, searched until he found twelve. Then we watched as Bobby slid Kevin's remains into the cremulator, which would pulverize them into a fine powder—the ashes most people are familiar with. Ryan looked tense; I took his hand.

"It's so fucking final!" he whispered fiercely. "I can't do this."

"Yes," I said. "You can do this. I will walk you through it, I promise."

"I'm glad we came here," Ryan says. "You know at the end, when he didn't want anybody to know?"

"Yes?"

"It was really because he didn't want to share the last of the time we had with anybody else. He said he knew it was selfish, but he wanted to spend every minute he had left with me, just the two of us." A continuous stream of tears flowed down Ryan's face. "It wouldn't have been right to send him off to strangers and let him go through this alone."

I pulled Ryan to me. "No, that wouldn't have been right. I'm glad you got to be here. He loved you so much."

Ryan nodded against my shoulder and said miserably, "I love him so much, too. He said he wanted me to be happy after he was gone, but I just wish I could die and go with him."

How well I knew. "You'll see him again one day," I said. "But in the meantime, you will be his living memorial."

"I don't think I can."

"You will grow into it," I said. "Trust me."

The cremulator finished its work and Bobby carefully placed the ashes in a plastic bag, attached the metal identification tag that had ensured Kevin's cremains would not be mixed up with anyone else, and sealed everything into a small box. Soberly, he presented the box to Ryan, who wrapped his arms around it as if he were cradling a baby.

"Thank you for letting me be here," Ryan said to Bobby. "You'll never know how much this meant to me."

Bobby told us he was glad to help. "I wish more people knew they could be here during this whole thing," he said. "It doesn't happen very often, but when it does, it feels . . . I don't know, right, somehow."

We thanked Bobby profusely, and he escorted us back to our vehicles. Willow rode with me and Ryan this time, so I could take them to Ryan's house. Michael took Sofia home.

264 🦋 Elizabeth Fournier

At the house, we tucked Ryan into bed with the box of Kevin's cremains. Willow and I set to the task of calling friends and family to organize the wake. Finished with that, Willow volunteered to clean the house for company while I did the necessary paperwork. It was late before I left, but Ryan seemed reasonably peaceful and had been able to nap. Willow planned to spend the night with him.

With everyone settled for the evening, I crossed town to Dad's house to embark upon an archeological dig for the precious gelatin mold. Dad put the coffee on and asked if I was okay.

"I will be." I told him about our vigil at the crematorium and the upcoming wake as I rifled through his cupboards. Suddenly, I realized Dad had stopped responding. He was asleep. Figuring he was worn out, I woke him gently and helped him to bed. He was oddly groggy and confused, but I put it down to being past his usual bedtime and didn't think much about it. He'd feel better in the morning. We'd all feel better in the morning, right?

I arrived home with the copper mold to find my daughter fast asleep in her bed and my husband running a bath for me. I told Michael he was the most wonderful man in the world as he unveiled a little plate of nutritious finger foods I could snack on as I soaked and sipped. He aided me into the hot, sudsy water and perched himself on the closed toilet, balancing my snack plate on one upturned hand. He had a white towel over his forearm, like a cartoon butler, and held out a cold beer for me—it was quite a sexy scene. I had a wee notion to act on that thought, but my sore muscles shut down the idea immediately. My number one goal, as the hot water swirled around me, was to unwind from this brutal day.

"I'm so grateful for everything you did today, honey. I don't think I could have pulled it off without you."

"I got your back," Michael whispered.

I looked at him and realized to what depth that was true. "I take you for granted sometimes. I'm sorry about that," I said. "But you always come through for me, even when you think I'm loony."

Michael chuckled. "You do keep me on my toes, but I like it."

"Really?"

"Yeah! Hell, everybody said this was impossible. I thought it was impossible, but we're pulling it off. It's pretty damn amazing."

"Even when I don't charge enough or let somebody make payments?"

"Well . . ." he frowned, "we do have some things we need to work on."

"I don't want to raise prices," I said gently.

"And, I don't want you spending so much time working to make ends meet and so little time with me and Sofia," Michael said, in his own gentle voice.

"I hate that, too," I admitted, "but I don't know how to square it with how I want to serve this community."

"We'll figure it out together," said Michael.

I love that word: together.

ↄ⳩

Two days later we held a tender but joyous wake at Ryan's house. In honor of our favorite party boy, mourners went to special lengths to add 1950s touches to their funeral wear. The table was loaded with vintage Pyrex and noodle-y casseroles, ham sandwiches and starchy side dishes. It was a good old-fashioned "Mom is here to take care of you" comfort food feast for a difficult day.

Ryan lovingly planted Kevin's cremains under a tree that gracefully draped across the yard to brush the bedroom window. He insisted on digging the hole himself. Once it was refilled, he placed the grave marker with his own hands—a simple granite stone with raised letters I'd had a local shop engrave.

A musician friend sang James Taylor's "Fire & Rain," and played his acoustic guitar so movingly, I was, as usual, left stripped of my mascara. As we concluded, I passed around a basket of bulb planters and assorted flower bulbs. Everyone helped plant the bulbs; both the tree and Kevin would be surrounded by flowers that bloomed throughout the year. Sofia planted winter aconite and snowdrops, because she especially wanted Kevin and Ryan to be happy when it was cold outside. Touched by her sensitivity to the added gloom that gray winter days can bring to the grief-stricken, I added some cyclamen to her mix for an extra shot of color.

When we finished, the guitarist sang a slow, delicate rendition of "A Satisfied Mind." The few who were not yet teary-eyed lost it when he hit the stanza about leaving life and loved ones in "this old world" with a satisfied mind. Still weepy myself, I invited everyone to take as much time as they needed next to Kevin and then gather in the house to celebrate his life.

Slowly, one by one, people broke away from the burial site and returned to the house. At last, it was only me and Ryan. I put one arm around him and we gazed at the newly planted garden for a few more minutes. Then he took a deep breath and said, "He wanted a party. Let's go inside and give him one."

And so, together, we did.

Chapter 36

A Father's Heart

THE SECOND TIME DAD FELL ASLEEP IN THE MIDDLE OF A CONVERSA-
tion with me, I got suspicious and called Nick.

"He did that last week, too," Nick said.

"So, this is not an event, it's a pattern. I think he should see a doctor, don't you?"

"Couldn't hurt," Nick agreed. "It's not like him."

To my surprise, Dad agreed as well. He said his heartbeat seemed irregular and promised me he would make an appointment with his primary care doctor. Before he even got to his checkup, he started having hallucinations.

"Who are these people in the house, Elizabeth," he demanded one morning on the phone.

"I don't know, Dad. Do you have people over?"

"Look at them! Who is that?"

"Dad, I'm not there, I'm at my house. Who is it?"

"Why are you saying that? Why are you pretending you're not here? Why won't you help me?"

My heart broke at the sound of his fear and frustration. Since Nick was closer in proximity to him that day, I asked him to get over there as soon as possible. I made my way over as soon as I could. An hour later, I found my brother and father together. Dad seemed normal. Nick had made an urgent appointment with the doctor, and they were just about to leave.

"Do you think its dementia?" I whispered to Nick in the kitchen while Dad located his jacket.

"I don't know, but something's not right. I guess, given his age, it might be."

The doctor wasn't sure. He said he'd need to run some tests.

That night, Michael and I agreed Dad should come live with us, but my father wouldn't hear of it. My worry about Dad's strange phone calls continued.

One afternoon, Nick called me at work. "Dad was doing his volunteer shift at the hospital today and he passed out."

Grateful he'd been at a hospital when it happened, I said, "I'm heading straight there."

The drive took forever. City-dwellers tend to believe that one of the greatest rewards of living the country life is the lack of traffic jams. Most days that's true, but there are plenty of times when a car slows in front of me and I can't see what's going on because of the long line of cars, or maybe the sun is in my eyes—I try to be patient. At some point, I'll be winding slowly around a turn wide enough for me to see a large piece of agricultural machinery up along the way. Somehow, this always seems to happen when I need to be somewhere sooner rather than later.

"Move," I snarled at the ratty pickup truck in front of me. I knew it wasn't helping to get so frustrated, but my anxiety levels were a tad high. After fifteen agonizing minutes, I checked in with Mom on high, to see if there was anything she could do. Lo and behold, the line of cars stopped and I could see way in the distance a huge farm implement creeping through a right turn into someone's private property. We'd been set free! I sent up a grateful prayer and followed the line of cars into town at a much more satisfying speed.

I still felt like I was crawling out of my skin when I got to the hospital, but this did zero good since the doctors were putting Dad though a battery of tests. There was nothing to do but wait. Finally, a doctor told us Dad was a strong candidate for a pacemaker. Compared to everything I had imagined, that seemed like good news.

Two months of heart monitors and doctor appointments followed for the necessary gathering of data. Dad wasn't allowed to drive, so we put together a complicated plan organizing rides from one of us or a volunteer organization. I fussed and worried the entire time, afraid Dad's heart would fail before we could get the pacemaker, and tried everything I could think of to get him to live with us. Dad was maddeningly resolute: he was determined to stay in his own house. I started spending as much time as possible with him there.

The upside to the arrangement was that Dad loved regaling me with stories of his farm life, growing up in Paw Paw, Michigan. I loved listening as much as he loved telling. I'd go over for a few hours to tidy up and cook a few meals so I knew he would eat nutritiously until my next visit. He repaid the favor with tales of his younger days and our family. My father is such a light in my life, he is so kind and such a gentleman that our time together, unexpectedly, became something of a respite from my constant fear I would lose him.

Finally, the day came when Dad received a phone call telling him a pacemaker would be his in two days' time. He called one crisp Monday morning with the news as I was leaving for work. I told him when I'd arrive to drive him to the hospital and left, feeling lighter than I had in a while, to pick up a body. The deceased, Betty, had to be transported to a Catholic church in the county for a visitation later that day.

I was on deck an hour early—I didn't want to take any chances I'd be late over some random farm implement on the road. The white casket was open with Betty inside, ready to receive her fond farewells. I tugged at the bottom of my black dress to make sure it hit my knees at a pious length as I headed down the back stairs to talk with Father Ben.

One of the perks of an evening visitation is the leftover donuts from staff meetings, all mine for the devouring. That day I scored big. In the kitchenette, I found the celebrated pink box and fluffy pride of Portland's famous Voodoo Donuts. I gave my hands a holy scrub and then ceremoniously lifted the lid to make my choice. I was somewhat amused to find this brand in a Catholic church. Voodoo Donuts secured their place on our nation's sugar-coated, fried batter map with such edgy confections as "Voodoo Doll" and "Cock-N-Balls" donuts. This particular box held tamer delights, however. I decided on an "Ain't That a Peach Fritter Donut."

My holy gorge had commenced when I heard, "Knock, knock!"

"Um, who's there?" I responded, chewing quickly.

"Justin."

"Justin who?"

"Justin time for a donut!" Father Ben exclaimed with a throaty laugh. He emerged from behind the door and headed straight to the pink treasure trove. "Only plain left? Nards!"

"Nards? Father Ben?"

"It's my swear word. That and 'sugar bakers.' Or if the diocese really cooks my grits, I go in the office and yell, *'Mother Fluffers!'*"

I was thunderstruck by his full disclosure. After I regained my footing, I said, "Knock, knock."

Father smiled gamely. "Who's there?"

"Donut."

"Donut who?"

"Donut let anyone cook your grits but you."

Father rewarded me with a hearty laugh, and we went over a few funeral details while munching on our donuts. He asked after Dad's health and I told him our good news, but confessed how worried I had been and how terrified I was going to be when Dad was in surgery. Father Ben asked about my faith.

"Well," I said, taking my time before continuing, "when I go to church, I'm full-on smorgasbord—a Cafeteria Catholic."

He nodded his head, familiar with this nutty term applied to Catholics who pick and choose aspects of the Catholic doctrine, but do not buy into the whole package. Catholics who dissent from Church teaching in regards to abortion, birth control, divorce, pre-marital sex, or the moral status of homosexuality.

I picked through the donut box devotedly for seconds as I tried to explain myself. "I like God and religion and spiritual stuff. Walking home to my Jeep at three in the morning many years ago in San Francisco and hearing a lone saxophonist playing 'Amazing Grace' in an alley was one of the most spiritual moments in my life, but I'm not a fan of Catholic politics."

Father Ben didn't say anything. He just nodded and let me go on.

"I have a really hard time when I hear of any cover up of the priests and their misdoings, but I love the stained glass and the audience participation: sit, stand, kneel. I always look forward to the next position, and I dig the smell of incense wafting past the statues."

Father Ben smiled but remained silent.

"But I also have no issue with people making their own life choices." Feeling a little foolish, I finally shut up.

After a moment of silence, Father Ben said, "How do you feel about prayer candles?"

"I love them. I especially love the ones with saints on them. I like to read the prayer on the back, light the candle, and know good things will happen. I am a believer, truly."

Nodding, Father Ben said, "We still have some time before anyone will arrive. Why don't you go up to the sanctuary and light a candle for your father?"

"I will," I said in gratitude, and got up immediately. "Thank you."

"I'll be praying for your dad this week, too," Father Ben said, placing his hand on my shoulder. "Take your time; I can watch Betty for a while."

Upstairs I had the church to myself. I unobtrusively made my way up the side aisle under the Stations of the Cross and slipped onto a kneeler. After praying, I watched the candle flame and wondered what I would do if I lost my dad. I imagined the funeral and laying him to rest next to my mother. In my mind's eye I was bereft again, worse than I had felt when Kevin died. Worse than I had felt when my grandfather died. This would be as bad as when Mom died. I saw myself weeping, and Sofia trying to comfort me with her snuggles, Michael steadying me with an arm around my waist at the graveside. Then it occurred to me: they were the answer. I would grieve, yes, but I wouldn't do it alone. I would not be a pathetic, lonely little girl. I was not that tragic, pitiful child any more. I had everything that girl had needed way back then, with some baby goats thrown in for good measure.

I stood up, respectfully took my leave, and went to take up my post next to Betty. Her family would be arriving soon, and I was going to be there for them.

When I stood next to the white casket, Father Ben didn't say anything. He just nodded and gave me a knowing little smile.

❧

Two days later Dad got his pacemaker. He began sleeping better immediately and stopped dozing off every ten minutes. His memory wasn't the sharpest, but it was better than before the pacemaker. He functioned pretty well on his own, although it would be a while before he was released from medical observation. He started volunteering at the hospital again. I agreed to stop nagging him to move in with us, but decided to keep up my frequent visits for a while.

One day, I told him about my upcoming trip to the Natural Burial Co-Operative Board of Directors retreat. Although the retreat was in Three Oaks, Michigan, I would be flying in and out of Chicago and was excited about the possibility of meeting up with a friend before my flight home.

Dad perked up at the mention of Chicago. Very casually, he told me that when he was a kid he went to St. Salomea Church at 118th and Indiana Avenue, and his family house was at 134th and Indiana. Oh, and that his aunt and uncle owned a funeral parlour in a Polish neighborhood.

"Wait, what? Your family owned a funeral home on Chicago's South Side?"

He explained the parlour had been handed down from generation to generation. "It skipped a generation with me," Dad said, "but you should know you are the eighth generation of morticians on my mother's side of the family."

Was he kidding me with this . . . with this earthquake, tsunami, and biblical flood of astonishing information? "I've been an undertaker for years. Why didn't you ever bother to tell me?"

Dad looked at me squarely. "I guess it never came up."

I shook my head in disbelief. "So why did you discourage me so much when I wanted to become a funeral director, if this is one of your family's legacies?"

Dad shrugged. "It's a lot of hard work, and the pay is lousy. I thought your life would be better if you did something else. I guess I was wrong."

That surprised me. "You think now that I made the right choice?"

"Oh my, yes," Dad said. "Just look at you. You've done so much and come so far. I'm so proud of you."

My eyes welled up and I hugged my sweet, wonderful Daddy. "It means so much to me to hear you say that."

"Didn't you know?" he asked.

"I never know for sure," I said, opening the blinds to let some light in. The windows were outrageously spotty, like a dot-to-dot picture. I wondered how long he would be able to live alone in this house. We had moved into this house when I was five and my brother was six. Our bedrooms were still waiting for us down the hall. Pictures of me and Nick as little kids covered the wall. My mother died in this house. Now, my father's heart was slowly failing in this house.

It was too much to think about, so I said cheerfully, "Hey, can you please tell me where you hide your window cleaner? You realize these windows look pretty bad, right?"

He led me to where the household cleaners have been kept for forty years. It was good to know he could remember. He pulled out a squirt bottle with blue-gray, foamy liquid inside which had to have been there since the Clinton Administration.

"Here it is, just used it last week. Good to the last drop." I grabbed some old newspaper and scrubbed the hell out of those windows. While wiping with newspaper in one hand and Windex in the other, I was painfully aware that I would be washing these windows in the not too distant future, when he was no longer in our lives; yet this plastic bottle of Windex will still exist.

"Why don't you know?" Dad asked a few minutes later.

"Know what?"

"That I'm proud of you."

"I don't know. Sometimes, in my heart, I'm still that odd little girl who worried you. I guess I wonder if you still see me that way."

"You know you're not anymore, right?" Dad asked.

"I do," I said with a smile. "I honestly do."

Epilogue

OPEN MY EYES TO A SUNNY DAY, A VERY SPECIAL SUNNY DAY. LITTLE
Sofia came into the world eight years ago this morning, and this afternoon children from all over town will arrive at our funky log cabin to
celebrate her next year's trip around the sun. She is drawing pictures for her
guests, excited to hug and kiss everyone, to share her art, to wear a pretty
dress, to blow out her candles. And she is excited to have another year. She
grew up in a funeral home and clearly gets that not everyone has the gift of
even one more day.

I was eight when my mother died. In this present moment, I am living the full circle of life and death. It is happening right before my eyes,
observing my eight-year old daughter quietly as she draws, in awe that this
is the same child who long ago asked me to tell Big Bird that Mr. Pooper
was safe in my care at the funeral home; the precious lamb who sat in the
field and played Schoolhouse with her farm babies; the precocious girl who
carried on a long-term relationship with the former lady of our house in
ghost form.

I have learned from observing Sofia that being a good mom has nothing to do with getting her to eat vegetables or having her sleep through the
night. There is a difference that looms large between me and many other
mothers I know, a difference quite akin to my work life as the Green Reaper.
Rather than bothering with naptime and bedtime regiments, I was more
concerned with teaching simple eco-conscious behaviors like recycling and
reducing energy usage. Michael worked his magic with her during reading
and arithmetic lessons; I presented kindly green lessons which were, in
some form, taught to me through my own mother's love.

My mother taught me to walk in compassion. Compassion is an attitude, a philosophy, a way of life, and sustainability is rooted in the basic compassion of being kind to others; a gift that keeps giving. I was taught to not hit, bite, or call other's names. Sharing earned a gold star, because we had more than we needed. Good things should be shared with everyone, especially if these good things can change at least one person's life.

Children are born with a sense of wonder and an affinity for nature. My mother was inspired by Anne Frank's ability to breathe in nature any chance she could, and in turn passed that gift to me. This is a passage written by Anne in her diary: "The best remedy for those who are afraid, lonely or unhappy is to go outside, somewhere where they can be quiet, alone with the heavens, nature and God. Because only then does one feel that all is as it should be and that God wishes to see people happy, amidst the simple beauty of nature."

With Sofia, I created an expanded scope of concern for nature's creatures. Those innocent-looking soft plastic holders for soft drink cans and other products can entangle birds, fish, and small animals. We snipped apart each ring before throwing it in the trash. We didn't throw rice at weddings in order to protect birds that might pick up the grains and have their tummies explode.

My mother knew we needed to cut the meat habit for a more sustainable outlook, already a built-in eco-trait of being Catholic—Sunday was pasta night. Momma was a fan of adding artificial bacon-flavored bits to give pasta more zing. Obviously, she was visualizing the importance of a vegetarian future. Sofia and I turn off the faucets when brushing our teeth, rather than watching nearly ten gallons of water slide down the drain. There is no way we would leave the car running while waiting for someone. We turn down the heat, only wash full loads of laundry, set the freezer temps exactly between zero and five degrees, always lather and rinse just once.

And the most important way I am teaching her to visualize the future: Always say your prayers before you go to bed. No one gets out of here alive.

About the Author

ELIZABETH FOURNIER BEGAN WORKING IN THE FUNERAL INDUSTRY twenty-seven years ago, back when it was truly an anomaly to walk into a funeral home and be greeted by a woman. Working hard to prove herself came natural, and Elizabeth takes great pride in knowing that her community has entrusted her funeral home with providing unparalleled service. She is renowned for burying her townsfolk in their backyards and is a self-described "gardener of people."

She is the author of *Green Burial Guidebook* and is the voice of the autopsy exhibit in the forensic wing at the United States National Museum of Medicine. She owns and operates Cornerstone Funeral Services in Boring, Oregon, where she lives with her husband and daughter.

Baby Elizabeth and Mom

Acknowledgements

MY CHERISHED HUSBAND, MICHAEL: SOMEHOW I SHOULD HAVE guessed I would meet the love of my life at a funeral.

My precious daughter, Sofia: I watch you sleep at night sometimes and can't believe you are mine.

My devoted father and celestial mother: I am truly nothing without you.

My literary agent, Sharlene Martin: You believed in me.

My editors, Shantell Booth, Karen Gowen, and Shelley Diamond: You took such profound care to make my words shine.

And to those who continue to shine their light on my life, I thank you.

www.ingramcontent.com/pod-product-compliance
Lightning Source LLC
Chambersburg PA
CBHW031127090426
42738CB00008B/993